SUSTAINING

Knock Your Socks Off

SERVICE

THOMAS K. CONNELLAN and RON ZEMKE

SUSTAINING

Knock Your Socks Off

SERVICE

American Management Association

New York • Atlanta • Boston • Chicago • Kansas City • San Francisco • Washington, D.C.
Brussels • Toronto • Mexico City

This publication is designed to provide accurate and authoritative information in regard to the subject matter covered. It is sold with the understanding
that the publisher is not engaged in rendering legal, accounting, or other
professional service. If legal advice or other expert assistance is required, the
services of a competent professional person should be sought.

Library of Congress Cataloging-in-Publication Data

Connellan, Thomas K., 1942–
    Sustaining knock your socks off service / Thomas K. Connellan and
Ron Zemke.
      p.   cm.
    ISBN 0-8144-5159-4 : $22.95. — ISBN 0-8144-7824-7 : $17.95
    1. Customer Service.   I. Zemke, Ron.   II. Title
HF5415.5.C66   1993
658.8'12—dc20   93-1271
                                                       CIP

Printing number

10   9   8   7   6   5   4   3   2   1

Contents

Our Thanks

From a thought in the head to a word on the page is truly a team effort. Many people deserve thanks for their contributions to the book you now hold in your hands.

Kristin Anderson's keen insights and helpful additions contributed greatly to the finished product. Jill Applegate's and Karen Revill's stern reminders and organizational skills helped keep us on target on time.

Craig Westover's "wordsmithing" and editorial support helped transfer our customer retention research and experience to the printed page.

Andrea Pedolsky, our AMACOM editor, was like a rock in our parade of ever-changing deadlines and manuscript lengths.

Special thanks go to Susan Zemke and Pamela Dodd, who not only endured our frenetic pace necessary to complete this book, but also gave us love and support throughout the process.

Finally, we wish to thank the many client organizations and workshop participants who gave us the opportunity to test and refine the techniques in this book.

Ron Zemke   Tom Connellan
Minneapolis, MN   Ann Arbor, MI

Preface

If you picked up this book looking for a one-size-fits-all, step-by-step guide to starting a service quality program (or a total quality program, for that matter), you're about to be disappointed. The last thing we intend here is to give you yet another book on service quality basics, answering questions such as, Where and when do we throw the kickoff party? What kind of training should we buy? What is the supervisor's role in empowerment?

The basics are the basics—and are critically important. But they're not enough. A journey may start with a single step, but if you expect to get somewhere, it takes time, attention, direction, and *sustained* effort. So our focus here is on the things you have to do *after* the foam is off the beer, the confetti is swept up, and the last "Quality Are US!" banner has been replaced with some new preoccupation, like back safety or data integrity.

Though quality purists may quibble, we don't have a big problem with "programs." They help focus attention. Any program that gets people excited—whether it's well conceived or not—can focus company attention for three months to a year. And that's fine. But that's also precisely where most programs (with a bang, a yawn, or a whimper) end. The task we've set for ourselves here is to show you how to avoid the traps of yet another three-month to one-year program—the familiar "flavor of the month" initiative—that has to be replaced with another program just to keep people's appetites whetted. You can't afford to do anything less than adopt what we call a *Knock Your Socks Off Service* focus—a new way of business life, not a passing fancy or fad.

What is Knock Your Socks Off Service? In truth, it's what-ever your customer says it is. But short of the chaos that nondefinition creates, we see Knock Your Socks Off Service as "making sure you know what your customer wants and ex-pects from you; being flexible in meeting those demands; treating the customer like a partner rather than an adversary or an end-user; and working like heck to make it easy for a customer to do business with you."*

One assumption of this book, then, is that you've already started something—a process, an effort, an initiative, even a program—designed to improve the quality of the service you provide your customers over the long haul. This book is de-signed to help you *sustain* those service-quality-improvement efforts and to keep you competitive in the long run.

We're not about to ignore, overlook, or belittle the impor-tance of the next thirty days or six months. Events in these time frames are all necessary for long-term success, but they are not enough. Our experience in building high-performing service cultures shows that organizations have to be considered living things, capable of learning and changing in keeping with changes in their environment. Events in the short term have profound immediate consequences, but as time passes, how you handle these short-term challenges should blend together into longer-term efforts. We'll show you how to build on the next thirty days, the next three months, the six months after that, and the two years after *that*.

In particular, we'll give you a framework and a reason for thinking in years rather than just months. Consider Tennant Corporation, a manufacturer of something as mundane as industrial floor-care equipment. One of the early leaders in improving both product and service quality and sustaining it, Tennant spent *thirteen years* getting the processes right and the wrinkles ironed out. Today it is confident that it is constantly improving quality at the rate and speed needed to keep the company globally competitive for the next 100 years.

Not every company needs thirteen years, nor is every

*For more on the nature of Knock Your Socks Off Service, see *Delivering Knock Your Socks Off Service* (AMACOM, 1991) and *Managing Knock Your Socks Off Service* (AMACOM, 1992).

company prepared to measure its future in century-length increments. But the sheer scale of Tennant's calendar is noteworthy. You don't create a culture that sustains Knock Your Socks Off Service overnight. It takes time, constant adjustment, and a level of customer-centered leadership not enough businesses have experience creating, let alone sustaining. But it can be done. If you apply the steps outlined in this book, you'll start seeing behavior change in thirty days—and more in sixty to ninety days. The examples are all around us. Just don't plan on getting it *all* done in ninety days.

A disclaimer: The effort involved in sustaining Knock Your Socks Off Service is not an addition to your job. If the first feeling you have as you look at this book is, "Gee, these folks are trying to add an awful lot to the way we do things here," look again. The truth is, we're not adding anything to the job of satisfying your customers. We're suggesting new ways of getting it done—ways that probably build on things you're already doing right. Knock Your Socks Off Service is not communication theory; it's a practical way of continuing to improve the way you communicate with people. It's not management theory; it's a functional way of managing systems on the customer's behalf.

The second thing you may notice is that much of what we've compiled in the pages that follow is organized common sense. On that count, we're guilty as charged. Most things that work are common sense—but that doesn't necessarily mean they are common practice. Our goal is to make into common practice those things that are already common sense, based on solid research that proves these ideas really work. Sustaining Knock Your Socks Off Service is not a box of cure-alls. It is a way of organizing things to increase customer retention, enhance customer satisfaction, and in doing so, to build the kind of long-term organizational results you are looking for.

Research shows that good companies continually try to get better while mediocre ones seldom try anything to keep from getting worse. The surest way to build a marketplace edge is to build a service edge. We know it. So do you. It's the one consistent differentiator in today's economy, no matter what field you're competing in. We're going to show you how to do some of the things you are already doing well even better—how to combine customer-focused standards with your systems, how to promote consistent behavior toward customers, how to further distinguish yourself in the eyes of your customers.

We also do some problems prevention for you. If you have been successful in getting some systems in place, you don't want those to be a short-term, shot-in-the-arm kind of thing. We give you both the strategy and the tactics by which you can ensure that your service quality and customer retention efforts pay off in the long run as well as the short.

There is an axiom: Give a man a fish and he can eat well that night; teach him how to fish and he can eat well every night. We hope not only to teach you how to fish better, but to throw in lures, a tackle box, and tips on where the big ones are biting as a starter kit. If you truly accept the premise of sustaining Knock Your Socks Off Service, your job will never "finish." Three years from now, five years from now, seven years from now you will still be improving. You will be raising the ante on your competition—and, we trust, you will still be setting the standard in your industry.

SUSTAINING

Knock
Your
Socks
Off

SERVICE

1

The Case for Service Quality

"Quitting smoking is easy," said Mark Twain. "I've done it hundreds of times." His observation provides a useful metaphor for organizations confronting the conundrum of service quality: *Starting* service-quality initiatives is easy, but sustaining continuous service improvement is anything but. That's why service-quality initiatives inevitably pass through three phases.

1. *The awareness phase.* Someone in the organization, usually a group of someones, comes to the realization that there is a benefit to be reaped from better service—whatever that might mean.
2. *The evangelical phase.* This is characterized by speeches, noise, banners, pledges of personal commitment, and the formation of from one to a dozen committees, task forces, or teams charged with everything from reviewing training programs to doing surveys of customer expectations to fashioning service awards.
3. *The frustration phase.* Inevitably, the frustration of instituting change brings the questions, "So what do we do now?" "How do we keep this going?" "How do we sustain what we've started?" Helping you through this phase is why we have written *Sustaining Knock Your Socks Off Service*.

No Easy Answers

You'll find plenty of material in serviceland literature about starting and managing a service-quality initiative. We have contributed several tomes to that body of knowledge ourselves, not the least of which are *Delivering Knock Your Socks Off Service* and *Managing Knock Your Socks Off Service*, the predecessors to the book you hold in your hand. But all these works, including our own, are concerned with getting your service-quality initiative started off right. They help you take advantage of your enthusiasm, point you in the right direction, and teach you enough to start down the path to Knock Your Socks Off Service.

Unfortunately, a few quick successes do not add up to a sustained service-quality effort. Would that it were so easy. We've been beaten on the head and shoulders more than once in the past few years for not having "five easy steps" to Knock Your Socks Off Service—a trump card tucked up our sleeves to play at the opportune time. Our experience in helping clients think through their service-quality efforts has biased us against easy answers, simply because there aren't any. But as renowned industrial psychologist Gary Latham notes, if you just stay on the problem until you understand it, the solution recommends itself.

Sustaining Knock Your Socks Off Service is about sticking with the problem of providing superior service. In concise language, we provide you with three valuable tools: first, a brief conceptual framework of the *systemic* approach to service quality; second, techniques that translate that framework into *action;* third, examples—not so you can do the exact same thing (because your needs are different), but so you can jump-start your thoughts and spark the ideas that will lead to your unique brand of Knock Your Socks Off Service.

Money in the Bank

Why bother? Because it's the "right" thing to do—providing your customers with the kind of service you'd expect if you were in their place? Certainly. But providing superior service is far more than an altruistic gesture. Companies that systematically sustain their service-quality initiatives find that their investments pay high dividends. From Stew Leonard's far-from-simple two dairy stores in Connecticut and Carl Sewell's bustling Dallas Cadillac dealership to multinational pacesetters like Federal Express, Marriott, and Ritz-Carleton Hotels, there is growing testimony that improving service quality improves the bottom line.

Marriott, for example, found that each percentage-point increase in the customer satisfaction measure-of-intent-to-return was worth some $50 million in revenues.

At IBM's AS/400 computer manufacturing site in Rochester, Minnesota—where the Malcolm Baldrige National Quality Award earned in 1990 is proudly displayed—a one percent increase in customer satisfaction is worth $257 million in additional revenues over the ensuing five years. (That, by the way, is just for business through IBM Rochester, not IBM as a whole.)

When Frederick Reichheld of Bain and Company and W. Earl Sasser, Jr., of Harvard Business School contrasted the consequences of improving customer retention versus cutting costs, they found that improving customer retention had significant economic advantages over trying to cut costs. In the credit-card industry, for example, they found a 5-to-1 net revenue advantage. In other words, on a percentage-point basis, increasing customer retention by 2 percent is the bottom-line equivalent of lopping 10 percent off of every operating budget.

The PIMs (profit impact of market strategies) database compiled by the Cambridge, Massachusetts–based Strategic Planning Institute shows striking differences between a high and low emphasis on service.

High vs. Low Emphasis on Service

- *High-rated* companies gain market share at the rate of 6 percent per year; *low-rated* companies lose market share at the rate of 2 percent per year.
- *High-rated* companies average a 12 percent return on sales; *low-rated* competitors average a 1 percent return.

- *High-rated* companies charge 107 percent of the industry average; *low rated companies* charge 98 percent of average.

Separate studies by both IBM Rochester and Motorola—both Baldrige Award winners—found that the difference between 4 Sigma quality and 6 Sigma quality (12,000 versus 3.4 defects per million opportunities) is equal to 16 points of return on controllable assets and 10 points of margin. Larry Osterwise, the site general manager at IBM Rochester when it earned the Baldrige, says, "If you have 10 points of margin to play with, and I don't have those same 10 points, if I try to follow you down 9 of those 10 points, you would still have 1 point to play with, and I would be a not-for-profit corporation."

Need a more personal example? The average strip mall does $162 a square foot in annual sales; the average regional mall, $350 to $450; a really strong retailer as much as $700 a square foot. Industry average in the food business is about $520. By comparison, Stew Leonard's now legendary dairy store in Norwalk, Connecticut, does *$2,700 a square foot.* Superior service drives incredible volume through his store—over $100 million a year. Because he's doing such an incredible volume, Stew can charge lower prices. Lower prices *plus* higher service build bedrock-strength loyalty among Stew's customers. He knocks their socks off and profits accordingly.

Service as a Marketing Edge

Service quality *is* catching on. In the insurance field, six of the eight fastest-growing companies are specifically following customer-retention strategies rather than customer-acquisition strategies. The basis of their operation is service quality. Service quality is the only true differentiator in an industry where a company can duplicate a new "product" within a week of when a competitor writes the first policy.

Similarly, 20 percent of Ford Motor Company's major R&D budget is spent on customer satisfaction—features and functions not required for quality or reliability but that give the rise and delight. And speaking of the ...en't purchased a new car lately, you ...—if not an outright shock—when you ...om. In response to customer desires, ...oving to no-haggle policies. Negotiat- ...car is, for most people, an unpleasant ...e unpleasantness, and the customer is ...or his or her next auto purchase and ...nd the dealership to friends.

...owns a number of auto dealerships, ...y Dallas Cadillac outlet, understands the ...tention. He gives the example of the ...s from out of town only to find his keys ...he customer calls the dealership. The ...ruck and waives the usual $25 fee. That ...cements the buyer-seller relationship and ...er for life. Conversely, Sewell notes, he ...wenty-eight new customers through a $700 ...to equal the cost-effectiveness of retaining ...nd one ad is unlikely to draw that many

...fecting external customers, a high-quality service focus ... an impact on the internal workings of your organization—an impact that carries over to your external customers. People who feel they are doing a good job, providing a service that is considered valuable by a customer, tend to enjoy what they're doing. They are more productive, stay with the organization longer, have lower rates of absenteeism, and have higher satisfaction with themselves, their colleagues, and their employer. Organizations with secure, satisfied people serving their customers typically have more satisfied customers.

Sustaining Superior Service

As we noted in *Managing Knock Your Socks Off Service*, organizations create superior service through a combination of eight tactics and practices:

1. Finding and retaining quality people
2. Knowing their customers intimately
3. Focusing their units on organizational purpose
4. Creating easy-to-do-business-with delivery systems
5. Training and supporting employees
6. Involving and empowering employees
7. Recognizing and rewarding good performance and celebrating success
8. Setting the tone and leading the way through personal example

With these elements in place, the task becomes one of sustaining the initial enthusiasm and focus of the organization. Delivering high-quality service must move from the realm of a special event to normal, everyday operations. To facilitate that move, a manager must integrate the concepts of Knock Your Socks Off Service with the organization's basic business practices, with service-system design, and with human resource management.

Chapters 2 through 4 put the business of providing service quality into perspective. Chapters 5 through 8 set the systemic framework for integrating quality into business practices. In Chapters 9 through 11, we look at behavioral issues that influence service quality. Chapters 12 through 19 examine the critical role of feedback in sustaining your service-quality effort, and Chapter 20 deals with nonperformance.

2

The High Cost of Losing Customers

A colleague of ours once sat through a management review meeting at which the group spent five minutes deciding whether to kill a product line and forty-five minutes deciding whether to have scooter races as part of its United Way campaign. "That's because," says our colleague "the management team knew something about scooter races."

That is typical of what is happening in business today. Despite evidence that customer retention has a far more positive impact on the bottom line than does arbitrary cost-cutting, too many managers continue to wield the cost-cutting ax. Why? Because management knows something about cutting costs (it's had plenty of practice in the past few years), and cutting costs is, from a financial perspective, a fast and rewarding effort. Wall Street is quick to cast kudos to the company that increases profits by reducing operating costs.

Neither management nor Wall Street is nearly so sophisticated when it comes to the economic value of customer retention. It's a comparatively simple exercise in mathematics to take 10 percent out of a budget line item. To analysts and managers reared on control-centered management, it *seems* esoteric and wasteful to spend time calculating the cost of the *x* percent of customers who leave every week, quarter, or year to do business with someone else. To others, it borders on clairvoyance to spend time figuring out *why* they left. Taking tactical action to recover those defections or planning strategic actions to prevent them—well, that must be voodoo.

Not so.

Understanding the impact of customer retention is simply a matter of defining and measuring proper variables. The homework involves knowing who your customers are, knowing your company, and understanding the crucial points at which your company and customers interact. We call these customer-sensitive transaction points Moments of Truth—a phrase borrowed from the corrida (bullfight) by Jan Carlzon, president and chairman of Scandinavian Airlines Systems, to describe the importance of certain customer transactions. Your assignment is to get to know your customers, not just in terms of individual sales but as lifetime assets who see you and your company through these Moments of Truth.

The Dollars and Cents of Service Quality

We believe it is an economic necessity for American business to change its attitude toward service quality. We believe that attitude is changing, and for the simplest of reasons: That's where the money is.

The Good, the Bad, and the Ugly

Study after study, plus more anecdotal evidence than anyone has time to recount, shows that there are substantial bottom-line returns for just *meeting* customers' basic service expectations. *Significant competitive advantage* awaits those organizations that consistently delight their customers. Consider these examples of the good, the bad, and the ugly of service.

Let's start with the ugly. Tom Carns, owner of PDQ Printing, a Las Vegas–based quick printer, says 60 percent of all printing done in the United States is either "screwed up or late." He says one printer in his town even has a sign in his office that says THIS IS NOT BURGER KING. HERE YOU GET IT MY WAY, OR YOU DON'T GET IT AT ALL. That's ugly.

Such an attitude may irritate Carns, but it is also the reason his service-conscious quick-print business is so successful. Among other things, PDQ delights its customers with such "extra" services as proofreading and typesetting. With every job, PDQ sends a questionnaire asking customers to detail their needs. And it responds. A few years ago, Carns found "continuous forms" cropping up frequently as an answer to that question. So PDQ bought a short-run continuous-form press in December 1989. Today it sells continuous forms to 60 percent of its commercial accounts. A nice return for asking customers to detail their needs.

How about bad? A Minneapolis woman and her husband renewed their membership to a local Bally's Health and Tennis Club via credit card in mid-October 1991. Although the credit-card purchase was processed just a week later, early December rolled around without any confirmation from the health club. The woman called an 800 number to inquire about the status of the membership. The customer service representative informed her that there was no record of the renewal and implied that nothing further could be done. Another call to a different representative the next day yielded the same result. A third try, same result. Finally the woman shot off a letter to Bally's Chicago-based president, Don Wildman. In a better-late-than-never gesture the couple was given a refund for the renewal and a complimentary membership *through* 1995.

Outstanding recovery and response? You bet. But what do you think the Minneapolis couple was telling their friends about Bally while this was going on? What's your reaction to this story? Does it sound like an organization you'd want to risk doing business with? Contrast the couple's experience with that of a woman who wrote to L. L. Bean.

L. L. Bean's reputation for service has reached mythical proportions, but it is firmly rooted in reality. Karen Larson, a consultant in Maple Grove, Minnesota, returned a shirt to L. L. Bean that had worn out after many years of hard service. The shirt cuff had frayed in an unusual way, and Larson thought the company "might be interested in that kind of product information from a customer." Larson made it clear in her letter that she was not looking for any kind of compensation.

Not long after, Larson received a phone call from an L. L. Bean customer service rep, who told her the company would like to replace the shirt but no longer carried it in the color she had purchased. Again, Larson made it clear she wasn't looking for compensation, but the rep insisted, so Larson gave her color preference. The rep then told her the new shirt was on sale for half-price, so she'd send her *two* shirts at no cost. End of story? Not quite. A few days after the shirts arrived, Larson received a check to cover her postage for returning the original shirt. That's not "good" service—that's Knock Your Socks Off Service.

The Value of Retaining Customers

True, these stories provide only anecdotal evidence of the bottom-line benefit of quality customer service. But there are also hard facts that substantiate the value of retaining customers. In the credit-card field, for example, the $54 cost of acquiring a new account isn't fully amortized until the second year the card is held. If a cardholder cancels in the first twelve months, odds are the company loses. Over a five-year period, however, the average account generates more than $200 in net profit—recouping the initial acquisition cost plus all the accounting costs later on.

Lifetime Customers

In the examples of good, bad, and ugly customer service, we saw that while bad (or even downright ugly) service will drive customers away, superior service will keep them loyal, and *sustained* superior service adds a whole new dimension to the buyer-seller relationship.

Loyal customers are more than just today's sale—more, in fact, than today's sale *and* tomorrow's sale. A committed customer spreads the good word about your organization. He or she takes an active interest in your success, perhaps offering constructive suggestions on how you might improve your product and/or your service, as Karen Larson did with L. L. Bean. They become a source of new product ideas, of instant market research. Loyal customers are indeed invaluable. But frankly, too few companies take the time to tap this resource or maximize it into a systematic, sustained advantage.

Faced with the choice of either building or satisfying relationships or churning the account base to find new customers to replace ones who have fallen away, too many companies opt for the latter to their inevitable financial detriment. They have not yet learned to think in terms of lifetime customers; they still believe that customer attrition is both normal and inevitable. But if you're going to sustain Knock Your Socks Off Service beyond the first month or two, you'll have to institutionalize the concept of lifetime customer value. Just what does that mean? Let's look at the incomparable Stew Leonard's deceptively simple approach.

For a "small" dairy store operation (if you call an annual volume well in excess of $100 million small), company president Stew Leonard, Jr., does an incredible amount of hands-on customer research. What he's learned, and what he passes on to his employees, is that his typical customer visits the store twice a week and spends $50 per visit. In his area of Connecticut, it's common for people to live in the same region for 10 years. Do the math: $100 per week times 50 weeks per year (two weeks for vacation) times 10 years is $50,000. So what do Leonard's checkout clerks and shelf-stockers do when a customer wants to return an 89-cent tube of toothpaste or a $34 ham? As they've been trained, they see a business asset worth $50,000 and respond accordingly. And the customers reciprocate with unparalleled loyalty.

Money talks. The Leonards understand that and use the $50,000 lifetime value to help their people understand why their brand of service is so important—Knock Your Socks Off Service that delights customers. You see, the Leonards also understand a second point about their customers and their attitude toward service: Merely good enough isn't . . . well . . . good enough.

AT&T reports that 10 percent of the customers who rate the company's service as good will not repurchase, and 50 percent of those who rate it good are undecided. In other words, at the "good" level, 60 percent of AT&T's customers are at risk of defecting to someone who does it better. When you drop down to "fair," 97 percent of AT&T customers say they will not repurchase. The data go on: It costs five times as much to win a new customer as it does to retain one you already have. The brand-loyal automobile customer is worth $100,000 in total purchases to the company. Fourteen percent of car buyers switch makes because of product; 68 percent switch because they are disappointed with service.

The case for sustained Knock Your Socks Off Service is simple dollars. And sense. You've picked up this book, so we can assume your heart is in the right place. No doubt you've already put a number of service-quality initiatives in place. You're on the right track, but as Will Rogers noted, even if you're on the right track, you'll get run over if you don't keep moving. Keeping on the move means not just starting service-quality initiatives but *sustaining* Knock Your Socks Off Service.

3

What Can Go Wrong

During the past three years, we have created a database, called the Service Management Practices Inventory (SMPI), to assess internal and external aspects of service quality. The SMPI includes more than 60,000 surveys from 200 organizations of varying sizes across a spectrum of industry. Using these data, we have identified the most common barriers to sustained high-quality customer service.

Eight Major Barriers to High-Quality Customer Service

1. **Inadequate communications between departments.** We invariably give higher marks for service commitment to ourselves than to our coworkers, and to our departments than to other parts of the company. We also tend to focus on our own tasks and departments and fail to see the big picture. Typical is the case of the X-ray department at the University of Michigan Hospitals.

It seemed as if everybody was always screaming at the X-ray department: "How come I can't have this? Why can't I have that?" Trying to explain to each person making a demand why his or her particular want was delayed proved futile. The ultimate solution was elegant in its simplicity: The X-ray department posted a graph that tracked incoming and outgoing work per hour. Suddenly, complaints all but disappeared. Once people realized the amount of work that went through the department, they became a lot more tolerant of delays.

2. **Employees not rewarded for quality service or quality effort.** The axiom of motivation is, "What gets rewarded gets repeated." Companies that preach service quality but reward something else get something else. Telling salespeople that

"Your job is solving customer problems" but making sales targets the basis of compensation sets salespeople up for an easy choice.

At D. W. Newcomers' Sons in Kansas City, Missouri, "bonus time off" is one small, low-cost way of rewarding employees for customer-service proficiency. The company, which manages funeral homes, cemeteries, and security businesses, found that many of its 3,000 employees couldn't properly answer questions about divisions other than their own. To correct the problem, the company prepared an extensive training session—but it didn't stop there. Employees are now rewarded for learning the material. Any administrative, professional, or sales employee who takes the course can earn a day off with full pay for knowing the answers to fifteen to twenty of the questions most commonly asked by customers about the business. Rewarding people for their newly gained knowledge reinforces its importance.

3. **Understaffing.** The best of intentions and the sharpest of skills can't be stretched indefinitely. Service typically is provided one-on-one. It's required immediately. If it's not available, chances are pretty good the customer will pick up her marbles and walk down the street. So why would any service organization understaff? Common wisdom would say to save money, but not all understaffing is the result of trying to save a buck. In many cases, understaffing results from not fully understanding customer requirements and/or not having service standards to measure performance—in short, from lacking a service system.

4. **Inadequate computer systems.** A computer system, from an enterprise perspective, is more than hardware and software. Inadequate computer systems are not necessarily made better by going out and buying bigger and faster processors or gigabits more memory. When your objective is delivering Knock Your Socks Off Service, you don't measure the effectiveness of a computer system by how fast it is. You look at the outcome you're after (from the customer's perspective), and determine if the service system is adequate to deliver the desired result. Only then do you look at the technology within the system.

Office automation is a prime example of the "technology from hell" syndrome. Today, desktop computers provide the average American worker with far more information than he or she can use. Rather than more computing power to sort, send, collate, and calculate, what most workers need is a process that defines the specific information they need to get their jobs done and to satisfy customers.

5. **Lack of support from other departments.** We're not talking about a conscious lack of support here. Often companies embark on a service-quality effort without taking into account how departments in the organization are going to interact with one another. This lack of preparation can have wide ramifications. SMPI data show, for example, that in organizations that share customer evaluations with customer-contact and support employees, customer-satisfaction ratings jump to an average of 81 percent (versus 50 percent for companies that don't share information).

6. **Inadequate training in people skills.** In a service situation, a customer experiences two results. The first is an outcome result: Did the customer receive what he wanted in the first place—a haircut, a correctly filled order, a physical examination? The second is a process result: What was the customer's total experience in getting what he was after? A person may have an order filled correctly, but if the clerk spends ten minutes on a personal phone call before waiting on him, the total experience is not likely to be perceived as satisfying. People skills make the difference. They can be the basis of Knock Your Socks Off Service, or they can send people running to the competition.

7. **Low morale; no team spirit.** Customer satisfaction is built on employee satisfaction. No company can satisfy its customers if it can't satisfy its employees. No company can do justice by its customers if it can't do justice by its employees. Employees tend to treat customers the way they perceive they are treated within the organization. Research shows that there is a direct relationship between people who feel good about the work they do and customers who feel satisfied about the way work is performed on their behalf.

8. **Bad organizational policies and procedures.** Organizational policies and procedures should be set up to meet the specific needs and expectations of customers. Good policies and procedures make your company easy to do business with. Bad policies and procedures hinder good service. Policies and procedures are rules of conduct written more or less arbitrarily to maintain an orderly business. They aren't laws or holy writs, but they are often looked on with such reverence.

A major metropolitan newspaper was on a quest for an improved image. It established a policy: 100 percent of all phone calls will be answered within three rings. (No one, by the way, checked to see if this was a real-world expectation.) To facilitate the policy, the newspaper installed a voice mail system. A news reporter could be on one call, place it on hold, and pick up a second call. At least in theory. In order to follow the three-rings policy, the phone system rolled unanswered calls over to the voice mail. And it really didn't give the caller three rings—calls rolled over between the second and third rings. That meant the moment a reporter heard a click on the line, he or she had to put the current caller on hold and pick up the second line, not a trivial event in a busy newsroom. So, in fact, the newspaper had put in place a policy that hindered its relationship with callers. Fortunately, it had the moxie to change the policy. Too many companies make a policy and then stick with it—even in the face of evidence that the new policy is inappropriate.

Need for a Service-Delivery System

The eight major barriers could be broken into component parts and further obstacles to delivering Knock Your Socks Off Service cited—inadequate product knowledge, inadequate equipment for the job at hand, high turnover rates that sap organizational skills and destroy continuity with the customer, poor facilities, ill-defined job tasks, lack of management support for service quality, inadequate technical skills, inadequate supervision, and a host of others. But doing so would commit the underlying sin that is at the root of all service-improvement-initiative failures—the lack of a systemic approach to service quality.

A major, if not *the* major, reason service-quality efforts fail is that companies launch them in an ad hoc manner and follow through on a piecemeal basis. Some departments get religion faster than others; they get frustrated because other departments are holding them back. A champion arises who gets frustrated when management balks at his suggestions or refuses to allocate resources for service-improvement projects. Everyone in the organization has a different idea of what Knock Your Socks Off Service is, and each department strives for different, sometimes conflicting goals. Service improvement becomes a series of tactical firefighting moves rather than a strategic, systematic effort. Quality service never gets integrated into the daily activities of the organization. It becomes an add-on, something to do along with everything else (usually *after* everything else).

In 1992, we conducted a study for a major telecommunications company that was pondering why its service quality was falling off. A survey of 2,000 employees found that they all understood the company's service strategy. The number-one reason they gave for not following through on it was that they were too busy "fighting fires." Lack of time to focus on quality improvement undermined meaningful and lasting results. Everyone was concerned with damage control; no one focused on fixing the system.

A 1992 study of total-quality efforts conducted by Ernst & Young for the American Quality Foundation found that many plans are too vague to generate better products and services. The plans lack the focus necessary to achieve realistic product or service improvement, which consequently limits the service-quality effort. Not all of the people who should be involved are. For example, Ernst & Young found that computer companies involve only 12 percent of their employees in any idea or suggestion program. Automakers had the highest involvement in the study—just 28 percent participation. Customer complaints—a key source of information for improving service—are treated as important by only 19 percent of the banks surveyed. Only 26 percent of hospitals used customer complaints as a source of improved service. Measurements like customer satisfaction are factored into compensation for senior management in fewer than one in five companies studied.

Instead of using informational feedback from customers to improve their service systems, most companies, according to the Ernst & Young data, keep their quality- and service-improvement programs at the "awareness level." They send their employees out with the vague charter to "make something better."The result is 937 quality- and service-improvement projects run by one percent of the people who should be involved.

To sustain Knock Your Socks Off Service, *everyone* in your organization must be involved. *Everyone* must be focused on the same service strategy and vision. *Everyone* must understand not only what the company means by Knock Your Socks Off Service but how the organization goes about providing that Knock Your Socks Off Service. The resources for providing Knock Your Socks Off Service must be available to people in the organization. You must understand your customers' expectations—what they are today *and* also what they will be tomorrow. You must have motivated employees. You must understand how to build a knock-their-socks-off-service attitude in your employees, and you must sustain it.

A big task? Certainly, but far from impossible as Disney, Marriott, Federal Express, Ritz-Carlton Hotels, Zytec, and countless other companies are proving every day. The key to sustaining Knock Your Socks Off Service is using a systemic approach to implement a service-improvement effort. That's what *Sustaining Knock Your Socks Off Service* is all about. However, before packing your good intentions and starting along the path you believe leads to customer satisfaction and loyalty, you should become aware of the many distractions that can lure you from a straight-and-narrow focus on the customer. We'll look at the dozen most common distractions in Chapter 4.

4

The Dangerous Dozen Distractions

There's the story about the fellow who saw his friend peering down at the ground, obviously looking for something. "Dropped my car keys," responded the friend when asked. After about an hour of scouring the area, which, being under a streetlamp, was well lit, the first man asked his friend,

"Are you sure you dropped your keys here?"

"Oh, no," said the friend. "I dropped them down the block. I'm just looking here because the light is better."

When it comes to service quality, too many organizations are "looking where the light is better" rather than in the areas of real importance. They are looking for tools without understanding what it is they have to fix. Someone comes back from a quality seminar and says, "Teams. I hear at Xerox they have lots of teams. We need some teams." Another person puts down the latest issue of the newest quality newsletter and says, "Leadership. That's what we're lacking around here. Too many managers and not enough leaders. Got to get some leaders."

Teams, leadership, empowerment, Total Quality Management (TQM), and the rest of what we refer to as the Dangerous Dozen have taken their turn in the quality spotlight. Are they good tools? Sure, if used in the right situation. A hammer is a good tool, too—for pounding nails. But if the copy machine repair person ever pulled out a sixteen-ounce ball peen, you'd show justifiable concern for your photocopy machine.

Today's hot management philosophy, TQM, used to be TQA, which used to be TQC, which used to be just QC, which . . . you get the point. Tools change over time. Their value changes as customer expectations change. QC (quality control) based on inspection was just fine until customer expectations of product quality changed. QA (quality assurance), was the ticket until customer expectations expanded beyond product into all activities of a company, including service quality. If you hope to *sustain* service quality in the face of changing customer expectations, you can't do it solely by relying on the tool *du jour*. You need more than tools. You need a method for evaluating and selecting the *proper* tools for your organization. You need a *system*.

Operating from that premise, we have resisted the temptation to look where the light is and simply put new twists on what everyone else is writing about—quality tools. This is not a book about specific tasks and tactics (although you'll find many examples of Knock Your Socks Off Service implementations). It's a book about sustaining a service focus and ensuring service systems work in the long-term best interests of the customers and the company. We didn't want to burden you with a lot of philosophical baggage. Lest you become tool-focused rather than system-focused, here are twelve areas where care should be exercised.

Empowerment

In most of the literature today, empowerment is treated as something new, something grand, something that must be granted to employees from on high. It usually is bounded by parameters; for example, employees are empowered to spend up to $500 to solve a customer problem. True, this type of empowerment has a place in delivering high-quality service and managing for high-quality service. However, companies that sustain Knock Your Socks Off Service don't empower through an endless list of policies and rules. They empower by creating a service vision, developing a service strategy, and establishing a service system that supports the vision and carries out the strategy. They empower by hiring good people, training them well, and making local heroes of employees who act empowered on the customer's behalf.

In a nutshell, *sustaining empowerment* are the words chiseled into a 6,000-pound rock resting just outside the front door of Stew Leonard's, the worlds largest and most profitable dairy store.

OUR POLICY

RULE 1: THE CUSTOMER IS ALWAYS RIGHT!

RULE 2: IF THE CUSTOMER IS EVER WRONG, REREAD RULE 1.

Stew Jr., and each of his employees know, live, and breathe the truth behind the slogan: CUSTOMERS ARE NOT ALWAYS RIGHT, BUT THEY ARE *ALWAYS* OUR CUSTOMERS. That knowledge is what empowers Leonard and his crew to knock the socks off their customers with unparalleled service.

Teams

It's in vogue today to put people on teams—self-managed teams, project teams, quality teams, ad hoc teams, temporary teams. The literature is full of theory supported by examples of why teams are a good thing. We support most of those notions. If grouping your people into teams improves service quality, great. But forming a team is an activity, it's not a result. Before you form a team, you need to know what it is you want the team to accomplish. Before you decide what you want the team to accomplish, you need to know if the accomplishment makes any difference at all to your customers. You can't make those decisions without a framework. It's having that decision framework, not forming a lot of teams, that enables you to sustain Knock Your Socks Off Service.

Total Quality Management

Total Quality Management (TQM) is a set of tools, a set of methodologies, a vague direction that says "do good and avoid evil." Quality is good, nonquality is evil; we couldn't agree more. But implementation of total quality in the product sense is different from total quality in the service sense. Products and services are different. Different services necessarily involve different tools, different methodologies. To say "I embrace the concept of Total Quality Management" says nothing about implementation. Implementation implies a system. *Sustaining Knock Your Socks Off Service* is first about systems. Until the service system is in place, it is premature to talk about tools and methods.

Product Quality

Today, high-quality products are the table stakes required to play the game. Product quality is the primary promise you make to your customers. If you don't have it, this book won't help you. Prompt delivery of a product that doesn't work is not a marketplace differentiator. Your core offering—the reason people come to you with open hands and open wallets—must be in shape *before* the quality of service becomes an issue.

Service Basics

If you're thinking in terms of *sustaining* service quality, you already understand what it takes to deliver Knock Your Socks Off Service. You can probably cite numerous examples of when your organization and its people did just that. You know good service when you see it, and more than likely, you're familiar with some service concepts like Moments of Truth, service strategy, cycles of service, and the like. Although this book provides plenty of examples of companies using these concepts, here we're more concerned with breaking new ground than rehashing information available elsewhere. This book looks at service basics not as isolated events but as activities that are part of an overall service system.

Gurus

There's value in W. Edwards Deming's fourteen points. Truth dwells in Joseph Juran's house of quality. Phil Crosby, Tom

Peters, Max DePree, Shigeru Mizuno—whoever your favorite guru is, whatever your favorite quality technique—they probably have a place in your service-quality effort. Not just because an article appeared in *Harvard Business Review* or the guru had his special on PBS, but because the philosophy fits with *your* service vision, *your* service strategy, *your* service system; most important, the philosophy helps you exceed the expectations of *your* customers. You know more about your business and your customers than do Deming, Peters, Mizuno, Connellan, and Zemke combined. This book shows you how to put that knowledge to work, making Knock Your Socks Off Service the signature of your company.

A Single, Exhaustive, All-Encompassing Plan

There are folks who believe such a plan exists. But every candidate for the "One Best Way of Improving Service Quality" award we've seen up close and personally is either hopelessly general—as in "Step One: Understand Your Customers"—or so detailed as to be useful to only one company in a million. Sure, you can copy the plans they used at Xerox, Motorola, or IBM. You'll probably end up with a great copier or microchip or computer company. Of course, if you're running a hospital, that might not be the way to go.

One way or another, your customers will tell you where to go. This book is about avoiding the path paved with good intentions in favor of the road less traveled—developing a systematic approach to service quality that drives a plan to meet *your* customers' expectations.

Technical Psychological Jargon

Although a great deal of this book deals with human psychology and motivational theory, you won't find a lot of psychobabble or complex theorizing as to why people behave as they do. That's not to say such theories of human behavior aren't important. They are, critically so. But rather than present straight theory, rather than lecture you that "random rewards beget regular behavior," we'd prefer to tell you about Macaroni's, a small, out-of-the-way Italian restaurant.

Like most restaurants, Macaroni's suffered from small crowds on Monday and Tuesday nights. The restaurant had a reputation for good food and good service, but that alone was not enough to draw more than minimal diners during the first part of the week. What the restaurant needed was high-impact behavior that could be sustained over time, not a one-time promotion. Owner Phil Romano, who later went on to found Fuddruckers, a national hamburger chain, could have chosen any number of activities to bolster Monday and Tuesday crowds. He could have offered reduced meal prices, free beverages or free deserts, held a special prize drawing, and the like—pretty ordinary experiences as far as dining out goes. Instead, Phil opted to give his customers a real knock-your-socks-off experience.

If you happen to be dining at Macaroni's on a Monday or Tuesday night, instead of a bill at the end of your meal you receive a letter informing you that, because Macaroni's mission is to make people feel like guests, once each month—on a randomly selected Monday or Tuesday—diners are not charged for their meals. That's positively outrageous service. It's random and unexpected, it's out of proportion to the circumstances, it invites the customer to play or be highly involved, it creates compelling word-of-mouth, and it results in *lifetime* buying decisions. And, by the way, it's based on sound psychological theory—variable interval reinforcement—which means that reinforcement for an action occurs after varying or random periods of time have elapsed.

But theory isn't what's important. What's important is that people are eating at Macaroni's on Monday and Tuesday when other restaurants are deserted. The free meals reduce Macaroni's profit margin about 3.3 percent, but the restaurant is full eight nights a month when it normally would be empty. Incremental profit more than makes up for the dip in percentage.

Research Methodology

It's not part of our plan to brief you on twenty-seven techniques for learning more about learning more from your customers. We assume you do some kind of market research and that you understand your customers' expectations. Perhaps you've even taken some steps toward delivering service that meets those expectations. What you'll learn from this book is how to *sustain* the efforts you have in place. How to keep your service quality efforts from running out of gas. How to keep your people enthused and motivated, not through gimmicks and promotions but by creating a sound service system that perpetuates your service vision and strategy.

Personnel Management

One of the basic tenets of Knock Your Socks Off Service is that you must start with good people, or you won't get started at all. If your problem is with people, your problem is beyond the scope of this book; however, be advised that poor service is more often the result of a poor service system than of poor people. A bad system is more apt to sap the motivation out of a dedicated employee than a dedicated employee is apt to change the system. Changing the system is *your* job.

Statistical Mind Control

We mention measurement a lot. There is only one honest place to start any quality-improvement program, and that is with proof. Data. However, to deliver Knock Your Socks Off Service, you have to look at data differently from how a statistical researcher might. Good data are not just quantitative; they are also qualitative. They are one or two sentences written at the bottom of a guest information report. They are the mumbled comment of a customer walking away from the counter. They are the phone complaint about a late delivery. You need a system that captures all kinds of data, not just numbers, and translates the data into information you can use to exceed the expectations of your customers.

Verbal Nit-Picking

We don't nitpick the distinction between leaders and managers, goals and objectives, outputs and results, or engage in other arcane linguistic arguments. We believe words shouldn't get in the way of meaning. That's why you'll find here lots of examples of Knock Your Socks Off Service. Sometimes a written "picture" is worth a thousand words of explanatory theory.

The point is simply that if you want to find your car keys, you look for them where you lost them, not where the light's the best. If you want to sustain Knock Your Socks Off Service, you start with the big picture—your service system—not ad hoc activities that are in the glare of current popularity. Let yourself get caught by the Dangerous Dozen Distractions or any other panacea, and you're in danger of losing focus on the *one* thing that really matters—sustaining Knock Your Socks Off Service for your customers!

5

The Five Elements of a Service System

The pilot's voice resonates over the intercom. "I've got good news and bad news," he tells passengers. "The bad news is all our navigation systems are inoperative. We're lost. We haven't the foggiest idea where we're headed. The good news is we've got a 200 mile per hour tail wind." Sitting in the aisle seat on this transatlantic flight, would you be comfortable with the pilot's announcement? Foolish question? Sure it is. On the other hand, having spent over a decade researching, writing about, and consulting on service quality, we've seen more than a few well-intentioned service-improvement efforts flying along with 200 mile per hour enthusiasm and an inoperative navigation system. Management has no idea where it is headed, and there's nary a nervous twitch.

Flying Blind

The late George S. Odiorne, management thinker par excellence, suggested that people sometimes become so immersed in "getting there" that they forget where "there" is. People, he said, can become so absorbed in their activities that they lose sight of what they're supposed to be accomplishing. He called this the "activity trap."

People caught in the activity trap include sales personnel who are so busy making calls and submitting proposals that they fail to address their customers' requirements, hotel clerks so concerned with the efficiency of putting people in rooms that they can't take the time to answer questions about entertainment options, and checkout clerks so busy uttering "Have a nice day" that they don't notice the shopper is harried, with a couple of tired and cranky kids hanging on her leg. Organizations caught in the activity trap include companies that "improve" processes without understanding the impact of those processes on their customers, companies that evaluate improvement efforts by counting the number of meetings held and the number of charts on the wall, and organizations more concerned with their people contacting customers than connecting with them.

For example, United Airlines plugged into the concerns of many American business leaders with a poignant "focus on the customer" commercial. In soft focus, shirt sleeves rolled up, tie loosened, head down, a contrite company president addresses his staff. A long-time customer, he tells the solemn gathering, tired of a relationship built on voice mail and fax has taken his business elsewhere. For the company president, the long-time customer's defection is a Damascus experience: He's seen the light. "We've lost touch with our customers," he tells his staff. "But that's going to change." He passes among them, handing out plane tickets.

We can envision the next working day: All across America, corporate executives gather their staffs, roll up their sleeves, and pass out plane tickets. "We've lost touch with customers," they parrot the commercial, "but that's going to change." Ultimately, what really changes? Unless there are in place specific customer-satisfaction goals, specific defined behaviors, established customer feedback mechanisms, and other systemic approaches to service quality, not much changes other than the size of the travel budget. *In most cases the people with the plane tickets are flying blind.* They have no objectives. There's nothing specific they're supposed to do with customers. They are charged with contacting customers, but have no plan for connecting with those customers. No one has thought through what information is important to gather from the customers or how that information will be used to improve service quality. There is customer contact activity but no customer retention *system.*

Too many companies trying to improve their service quality are also flying blind. Their efforts lack clear purpose and well-stated goals. They have defined no specific behaviors that enhance the ability of their people to satisfy customers. They haven't thought through what information should be gathered from customers, how they should survey customers to gather that information, where in the organization the information should go, or how they'll formulate action based on the information they gather. United's ad was partly right—customer contact *is* important—but it's not enough. You also need a system.

A Service System That Supports Excellence

Sustaining Knock Your Socks Off Service requires more than a swift kick from a dissatisfied customer or an immediate fix of enthusiasm. Events like these help, but they're not enough for *sustained* excellence. Sustained excellence requires a service system. A service system is all the apparatus, physical and procedural, that employees must have at their disposal to meet customer needs and deliver and sustain Knock Your Socks Off Service. The operative word is *sustain*. A rollicking meeting, clever slogans, and eye-catching posters provide a good start, but they go only so far in motivating people to provide outstanding service. Education and training add another dimension. You can have highly trained and motivated people but if you put them into a dumb system, then everyone loses—you, me, the customer, the staff, the stockholders.

Consider the Case of the Telltale Tray. Kathy Ridge, manager of training development and communications, TVA, Chattanooga, tells the story of going to a grocery store one evening to buy food for the family of a friend who was in the hospital. When she asked about getting a deli tray, she was informed that the woman who made them up had already left for the evening. "I didn't know making deli trays was such a specialized skill," was Kathy's first thought. But meats and cheese still seemed like a good idea, so she decided to create her own deli assortment. She asked the clerk to thin-slice a half-pound of ham. He did, wrapping the slices in butcher paper, writing the price on the package, and putting it on the deli counter. The process was repeated with turkey, then roast beef, Swiss cheese, and so on. About the time Kathy had more than $20 worth of food on the counter, she noticed a stack of empty plastic deli trays on a back table. She had a sudden inspiration: "How much for one of those trays with the plastic lid?"

"Lady," came the tart response, "you can't buy a tray unless you buy a tray."

"Excuse me?"

"You can't buy a tray unless you buy a tray."

Kathy's first surmise was that she was dealing with a front-line person in desperate need of a personality transplant and an IQ booster shot. Belatedly, she realized the real issue: The store's inventory control system was based on counting trays. It wasn't that the clerk didn't want to help her. He just couldn't see how to do so.

There are no bad guys in this story. The financial people who decided to use deli trays as an inventory control device harbor no evil intentions against friends of the hospitalized. They have a business to run—to run as efficiently as possible. The clerk wants to help, but there are company policies and procedures to follow. There is a system, albeit a lousy one. In the Case of the Telltale Tray, it's the *service system* that's the guilty party. The service system motivated Kathy to take her future business, not just for deli trays but for all her other groceries as well, to another store. The delinquent deli counter cost the grocery a customer, not because its people lacked enthusiasm or motivation, but because from the customer's perspective it has a lousy service system.

Having examined the service performance of thousands of people and hundreds of systems, we've concluded that there are far more dumb systems than there are dumb people. Put a good performer in a dumb system, and it's far more likely that the system will wear down the good performer than that the good performer will be able to sustain high-quality service. Unfortunately, the customer simply experiences poor performance. Most customers are unable to distinguish between poor *personnel* performance and poor *system* performance. So they get upset, not at the system, but at the person. They berate the front-line person and move on—to the competition.

The Five Elements of a Service System

Obviously, your goal is to create a sound service system. Service systems can become highly complex, especially in large and geographically dispersed organizations. However, no matter how complex the service, three functional elements (inputs, activities/behaviors, and outputs/results) and two guiding elements (goals and feedback) comprise the core of all service delivery systems.

The functional elements of a system are illustrated in Figure 5-1. Inputs drive activities/behaviors to produce outputs/results. *Inputs* are money, time, and people. They provide the resources to carry out activities such as calling on customers, analyzing markets, delivering goods, and greeting customers. *Results* are the measurable output of the activities. Market share, customer retention, product quality, cycle time, and profitability are all examples of results.

In a simple manufacturing system, for example, wood, nails, and glue (inputs) are transformed by the building process (activity) to produce birdhouses (result). In a simple accounting system, revenue and cost of sales data (inputs) are transformed by the accounting process (activity) to produce the financial reports (result). In a simple service system, time, money, and people (inputs) are transformed by service behaviors such as analyzing customers' needs and cheerfully greeting customers (activity) to deliver the service customers require (result).

Figure 5-1. Functional system elements.

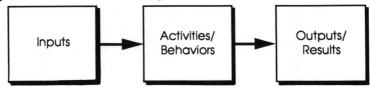

Inputs, activities, and results are the functional aspects of a system. As long as inputs are supplied and activities take place, some type of result will be produced. Recall the transatlantic flight described earlier. As long as the plane has fuel (input), it will keep flying (activity) and racking up miles (result), but it will move in no particular direction unless it has a destination and a navigation system. What about your service system? Is it heading in the right direction? To answer that question, you must add the two guiding elements to the system model: *goals* and *feedback* (Figure 5-2). Once our transatlantic flight has a goal of where to land and a functioning navigation system (feedback) to keep it on course, it becomes a complete system.

A system functions very much like a furnace. The heating system itself is neutral. A thermostat does not "care" if the temperature is 55°F or 85°F. It activates the furnace based on the temperature (goal) that we set. Then, at an appropriate time, it releases the resources necessary to maintain the appropriate room temperature. Goals and feedback are the navigation tools and temperature tools of your service system. Goals provide direction; feedback tells you if you're on course.

In common usage, people often confuse or interchange the various elements of a system. For example, "activities"—or what we do—are often confused with "results"—what we accomplish. Flying the plane (activity) isn't the same as landing

Figure 5-2. Service quality as a system.

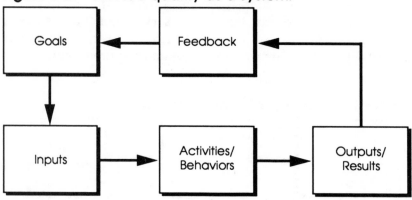

in Brussels (result). Visiting customers (activity) isn't the same as retaining customers (result). Smiling (activity) isn't the same as customer satisfaction (result). Customer service is a set of activities; it is neither a goal nor a result. In fact, if an organization emphasizes customer-service activities at the expense of the other four system elements, it lures people into Odiorne's activity trap—people can get so caught up in the customer-service activity that they lose sight of customer satisfaction, customer loyalty, and customer retention. They have no contextual framework for their assigned activities. You've no doubt experienced the result of this situation—a glassy stare from a disinterested sales clerk and a rote recitation of "Thank-you-for-shopping-here-and-have-a-nice-day. Next!"

Customer satisfaction, customer loyalty, and customer retention are examples of customer-service goals. The result of customer-service activities is the degree to which customers actually are satisfied, remain loyal, and stay on as paying customers. Just as activities and results are often confused, goals and results are often incorrectly equated with one another: Goals are what we want, results are what we get. If the system is functioning as we anticipate, goals and results will be one and the same; however, that equivalence cannot be an assumption. Goals and results must be continuously compared. Measuring, recording, comparing, and reporting differences between goals and results is feedback.

Continuous Feedback

Feedback is a key system element for sustaining Knock Your Socks Off Service. Goals provide people with direction; feedback tells them if they're on course. Without feedback, your service effort is a transatlantic flight with no navigation tools, flying along on auto pilot with no sense of direction until it inevitably runs out of gas.

Short-term motivational efforts, "smile training," and punishment of non-service-oriented behavior do not produce sustained Knock Your Socks Off Service. At best, the quick fix produces spikes in service activity. But because these spikes are based on short-term efforts rather than system changes, they seldom result in sustained excellence. Even instances of outstanding service characterized by employee performance above and beyond the call of duty may be indicative of serious service-system problems. "Above and beyond" is good; however, if you stop to think about it, many instances of above and beyond the call of duty service are necessitated by system breakdowns.

When a Nordstrom's sales associate personally delivers an item of clothing to a customer's home after business hours because in-store alterations weren't completed on time, that's outstanding service and a laudable act of customer service. From a system perspective, however, one must ask why the alterations weren't completed on time. When an airline reservations clerk dons a parka and boots to retrieve a piece of luggage misplaced on the tarmac, that's above and beyond her job description. But do we know why such action was necessary? The server who reduces your dinner bill because your steak arrived not to your liking may recover your good will. But the underlying issues are why was the steak cooked wrong in the first place and how the restaurant will ensure that the problem doesn't occur again.

Don't misunderstand. Recovery from system breakdowns will always be a fact of service life, and the potential for Knock Your Socks Off Service recovery should be part of your service-delivery system. Too many service systems are designed as if nothing will ever go wrong. That's not reality. However, the fewer system breakdowns that occur, the more resources are available to improve the system—to raise the consistent level of service on a daily basis and the level of recovery when things go amuck. Without continuous feedback—continuous comparison of goals and results—consistent levels of service quality are unlikely, if not impossible.

Uncovering Customer Dissatisfaction

Opportunities to more effectively use feedback abound. For example, a common financial measurement used by distributors is days sales outstanding (DSO), essentially the number of days customers take to pay their bills. Confronted with an unacceptable number, most companies concentrate on improving their collection process. In proceeding down that path, one of our clients started examining in detail the underlying reasons for late payments. She found some expected "reasons" of the-dog-ate-my-payment variety: "Tight cash flow this month"; "Mm, I'll have to check"; and "Thought that had already been taken care of." However, she also found a substantial number of late payments caused by customer dissatisfaction. Customers were not upset enough to complain, but they were unhappy enough so that they didn't get too upset if they missed the payment date by a day or week or month.

Noting the trend, our client quickly instituted some changes in the shipping process, which was accounting for most of the customer dissatisfaction. Over time, DSO started decreasing. By improving its shipping process, the company realized faster payment of its bills *and* improved customer satisfaction. The company also changed the way customer surveys were performed. Representatives now talk to customers more frequently in order to catch operational problems before they become customer-satisfaction problems.

When feedback indicates a gap between goals and results, you can adjust either the inputs to the system or the activities within the system. Change the inputs when feedback tells you they are inadequate to support the activities required to meet customer expectations. Alter activities when they don't result in meeting customer expectations. For instance, in our simple system for manufacturing birdhouses, feedback may tell you that the perches are falling off. The solution might change the inputs—use a higher quality brand of glue. It might involve a change in activities—change the depth of the holes in which the perches are mounted. It may mean both use a better-quality glue *and* change the hole depth. In the same manner, feedback from dissatisfied customers might indicate a change in inputs—hire front-line people with a different behavioral profile. It might require an activity change—don't use deli trays as an inventory control mechanism. Or it may again require a change in both—hire differently *and* use another method of inventory control. We'll see more about using feedback to improve service quality later in the book.

Revealing Service Defects

Sorting out what to change can be challenging under any circumstances. It can be particularly challenging in a service system where the customer is part of the delivery system, and even more so when you consider that there might be multiple "customers." For example, one of the reasons for Smoke Stoppers' (a program developed by The National Center for Health Promotion) unusually high long-term success rate is that one of the program developers realized the initial program ignored an integral part of its systems approach to quitting smoking—the people who interacted with the person trying to stop smoking. A segment was added to the program showing family members, friends, and coworkers how to help the person kick the habit.

Feedback is the "learning ability" of a system. Transforming feedback into action to correct the system enables you to both correct defects in the system and change the system as customer expectations change. Customers may stop buying from a company's mail order catalogue because its red sweaters are consistently "too pink," but they may also stop buying because red is no longer the "in" color. Without systematic feedback, the company is unable to detect either the defective dye process or the alteration in customer desires.

Most companies do a fairly good job of addressing product-feedback issues. They usually have a method for identifying when their internal processes are defective. Their market research and buying-trend information tell them when the market is changing. But they don't always have information that tells them *why* customers may be buying elsewhere. Companies don't often collect feedback on the customer's total experience. For instance, was the service too slow? Did questions go unanswered? Was the information given unreliable? Was the company just plain hard to do business with? Do customers perceive the sales and service people as not very helpful, unresponsive, or unreliable?

In order to sustain Knock Your Socks Off Service, you need to look beyond traditional feedback from only internal processes. Instead, think of feedback from a system perspective—information that helps your organization perform at peak levels.

Advantages of the Systems Approach to Service

For the company intent on sustaining Knock Your Socks Off Service, the service-system approach to an organization has some distinct advantages over the traditional organizational chart. An organizational chart is an administrative tool. It shows how people are grouped together—who reports to whom. It does not address how the organization functions to meet or exceed the expectations of its customers.

On the other hand, the service-system view shows how work gets done. It defines the inputs required to support the work activity that produces the outputs. Feedback tells us if the output is meeting our goals and if the goals are appropriate. If output matches the goals, but customers are not satisfied, the goals are inappropriate.

Consider the case of the California State Automobile Association (CSAA). When CSAA was founded in the early 1900s, clients with questions about their insurance were likely to walk down the street to see their agent. Some eighty years later, the company, with $3.2 billion in assets, was still organized to handle walk-in traffic. The company had not yet realized that most people today want to do business by phone when it's most convenient for them, which could mean late at night or early in the morning. In addition to a Monday through Friday 8:30 to 5:00 orientation, the company was organized functionally. It had insurance specialists, travel specialists, and so forth. If customers had more than one question, odds were they would be switched from specialist to specialist. Without a feedback system, CSAA could measure each of its activities, find it to be efficient, and still not satisfy its customers' expectations. In fact, to "satisfy" customers, the company added more people to improve customer service, not surprisingly with little success. Only recently has it started a massive redesign of its business system.

Every top service organization we've encountered in our research without exception uses a systems approach to sustain high-quality service. They align every element of their operation in both apparent and not so apparent ways to knock their customers' socks off.

- Disney does it when it touches up the paint on the horsehead hitching post on Main Street every night. It does it by building a culture that it calls personnel "casting." It does it by spending four days training grounds keepers to answer questions guests might ask. That's not piecemeal—that's using a systems approach.
- Ritz-Carleton Hotels does it when a frequent guest requests a foam pillow at one property and the next day every other Ritz-Carleton hotel can call up that guest's record and note the special request. That's not piecemeal—that's using a systems approach.
- Rally's Hamburgers (billed as the fastest takeout in the West) does it when it sets a goal and puts a system in place that allows it to deliver an order to a driver within thirty seconds of the car pulling up to the drive-through window. That's not piecemeal—that's using a systems approach.

Knock Your Socks Off Service is more than a string of occasional events. It's superior service that happens consistently, day after day. It's the result of a systems approach to providing service. When your concern is *sustaining* Knock Your Socks Off Service, you must build a system that consciously supports the level of service your customers expect.

6

Putting System Results in Perspective

In 1966, we created the Christopher Columbus Annual Better Leadership Award. It's presented in honor of Christopher Columbus, who started his venture not quite sure where he was going. Upon arriving, he did not know where he was. Upon returning, he could not describe where he had been. (We find it appropriate that Columbus's venture was a federally funded project.)

Too many organizations attempting to sustain high-quality service operate like Christopher Columbus. They're not sure where they're going. They don't know where they are when they get there. And if questioned, they can't describe where they've been. They set sail on a customer-service voyage guided only by a vague sense of "reaching the East by sailing west." They may use a service mantra, usually crafted by the corporate communications department—YOU DON'T GET TO BE #1 BY TREATING CUSTOMERS LIKE #2—or some equally clever but vague turn of phrase. They cast off with no explicit route in mind, just the misguided belief that if they treat customers "well," high-quality customer service lies just over the horizon.

With this approach, high-quality service will always be "just over the horizon." In Chapter 5, we discussed the need to take a systems approach to sustaining Knock Your Socks Off Service. A customer-service system consists of five elements: the three functional elements of inputs, activities/behaviors, and outputs/results; and the two guiding elements of goals and feedback.

The Importance of Goals

Although it's popular these days to bash goal setting, the truth is that all organizations that consistently deliver great service have purpose and goals driving their service-delivery systems. At Country Fair theme park, the purpose is to deliver fun. There are some specific goals that focus on cleanliness, friendliness, service, and show. Specific measures that tie into each of these four areas are also targeted.

At Ritz-Carleton Hotels, where the service vision was put into words before the first property opened in 1983, President and COO Horst Schultze notes that employees can't be expected to deliver first-rate, five-star service if management can't define it. And he backs that statement with a first-rate system. The National Center for Health Promotion, developers and deliverers of the highly rated Smoke Stoppers program, had as an early driving vision the concept that THE MOST IMPORTANT PERSON IN THE WORLD IS THE PROGRAM PARTICIPANT AND THE SECOND MOST IMPORTANT PERSON IN THE WORLD IS THE PROGRAM INSTRUCTOR. That purpose still drives every system, every policy, every procedure, and every goal the Center has. Fred Smith tells his Federal Express troops that they carry the most important cargo in the world. And they measure their service every day against twelve indicators that comprise their service-quality index.

In short, a sense of purpose and well-articulated goals are critical to sustain superior service. You can't sustain something you can't define. It's no accident that both Federal Express and Ritz-Carleton have strong service purposes and goals driving their service systems, and that both have won the Malcolm Baldrige National Quality Award. Granted, goal setting can be abused, but sooner or later a company has to go to the bank. Results are important. Goals, as the up-front expectation of results produced by a service system, provide indispensable direction for sustaining Knock Your Socks Off Service.

The Difference Between Outcome and Process

Service results can be divided into two categories: *outcome* results and *process* results. Getting a favorable mortgage is an example of an outcome. So is having your car serviced correctly the first time or having a nice room at a hotel. The hassle in obtaining a mortgage is a process result. How long you have to wait for a service writer is also a process result. Being treated courteously in the hotel restaurant enhances your hotel experience; it is a process result.

The outcome/process distinction is an important one for sustaining Knock Your Socks Off Service. The rash of quality literature on process management and Total Quality Management (TQM) has tended to blur the outcome/process distinction—to the detriment of service quality. The TQM approach takes a mechanical view of process, breaking down a system into measurable increments and micromanaging each segment to produce a tightly specified result. This approach may work for manufacturing a widget, but it is not adequate for ensuring superior service.

Process from a service perspective is *not* a technical series of steps that produces a tightly specified outcome; it's the customer's experience of the process he or she goes through to obtain the outcome. Although customers may initially come to you for an outcome—what you can do, create, produce, or deliver—the process by which that outcome is delivered is at least equally important. In some instances, it is even more important.

A Pathmark supermarket in Brick, New Jersey, created floorwalkers, or greeters, in stores where a large amount of business comes from senior citizens. All their stores have well-staffed courtesy desks where customers usually have their questions answered. But for a senior citizen, it can be an inconvenience walking the distance to the desk for an answer. So Pathmark has floorwalkers patrol the aisles, helping customers find what they need, reaching the top shelf when it is difficult, and making price adjustments if necessary. Seniors may *initially* shop at Pathmark for the products and prices (outcome), but the extra service (process) ensures that they'll *keep* shopping there. The combination of outcome and process means they'll probably recommend Pathmark to friends and neighbors.

The outcome sought by people who dine out is a good

meal at a reasonable price. But beyond that outcome, A Piece of Quiet restaurant in Denver provides a unique experience for couples with children. Recognizing that finding a baby-sitter can be a hassle, A Piece of Quiet uses child care as a drawing card. Within the restaurant are two separate dining areas—one for adults, one for children. The Kids' Cafe is more than a baby-sitting service; it's a place where children can be both entertained and educated about the dining-out experience. While the kids are being entertained, parents enjoy a quiet meal together. In addition to good food and service (outcome), the restaurant provides parents and children with a unique dining experience (process).

Smoke Stoppers has the highest long-term success rate in the country (outcome). Its program quality has been cited in two different surgeon general's reports (outcome). But the experience participants have going through the program (process) is so outstanding that even participants who later return to smoking, frequently recommend the program to others. Michael Samuelson, president and CEO of The National Center for Health Promotion, originally developed and guided the training program that turns out the high-caliber instructors able to consistently deliver that level of Knock Your Socks Off Service.

"Batteries not included" printed in a catalog ad generally means that the customer is responsible for picking up or ordering batteries. Not, however, when people order from the J. C. Penney Company catalog. Computer programmers search the Penney catalog for every item that needs batteries. Every time a customer-service operator punches in an order for a battery-powered product, a flashing message identifies what size and how many are needed. Items that need them are sold with batteries more than 90 percent of the time. That's a convenience for customers (process) beyond the purchase of the initial product (outcome), and it helps sales.

Complete Customer Satisfaction

Companies that retain customers pay as much attention to the process customers experience as they do to the outcome expected. A company's purpose encompasses both process results and outcome results. And both are tracked in *measurable* terms.

While many companies talk about service systems, few of them develop all five elements of a system. Rhetoric does little to cause long-term behavior change. A properly designed system, however, can produce the kind of changes necessary to sustain Knock Your Socks Off Service. And the starting point of that system is clearly articulated goals that take both outcome and process into account. Our experience with a wide variety of companies and the way they measure service results has led us to three conclusions:

1. **When a company talks about complete customer satisfaction but measures only service outcome, customer-satisfaction evaluations will be misleading and often inconsistent.** Because the company does not measure the customer's experience in obtaining the desired outcome, it has no insight into the customer's experience. If you can't stipulate how you want a customer to feel about having done business with you, you can't create the feeling.

2. **When a company talks about complete customer satisfaction but measures only the process (experience) customers go through in obtaining their outcome, customer satisfaction evaluations will also be misleading and often inconsistent.** If you don't track outcome quality, you can't improve it and will probably miss shifts in the marketplace. (Note: many firms fool themselves by measuring only internal process to the exclusion of measuring how customers experience the company's processes. The company that does this receives no feedback on customers' changing expectations.)

3. **When a company measures both outcomes and process, it will deliver and sustain Knock Your Socks Off Service.** Sustaining high-quality service is the result of keeping focused on changing customer expectations and continually modifying internal processes to maintain a leadership position.

An interesting consequence of the above conclusions is that when either outcome or process is emphasized at the expense of the other, customer surveys—the most common means of evaluating service performance—will be inconsistent. Customers will provide conflicting evaluations of a company's service, which prove to be of little help for improving service levels. Wess Rydell, who owns or has a major interest in ten auto dealerships in the upper Midwest, is an evangelist for outstanding service. Ask him to define his job, and he says his mission is simply to "create customer enthusiasm, employee satisfaction, financial performance, market penetration, and quality." Customer enthusiasm, employee satisfaction, and quality all contribute to the total customer experience. Financial performance and market penetration are derivatives of Knock Your Socks Off Service—customers buying cars.

The Customer Retention Grid

What an organization chooses to measure and report not only determines the level of its service quality but also its ability to improve customer retention. In our work we use the Customer Retention Grid in Figure 6-1 to ensure that outcome and process results are equal partners in the service system. The two axes of the matrix are Outcome and Process; Outcome answers the question, "Did the customer get what he or she wanted?" Process speaks to the customer's perception of the service experience.

We've labeled the Outcome axis from 1 to 3, with 1 being a value-added outcome—the customer not only got what he or she expected but something extra besides—and 3 being the outcome did not meet the customer's expectations. The Process axis is labeled from A to C, with A representing a terrific experience that dazzled the customer beyond all expectations and C being a case when the customer is to a small or large degree dissatisfied with the process.

An A-1 customer is an Advocate: You consistently exceed outcome expectations and dealing with you is a rewarding and/ or interesting experience. On the other hand, chances are a C-3 customer isn't around anymore. Not only did you not deliver

Figure 6-1. The customer retention grid.

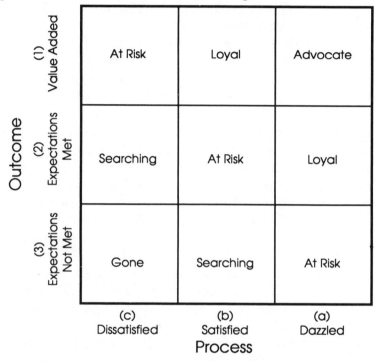

what was expected, you inflicted a lot of hassle and pain in the process of not providing what was wanted. The point of this grid is that customers do not view your business in only one dimension—outcome *or* process. A customer is looking for two things: the desired outcome *and* an experience that enhances the outcome. If a company sets only outcome goals and measures service quality only in terms of outcome, it gets a distorted picture of customer satisfaction, loyalty, and retention.

That's not the case at Carl Sewell's Village Cadillac of Dallas, where Sewell retains his perennial position as one of the top dozen Cadillac dealers in the country. When our friend Craig takes his Cadillac in for service, the service is done right the first time, every time. Additionally, small items needing attention but which are not on Craig's list are taken care of. (Level 1 outcome). Beyond Craig's service expectations, he's never had to hassle dropping off his car, picking it up, or paying the bill. Questions are answered in terms Craig understands. (Level A experience).

Craig's experience is no accident. Sewell makes a concerted effort to ensure that everything about the customer's buying experience is positive. Nearly 90 percent of his employees have incentive bonuses based on service quality. Computers track the time to deliver the car after the customer has paid the bill (average time is three minutes). Sewell conducts extensive customer surveys on *all* aspects of the service experience to find out what customers expect, what they want, and how what they get compares to competition. Our friend Craig is an advocate for Sewell. He feels personal loyalty to the dealership that goes beyond the Cadillac product line. That kind of loyalty is important, especially when things don't go as planned.

Another provider of Knock Your Socks Off Service, Longo Toyota of El Monte, California, measures the customer's total experience. Should a problem arise (Level 3 outcome), the dealership's customer relations team has authority to spend up to $500 to resolve the gripe, which means that scratched paint gets touched up without an argument and other minor glitches are taken care of before they can fester into lingering bad feelings. It also means that what started out as a Level 3 outcome can be converted into a Level 2 or even a Level 1 outcome. Longo has been known to dispatch a team of people to a customer's house to wash and wax a car in response to a complaint of a greasy fingerprint left on the dashboard after an oil change (Level A experience in response to a somewhat less than desired outcome).

Despite the occasional service snafu, customers of Village Cadillac, Longo Toyota, and other companies that deliver Knock Your Socks Off Service go away feeling good about their total experience. Studies have shown that customers for whom a problem is quickly and satisfactorily resolved are more likely to remain loyal to the company than customers who never experience a problem. They are also more likely to pass on favorable comments about the company to others.

Doing Business Should Be Easy

Unfortunately, most companies spend a great deal of time measuring outcome and not nearly enough time measuring process. As a result, their service systems don't function well, and they have an uncomfortably high percentage of customers who are at risk, searching, or gone.

Jim King falls into the *searching* category. Jim purchased a Ford Ranger pickup truck from the largest Ford dealer in his area. He was happy with the truck; the price was about what he expected to pay. He told the salesperson up-front that he wanted to pay cash for the truck. When it came time to close the deal, the salesperson proceeded to present both financing and leasing options, despite Jim's insistence that he wanted to pay cash, which the salesperson referred to as "a stupid idea." When Jim expressed reservations about the leasing program and asked questions, the salesperson could not respond directly, but had to ask the sales manager. The dealer had a policy that customers were not allowed to talk to the sales manager. After much negotiation, finally and reluctantly, the salesperson wrote up paperwork for a cash sale, and it was off to the cashier.

After waiting outside the cashier's office for twenty minutes while the salesperson and the cashier "went over the paperwork," Jim was finally ushered to a chair opposite the cashier's huge desk. The cashier also made a pitch for the financing and leasing packages, but she had a computer. Unfortunately, she couldn't make it work. After a fruitless fifteen minutes or so, she finally had her program running. "Now," she proclaimed proudly, she could show Jim "why it was stupid to pay cash." Jim probably would have ignored the comment if she had made good on her promise, but her calculations were so obviously slanted in favor of the loan and leasing program that, with one or two questions, Jim showed her his logic for paying cash. From Jim's perspective, the dubious savings weren't worth the inconvenience of a monthly bill.

Ironically, two weeks after taking delivery on his truck,

Jim received a customer satisfaction survey from the dealer. Ten of the questions dealt with the condition of the truck at the time of delivery (outcome). The balance of the twenty-five-plus questions were marketing items: How much money did Jim earn? What magazines did he read? What sports did he enjoy? There was not one place on the survey for Jim to express his dissatisfaction with how he experienced the closing process.

From its measurements, the Ford dealership won't recognize that Jim is a "searching" customer. He'll actively look somewhere else for his next vehicle. Although he is happy with the truck (Level 2 outcome), Jim obviously had an unpleasant experience buying the truck (Level C experience). Because the Ford dealer tracks only outcome, not customer experience, it can't even attempt to recover Jim's loyalty—it doesn't know that it's lost it. Unlike Longo or Village customers, the Ford dealership's unhappy customers are not inclined to give the dealership a second chance. When asked about the Ford dealership, he tells people "They have a good selection to choose from, but if you can find what you want someplace else, buy it. They're really a hassle to do business with."

7

Determining Performance Indicators and Setting Realistic Goals

An old proverb warns, BE CAREFUL WHAT YOU PRAY FOR; YOUR PRAYERS MIGHT BE ANSWERED. The modern corollary for the service professional is BE CAREFUL WHAT YOU MEASURE; YOU MIGHT GET THE RESULTS YOU ASK FOR.

In Chapter 6, we had the example of an organization that got the results it asked for. The people at the Ford dealership where our colleague Jim bought his Ranger pickup were probably sincerely concerned about customer satisfaction. However, they only measured how customers felt about Ford products and the dealer's new car prep skills. Jim was satisfied with the truck he purchased and the condition it was in when it was delivered. But Jim was also very *dissatisfied* with the sales process he had to endure. The dealership had no mechanism to uncover Jim's dissatisfaction with that process, however; there was no way to measure his degree of dissatisfaction, and no way to correct the root cause of that dissatisfaction. Unfortunately for the dealership, satisfaction with the sales process is significantly related to use of the dealership service after the warranty period, the probability of recommending the dealer-

ship to other potential customers, and the probability of returning there for future purchases—even somewhat related to the
probability of buying another Ford truck anywhere.

Too many organizations are in the same position. They
talk about service. They do a variety of things to try and jump-
start it. They sell it in ads. Top management believes in it. And
they get it in little spikes and spurts. But they don't ever
sustain Knock Your Socks Off Service because they never
measure enough things, they never measure the right things,
and they never measure the things they measure frequently
enough. As obvious as it may sound, if you can't or don't
measure something, you can't improve it. If you want to
continuously deliver Knock Your Socks Off Service, you need a
framework for determining what measurements give a true
picture of your service quality *as perceived by your customers* and
as compared to your goals.

The Customer's Five Criteria for Service

In our book *Delivering Knock Your Socks Off Service*, we introduced a framework for organizing customer requirements and
expectations. Developed by service researchers Leonard Berry,
A. Parasuraman, and Valarie A. Zeithaml, this framework can
logically be extended to a guideline for determining measurement factors for your organization. The framework consists of
five factors that customers use to evaluate service quality. In
descending order of priority, these are:

1. *Reliability*. The ability to provide what is promised,
   dependably and accurately.
2. *Responsiveness*. The willingness to help customers
   promptly. The turnaround time or response time.
3. *Assurance*. The knowledge displayed to customers, and
   your ability to convey trust, competence, and confidence.
4. *Empathy*. The degree of caring and individual attention
   you show customers. The warm feeling customers get
   when doing business with your organization.

5. *Tangibles*. The physical appearance of facilities and equipment. Your own and others' appearance.

Chances are, almost everything you do to and for your customers falls into one of these categories. Consider these common examples:

- When you fulfill a customer order on time, every time with no hassle, you demonstrate *reliability*. When Federal Express says your package will be there by 10:30 A.M. the next business day, it's there by 10:30 A.M. the next business day. That's reliability. Need to trace your order? Federal Express can tell you exactly where your package is in the system or when it was delivered, every time you call. That's reliability as well.

  Reliability is related to your core promise to customers. If you don't keep your core promise, nothing else matters. We tell our clients that in today's competitive market, keeping your core promise represents table stakes—it lets you stay in the game. An airline's core promise, for example, is to get you safely from point A to point B, close to the scheduled time. (We've concluded that luggage is not included in that core promise.) If they break that core promise by landing you in Atlanta instead of Mobile, no amount of courtesy, good food, or cabin attendant care can make up for that lack of reliability.

- Noticing a customer puzzling over a product and quickly offering help and information, shows *responsiveness*. MBNA America, the country's fourth largest bank credit-card issuer, processes requests for credit-line increases within an hour. That's being responsive. So is Domino's pledge of thirty-minute delivery or $3 off the price.

- Smiling and telling a customer "I can help you with that," and doing it, builds a perception of *assur-*

ance in the customer's mind. Infiniti, the luxury-car division of Nissan Motor Company, puts on a six-day "boot camp" for every dealer employee, including clerks and receptionists. Boot camp teaches a receptionist how to help customers beyond merely pointing them to a salesperson. This small action by the receptionist immediately starts to build a sense of assurance in the customer and helps set a positive tone for the entire sales process. After all, if the receptionist is knowledgeable about the product, think how knowledgeable the service technicians must be!

- Being sensitive to an individual customer's needs and treating them as individuals, shows *empathy*. Many companies focus service-improvement efforts on empathy with traditional "smile training" programs. Few follow up with standards that focus on how customers experience the people with whom they come in contact. Contrast that with AT&T Financial Services. This Baldrige Award winner has defined extensive internal standards for treating customers, and it continuously monitors employee performance against those standards.

- While fifth in priority, *tangibles* play an important role in how customers perceive your organization. A nice-looking office or store, attractive catalog, clean delivery trucks, a nicely laid-out proposal, and crisp uniforms all add to a customer's perception of excellent service. Receipts, order forms, bills of lading, invoices, and confirmations are all tangible artifacts of a service performed. Good tangibles remind customers of a service well done.

In short, customers want you to be reliable and responsive; they want you to act in a manner that inspires confidence in your ability to meet their expectations; they want you to treat them as individuals and their concerns as important; and they want you to maintain a physical environment that enhances their experience of doing business with you. These five factors form the foundation upon which customers base their perceptions of your organization's service quality. They also provide you with guidance in developing meaningful performance indicators and specific goals.

The Performance Indicators

Every time a customer comes in contact with your organization, it's a Moment of Truth. Think of the five factors—reliability, responsiveness, assurance, empathy, and tangibles—as a template against which you can examine each Moment of Truth and determine what you need to measure, track, or be concerned with. Your performance indicators define how the service performance will be measured and observed.

Typical performance indicators for reliability might be orders delivered when promised, call-backs on repairs, accuracy of orders shipped, invoice accuracy, and merchandise returns. Use these as thought starters, but to develop the very best measures, examine each Moment of Truth and *ask your customers what they think is important*.

Performance indicators for responsiveness are generally a function of time—turn-around time on help-desk questions, cycle time, the time between a customer call and the time a repairman arrives on site, response time on call-ins, average age of special customer requests. Use these as thought starters, but to develop the very best measures, examine each Moment of Truth and *ask your customers what they think is important*.

To measure assurance, you need to determine the degree to which customers have confidence in your organization. Many organizations attempt to measure customer confidence through customer-satisfaction surveys. Potential performance indicators for assurance include the percentage of customers who rank the sales representative as "significantly more knowledgeable than others in the industry"; strongly agree with the statement "the service representative handled my situation competently"; or, based on the knowledge displayed by the insurance agent, would "highly recommend to a friend or neighbor." Use these as thought starters, but to develop the very best measures, examine each Moment of Truth and *ask your customers what they think is important.*

You can also build assurance by combining customer feedback with internal measures. Once you've identified the substance of what your organization does that drives the customer's perception, you can, for example, define a core base of knowledge every salesperson should know, educate the salesperson, and test for mastery. A "periodic test score" is observable, measurable, and improvable. It is a partial performance indicator for the perception customers have of your organization. In addition to product knowledge, consider testing for mastery of other assurance-creating knowledge and skills—company knowledge, listening skills, and problem-solving skills.

Measuring empathy requires that performance indicators be expressed in definitive terms. Statements like "Treat the customer as an individual," or "Understand the customer's perspective" may provide useful direction, but the percentage of customers who strongly agree with statements like "I was treated as an individual" or "The sales associate understood my needs" or "Based on the way I was treated, I would definitely shop here again" really determine whether or not a sense of empathy is being created. Use these as thought starters, but to develop the very best measures, examine each Moment of Truth and *ask your customers what they think is important.*

Performance indicators for tangibles revolve around impressions people form as they drive up to the building. Is the parking lot cluttered or clean? Are the building and the grounds well kept? Is the dining area clean, warm, and inviting? Use these as thought starters, but to develop the very best measures, examine each Moment of Truth and *ask your customers what they think is important.*

You may have noticed that we think it's important to ask your customers what they think is important. That's because they—not you, not us, not your staff, nor anyone else—determine what Knock Your Socks Off Service really is. So use the five factors as a template in developing indicators, but be sure to *ask your customers what they think is important*. Then you're ready to set some goals.

Realistic Service Goals

Once you have identified the key performance indicators for your organization, you need to assign a specific performance expectation for each indicator—your service goal. Remember, a performance indicator is not a goal; the indicator is how you measure service quality. Goals establish the expected level of performance for the indicator. In essence, a goal is your organization's definition of Knock Your Socks Off Service. To properly communicate your vision of service quality, your organization's goals must be relevant, realistic, understandable, measurable, believable, and achievable (just remember RRUMBA).

For example, feedback at one restaurant indicated sporadic problems with keeping the parking lot clean and the grounds looking neat. Not surprisingly there were problems setting goals that met RRUMBA. The number of times per week to cut the grass didn't work because sometimes it frequently depended on the season. The height of the grass was barely understandable to the person doing the cutting, and who wants to measure the grass, anyhow? The number of times per day to clean the lot didn't work because the need varied with the day of the week, the traffic in the lot, and the season.

What did work was a set of twenty-one pictures for the grounds and twenty-one for the parking lot. For the grounds, the first group of seven was labeled "This is an ideal of what our grounds should look like. Our *goal* is to keep them looking like this all the time." The second group of seven was labeled "This is just barely acceptable. *Sometimes*, the lawn or flowers may end up looking like this because of something unexpected, but don't let things stay like this for one second longer than necessary." The third group of seven was labeled "Our lawn and flowers should *never* under any circumstances look like this." Standards for the condition of the parking lot were handled in a similar manner.

Now we have to confess that we love numbers. Most managers love numbers. There's something very satisfying about 3.6 or 2.75. And 9.875 is really exciting. But the truth is that the pictures in this case provided a much better set of goals than numbers. The way the restaurant used them also illustrates how to answer the age-old question of "How high do I set goals?" The method provides a way to improve the motivation of service deliverers and keep the system from beating them up. It's an approach that we've used for some twenty-five years, based on the relationship between motivation and probability of success, depicted in Figure 7-1.

The curve in Figure 7-1 suggests that if there is zero probability of success in achieving the goal (the goal is too high), there's not much motivation or commitment. It also suggests that if there's 100 percent probability of success (the goal is too low), there's not much motivation or commitment, either. Most important, the curve suggests that at the point where there is some risk of failure, there's also a relatively high motivation level. To sustain high-quality service, set your goals high enough so there is enough risk, but not so much risk that the effort becomes impossible. The level of a goal should depend on systemic factors—the people involved, the situation, the task being performed, and other variables.

Figure 7-1. Goal motivation curve.

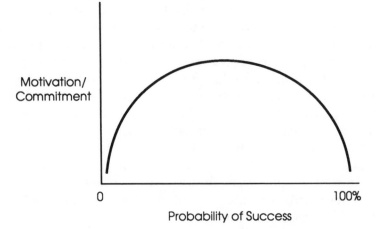

Motivation/
Commitment

0   100%

Probability of Success

As mentioned in Chapter 6, many well-known quality gurus claim that setting goals is a management technique that has outlived its usefulness. It is argued that goals and standards impede quality, including service quality. If you set the *wrong* goal, then goals can impede service. Give an airline reservations clerk a goal of forty-five calls per hour, and there's a good possibility that he will cut some callers short rather than fall short of the goal. But the dilemma faced by the airline reservations clerk (and many other service providers) is not caused by having a goal; it is caused by how the goals are viewed in the organization. Many companies take a single-target approach to goal setting. With a single goal, there's a tendency to use that target as an evaluation and punishment tool.

But if you set both a standard and a goal (for example, you set a standard of "at least twenty-four calls an hour" and a goal of "thirty-five calls an hour"); if you involve individuals or teams in setting their targets; if you empower individuals and teams to make decisions on their own; if you combine goal setting with measurements of customer satisfaction tracked back to both individuals and teams; if you add positive coaching; if you celebrate progress; and if you use regular positive reinforcement for the right set of behaviors, then goal setting is a powerful, positive tool for sustaining Knock Your Socks Off Service.

Organizations using this high-low standard and goal method of setting objectives find that it raises people's motivation and performance. The technique maximizes the probability that people will operate at the top of the motivation curve. It encourages people to set high goals because they know that their performance is going to be measured against an ongoing standard (twenty-four calls an hour) instead of an arbitrarily high goal.

Here are some examples of the standard and goal approach. Use them to develop your own.

Standard: 100 percent of all orders will be turned around in twenty-four hours.

Goal:	90 percent will be turned around in eight hours.
Shipping standard:	Zero days late.
Goal:	Three days early.
Standard:	80 percent will rate us as "would probably recommend" or better.
Goal:	92 percent will rate us as "would probably recommend" or better.

If you want to continually set the standard for your industry, over time both the standard and the goal should be raised, but not in an arbitrary fashion. Sustaining Knock Your Socks Off Service is the result of highly motivated people striving for successively higher goals, not people fearful of failing to meet arbitrary standards.

8

Allocating Resources to Meet Customer Priorities

A little knowledge is a dangerous thing.

The executives of a large midwestern insurance company gained a little knowledge from a survey they did of one customer segment: independent insurance agents. The survey clearly told the insurance company that it was not providing timely decisions when accepting or rejecting policies. The time required to approve a policy application was roughly four working days; agents said they wanted a decision in seventy-two hours.

It was obvious that the company wasn't performing up to agents' expectations. Eager to right the wrongs, someone (fresh from a quality seminar, we guess) suggested "If seventy-two hours is what agents want, let's really wow them with a forty-eight-hour turn-around!" A little investigation quickly made it evident that improving turn-around on policy decisions from four days to forty-eight hours would cost twice as much as going from four days to seventy-two hours.

Fortunately, one member of the executive team glimpsed the obvious, and asked agents what their *real* requirement was. The universal response was that seventy-two hours was the optimum turn-around time for a decision from the home office. Earlier meant nothing; before that, they were busy completing their own paperwork. The agents would receive no extra value for forty-eight-hour turn-around time *although the insurance*

company was prepared to double the cost of the improvement effort.
From the customer's point of view that's not adding value. It's
wasting resources. This is an example of one of our favorite
responses to clients who want to improve everything all at
once, without examining exactly what the customer wants.
Our response? A difference that doesn't make a difference isn't
a difference. The difference between seventy-two hours and
forty-eight hours didn't make a difference, so it wasn't really a
difference.

What Customers Really Value

Here's another example of a difference that doesn't make a
difference. Numerous articles on the "Disney Magic" have
focused attention on Disney's obsession with the cleanliness of
everything from sidewalks to parking lots. But how clean is
clean? Theme parks trying to emulate Disney often miss the
mark by a wide margin. How often do you sweep a parking lot
to have customers perceive that it is clean? Not that often, it
turns out. If you sweep twice a day, people will say it's a clean
parking lot. But wannabe Disneys continue to send out the
sweepers every two hours, eating up resources and adding
nothing of value to the customers' perception of cleanliness.

   The problem is that organizations often set goals and
create standards based on gut feel and professional judgment,
rather than find out from customers what they really want and
how they determine whether wants have been met. For example, in a recent survey of airline passengers, researchers from
the University of North Carolina at Charlotte posed a number
of questions to both passengers and airline management. The
researchers discovered a significant gap between what managers thought was important to customers and what customers
really valued. On a five-point scale, with 5 being most important or strongly agree, passengers rated receiving prompt information about delayed flights as 4.61; the airline managers
rated that same factor at 4.18. How important is it that airlines
assume responsibility for passengers on delayed flights? Passengers rated it 4.56, airline managers 3.66. How important is

knee and leg room? Passengers said 4.53, airline managers 3.86. Were comfortable seats important? Passengers said yes, by 4.43, airline managers 4.09. How important is it that a passenger obtain a preassigned seat? That was rated 4.15 by passengers, 3.59 by the airline managers. How about nonstop flights? Passengers rated the importance of a nonstop flight at 4.05, the airline managers at 3.77.

The absolute numbers in the survey are not nearly as important as the overall trend: Airline managers consistently underestimated the importance of certain services to passengers. Without understanding its customers, how can an organization effectively allocate resources? The simple answer is that it can't.

Putting Resources Where Value Can Be Gained

Let's look again at the five-element model of a service system introduced in Chapter 5 (and repeated in Figure 8-1). Note that *goals* are directly linked to *inputs*. Inputs are the raw materials transformed by system activities/behaviors to produce measurable outputs/results. We express that idea by saying "Based on our goals, we need to expend these resources (time, money, people) to support these activities and behaviors (the organization's standard processes and procedures) to produce these

Figure 8-1.   Service quality as a system.

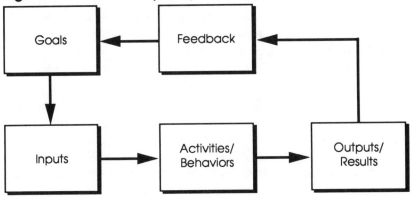

desirable outcomes and experiences for our customers (the end point of your service system)." Before spending a dime to improve service, an organization needs to make sure the processes and procedures in place are the *right* processes and procedures—that is, they are activities that produce results important to the customer.

At Taco Bell, the Irvine, California–based fast-food company, sustaining high-quality customer service is based on an intimate understanding of customer expectations. According to Leonard A. Schlesinger, writing in the September-October 1991 issue of *Harvard Business Review*, the company surveyed 800,000 customers to determine what they look for in a fast-food establishment. Customers asked for four things: quality products, fast service, an affordable price, and a clean environment. Factors assumed to be critical to the customer, such as preparing all food on site, were rated as non-value-adding services. Like the insurance company, Taco Bell discovered a key principle of sustaining Knock Your Socks Off Service: *More is not better unless it adds value for the customer.*

Sustaining high-quality service is not simply doing well whatever it is you do; it is understanding what is important to the customer and doing *those things* well. This concept is illustrated in Figure 8-2, the Performance/Importance Matrix. Any activity performed by your organization fits into one of the quadrants in the figure. Each quadrant has two dimensions: how well an organization performs the activity (horizontal axis), and how important that activity is to the customer (vertical axis).

The midwestern insurance company that was going for forty-eight-hour turn-around on policy applications was stuck in the lower right quadrant—overkill. It was going to spend a significant amount of money to provide a service that held no perceptible value for the agents who write the company's policies. Likewise, until they surveyed their customers, Taco Bell was also in overkill mode. Schlesinger points out that it believed that customers cared strongly about food being prepared where they could see it. It was using front-line resources to shred lettuce and chop tomatoes instead of serving customers.

Figure 8-2. Performance/Importance Matrix.

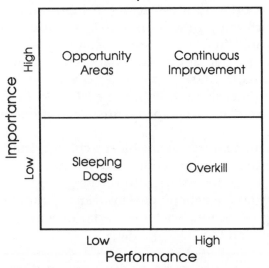

Based on its understanding of customer requirements, however, Taco Bell changed its procedures. Work that can be handled outside the restaurant is now done in advance. Such changes drove down costs and eliminated fifteen hours of backroom labor per day from the average operation. But perhaps more important, it shifted the focus of both front-line workers and managers from preparing food to serving customers. Now, while off-site facilities perform the tasks that lend themselves to economies of scale, Taco Bell's store employees are free to concentrate on customers and their needs. Taco Bell is successful because it has systematically moved from a manufacturing view of service to a human resource perspective. Competing against Taco Bell and other redesigned service businesses demands a shift in mind-set as well as a new appreciation for the real value of service and the value that service employees create.

Focusing on Importance to the Customer

The top two quadrants in Figure 8-2 are where Knock Your Socks Off Service companies spend their resources. Sustaining quality service means diverting resources from overkill either into areas of opportunity—factors of high importance where you don't perform very well—or into continuous improvement. The old saying "If it's not broke, don't fix it" doesn't work anymore. The paradigm of Knock Your Socks Off Service is IF IT'S NOT PERFECT, THEN FIND A WAY TO MAKE IT BETTER. If it is perfect, then reevaluate it with the customer. In today's competitive marketplace, a company must be continuously improving.

Continuous improvement means change, innovation, and experimentation. Organizations like Disney are consistently reinventing their organization to further delight their customers. The constant questioning—How can we improve?—has led to some marvelous touches for everyday experiences, like parking your car with the "Disney Magic."

- Employees cruise the parking lots at Walt Disney World in golf carts, looking for cars with lights on and engines running—and leave "Don't worry, we have your keys" notes for guests.
- Tram drivers repeat the pickup point three times to give guests a better chance of remembering where the family car is parked.
- A full-service repair shop operates in one corner of the lot so that if anyone needs help starting the car or changing a tire, Disney supplies no-charge assistance.

Asking "How can we improve?" led Saturn, a division of General Motors, to pioneer low-key, no-haggle selling. Saturn's research showed that customers disliked haggling with salespeople more than any other aspect of car buying. They hated the anxiety of wondering whether someone else got a better deal on the same car. The new approach is paying off: Saturn dealers are selling an average of 100 cars each month—more than any other brand sold in the United States.

Asking "How can we improve?" prompted Best Buy Co. to replace commission-motivated salespeople with answer centers staffed by employees who have all the product knowledge of the former sales staff but are on salary. Through customer surveys, Best Buy found that customers did not like the pressure that consumer electronics salespeople typically apply. Sales pressure was virtually eliminated by changing the commission structure; it also allowed for a 20 to 25 percent staff reduction *and an incremental revenue gain* because customers are more comfortable with the buying process and want to come back.

Letting Sleeping Dogs Lie

The one quadrant of the Performance/Importance Matrix we have yet to discuss is the lower left, sleeping dogs. As the saying goes, "Let sleeping dogs lie." *Sleeping dogs* are those activities your organization doesn't do very well, but which are of little importance to customers. Improving performance on sleeping dogs adds little value for customers. It is a black hole for resources better spent on areas of opportunity and continuous improvement.

For example, according to a recent survey by Wyndham Hotels & Resorts, hotel luxuries like breakfast in bed, a long, luxurious soak in a bubble bath, or having the room made up twice a day are sleeping dogs—not nearly as important to guests as are factors like efficient and friendly service, free parking, and longer weekends. If you managed a Wyndham hotel, where would you commit your resources?

In today's lean and mean business environment there are no extraneous resources. There are no people sitting on their hands with nothing to do. Bearing that in mind, look at the concept of zero defects. This concept holds that for any given process, the only acceptable goal is perfection. From the customer's perspective, "no errors" *is* the only acceptable objective. Given unlimited resources, an organization should strive for zero defects in everything it does.

However, no organization has unlimited resources, and therefore setting priorities in the pursuit of perfection is an economic necessity. If you're a computer-chip manufacturer and you say everything has to be done at 6 Sigma quality (3.4

errors per 1 million steps), then you run the risk of allocating equal resources to making sure that shipping labels are applied straight as well as to improving the quality of your chips.

One word of caution about sleeping dogs: There is a minimum level of service below which sleeping dogs will rise up to bite you. Twice-a-day room cleaning may be a low value-add for hotel guests, but if the once-a-day service doesn't pick up dinner trays, leaves dirty towels in the bathroom, or doesn't restock the toilet tissue, hotel management is going to hear some barking from the guests.

Revolutionizing, Reinventing, Reengineering

Time, money, and people are always in short supply. Once customer expectations are defined, immediately the questions arise: Is there enough time? Do we have enough people? What's it going to cost? In most cases, the first response is no. And the second response is, "We don't know where we're going to get them." Any effort to sustain Knock Your Socks Off Service is doomed if it is based on meeting requests for more and more resources. The path to service quality takes you through not more resources but more creative use of existing resources.

The panacea *du jour* is technology, from 1-800 numbers to elaborate voice mail systems, to notebook computers, to fax machines, to cellular phones, to expert systems. Everywhere we turn there is another productivity tool. There is no question that appropriately selected and strategically used technology can create a tremendous service-quality advantage. The organization that doesn't take advantage of new labor-saving, customer-pleasing technology won't be around long. And technology has been put to good use by a number of companies.

- When a customer phones the Chevrolet Customer Assistance Center, after just a few questions, the operator can call up a complete history of the customer's car, including the plant where it was manufactured. If the customer is stranded out of town, the adviser can give the name of the nearest dealer, the name of the towing company used by that dealer, and the name of the service writer in the dealership. Ninety percent of the customers who use Chevrolet's Roadside Assistance report that they intend to purchase another Chevrolet—more than double the national average of 38 percent.

- Kmart is piloting a system called ShopperTrak, which gives each store manager a minute-by-minute customer-traffic profile of the store. Armed with this information, the manager can dispatch additional floor assistance to crowded areas or open additional checkout lanes.
- If a customer calls Metropolitan Life with a question that falls beyond the salespeople's expertise, a specialized computer system enables the salesperson to simultaneously transfer the caller *and* the data to a specialist. Prior to installing the system, the salesperson had to create a back file so the specialist could call the customer later, resulting in a decrease in customer satisfaction.
- Arby's is testing Touch 2000, a computerized system that allows customers to order food from a touch-sensitive display screen. As the food selection is touched on the screen, it is displayed on monitors in the food-preparation area. The system's screen automatically indicates the selections and keeps a running tab of the order.

As these examples vividly show, technology has revolutionized the way we approach service and maximizes the use of resources, especially human resources. At the same time, technology has in many ways been a disappointment, largely because companies use technology to mechanize old ways of doing business. They speed up existing processes rather than revolutionize, reinvent, or reengineer those processes.

Simply speeding up an existing process does not address the flaws in a system. One of the best examples of this is the accounts-payable process at Ford. In the early 1980s, Ford's North American operation employed more than 500 people in accounts payable. Management was enthusiastic about a plan that would cut that number by 20 percent—until it bench-marked its partner, Mazda. Mazda's entire accounts-payable organization consisted of 5 people. Even after adjusting for Ford's size, the difference was astounding. Even with the planned improvements, Ford was by Mazda's standards five times the size it should be. Consequently, Ford realized that it had to reengineer the entire system. The old rule was to pay when it got the invoice. The new rule was to pay when it got the goods. Thus Ford's new view of its acquisition system— purchasing and receiving as well as accounts payable—paid off.

Reengineering a process involves constantly asking why and what if. Why do customer returns require a manger's signature? Is it a control mechanism or a decision point? What if employees are authorized to spend up to $500 to resolve a customer problem? Only by wrestling with questions such as these can companies separate the essential purpose of a proc-ess from the tasks associated with it—the essence of allocating resources to the right place.

9
Service Behavior That Makes a Difference

Behaviors are human activities that can be seen, measured, or described. In a well-performing service system, organizational resources (time, money, people) are used to carry out behaviors (analyzing customers' needs, for example) to produce desirable outcomes and experiences for the customer (the organization's service goals).

The ability to describe and specify behaviors is critical to the continuous improvement of service quality. General descriptions like "good attitude," "motivated," "friendly," "courteous," "neat," "angry," "cheerful," "pleasant," and "irritating" are seldom useful. Tell ten customer-service reps to be "more friendly," and they will walk away with ten different ideas of exactly what to do. Similarly, phrases like "We need to be more motivated to provide quality customer service" and "We have to be more responsive to our customers' requests" may be useful from a conceptual viewpoint, but they are not helpful to the organization trying to sustain Knock Your Socks Off Service.

We are not against "good attitude," "motivated," "friendly," "courteous,' "neat," "angry," "cheerful," and "pleasant." We're all for them. It's just that those terms don't provide the precision necessary to create and sustain service quality. When employees have only a vague idea of what quality service is, they have no guidelines for relating customer service to their own job. Customer service and customer satisfaction then become inconsistent. Conversely, our Service Management Practices Inventory (SMPI) studies show that

69

when employees recognize the day-to-day behaviors important in a successful delivery of services, customer-satisfaction rates are more than double those of organizations in which such behaviors have not been clearly defined (76 percent versus 35 percent).

Managing Employee Behavior

Specific actions like thanking a customer, saying good morning, answering the phone, submitting reports on time, and submitting accurate reports are "good" behaviors in the sense that they presumably lead to desirable outcomes and experiences for customers. In a systematic approach to service quality, these behaviors are defined as desirable because they contribute to the ultimate goal of Knock Your Socks Off Service—loyal and delighted customers.

The best way to sustain Knock Your Socks Off Service is by managing specific behaviors within the service-system model. Although the idea of managing behavior bothers some people, who view consciously changing people's behavior as a manipulative Big Brother technique, all managers "manipulate" behavior every day, whether they realize it or not. They just don't do it systematically; accordingly, they don't achieve consistent results. Failure to manage for behaviors that sustain Knock Your Socks Off Service ensures that the service level of the organization will slip.

You are far better off, and will be ahead of your competition, if you set out to change specific behavior instead of giving your people general instructions like "be cheerful." Service-quality efforts fail to sustain their early momentum when people lack a specific understanding of how they should behave.

For example, an employee may say "Customer service is important," but that does not ensure that he or she will promptly return customer calls. It doesn't even ensure that the employee knows what behaviors facilitate taking care of customers. On the other hand, an employee who says "It helps retain customers when we return their calls within one hour,

because that shows that they can count on us to be prompt"
has demonstrated an understanding of three things: (1) the
overall goal (customer retention), (2) a customer requirement
(promptness/responsiveness), and (3) the related behavior (calling back within one hour). To sustain Knock Your Socks Off
Service, you must translate the intent of your statement into
specific behaviors that contribute to the end result of building
customer loyalty.

Ask yourself, How can people demonstrate that they are
motivated to provide quality customer service? Well, a retail-
store employee might demonstrate that desire by greeting
customers as they enter the store. That's a specific behavior
you can see, describe, and measure. The athletic footwear
company Foot Locker has among its list of defined behaviors
that all customers will be greeted within thirty seconds of
when they walk into the store. The impact of that policy on
customer satisfaction is reflected in solid sales and profits.
Likewise, bank tellers might use their down time to telephone
long-time depositors to thank them for their loyalty and ask
how service might be improved. That's a defined behavior at
First Hawaiian Bank.

Linking Behavior to Customer Requirements

A word of caution. Keep the customer in mind when specifying
these service behaviors. If you don't, you run three risks.

1. The potential always exists for "I'm-supposed-to-greet-
   each-customer-within-thirty-seconds-so-here-goes-Hi-
   wecome-to-our-store-how-are-you-today-can-I-help-
   you-with-anything?" If you're anything like us, this
   behavior produces the opposite reaction of what's intended. Instead of feeling welcomed, we feel irritated
   at being treated like a robot being greeted by a robot.
2. A lack of customer focus takes responsibility and flexibility away from your front-line service team. Each
   customer *is* different and should be treated appropriately. For example if three male teenagers in varsity

jackets, wearing baseball caps backwards and laughing loudly, enter a Foot Locker store, they are greeted promptly, but differently from how a middle-aged man with a tennis racquet in hand is greeted or from how a grandmother with two grandchildren is greeted. All three customers are greeted promptly, however, and that's what you would want if you owned the store.

3. If service staff lose their sense of responsibility for how the customer feels, and cannot be flexible in meeting customer needs, customer satisfaction will decline (and staff turnover will probably go up as well).

Instead, use statements like "Greet customers within thirty seconds in *a fashion that makes them feel comfortable and welcome.*" That's a specific behavior description that puts accountability for behavior and for making the customer feel welcome where it belongs—at the front line. As part of your coaching and training, provide your personnel with examples so that they have some idea of how to be flexible or treat customers as individuals.

Once the service behaviors are specifically defined, you must incorporate those behaviors into the service system. If the desired behavior is that bank tellers make thank-you calls to long-time depositors, then the rest of the service system must support that behavior. Tellers need time to make calls. They'll likely need some training in how to handle the calls. They will need to understand how the calls produce desirable outcomes and experiences for the customers.

The 20-80 Principle

In the previous chapter, we noted that to sustain Knock Your Socks Off Service, an organization needs to allocate time, money, and people on customer priorities. There is a corresponding application to service behaviors. The 20-80 principle was first proposed by Italian sociologist and economist Vilfredo Pareto. Studying income distribution in various countries, he discovered that no matter what economic, political, or social system was in place, about 20 percent of the people controlled about 80 percent of the wealth. The 20-80 principle still applies in many areas of business. We know, for example, that:

- 20 percent of employees are responsible for 80 percent of absences.
- 20 percent of accounts generate 80 percent of the dollar volume.
- 20 percent of a product line produces 80 percent of the gross margin dollars.

Of course, it's not always 20-80. In reality, 27 percent of employees might account for 91 percent of absences. Or maybe 35 percent of the product line accounts for 77 percent of the gross margin dollars. But in these forms, the 20-80 principle is well known and fairly widely applied. What is less widely known and less widely applied is 20-80 principle in regard to *behavioral leverage*. Behavioral leverage is illustrated in Figure 9-1.

Figure 9-1 suggests that very small changes in behavior can have very large changes in results. Think, for example, about the difference between a top service rep and a marginal one. From a behavioral point of view, there is usually very little

Figure 9-1. Leveraged behavior and service results.

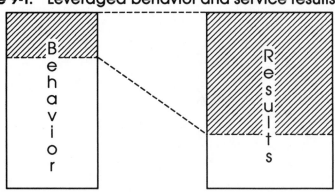

difference. The marginal rep does 90 to 98 percent of what the top rep does. But in terms of customer satisfaction, there's a world of difference. And if the marginal rep did an additional 10 to 12 percent more, that world of a difference would be made up.

Let's step away from customers for a minute and apply the 20-80 principle to golfers. Watch two golfers—Arnold Palmer and our friend Billy Jack—with regard to three dimensions of their performance—their club grip and stance, their score, and their earnings. Both men tee up on the first hole, grip the club, and address the ball. You see very little difference. Jack has played more than a few rounds of weekend golf in his life, and on the first dimension, club grip and stance, he and Palmer are pretty close. In fact, at that dimension Jack might even be able to fool you into thinking he really *is* a professional golfer.

What about score? Palmer shoots a 70. Jack's average round is 84. That's certainly not an embarrassing score; it's only 20 percent off of Palmer's mark. But now we come to the bottom line—earnings from professional golf. What difference do you see there? A lot. Palmer and Jack are at opposite ends of the earnings spectrum. The figure below shows how Arnold Palmer and Billy Jack rate on the three dimensions.

(a)

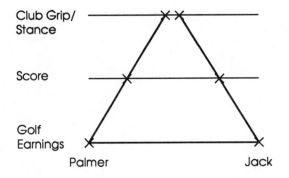

Let's say Jack starts working with a good pro. The pro fools with his grip, works on his follow-through, counsels him on club selection, and—lo and behold—Jack cuts his average strokes per round down to 77—a 50 percent reduction in the difference between the scores. Any change in earnings? No. Nothing goes to the bottom line. The result is illustrated here:

(b)

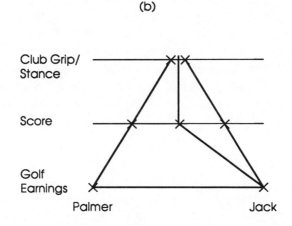

Palmer   Jack

Not discouraged, Jack keeps working and cuts the difference between average scores another 50 percent. He's now averaging 73.5 strokes per round. Any change in earnings yet? Maybe $125 in a club tournament, but Jack's not ready to quit his day job:

(c)

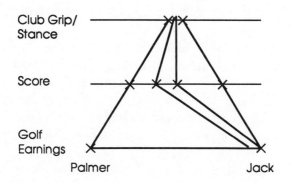

Palmer   Jack

But he keeps practicing. He eliminates those 3.5 strokes. He can now shoot even with Palmer, Trevino, Lyle, Norman, Strange, and the rest of the PGA tour. Suddenly, there's a big change in Jack's earnings from professional golf (see figure below). Billy got tremendous earnings leverage in the last little grip change, which cut those last 3.5 strokes off his score. Thus even very small changes in behavior can have tremendous results. This is the power of behavioral leverage. If truth be known, in any given year the difference between first place and fortieth or fiftieth place in earnings is about ⅒ stroke per hole. It's that metaphorical ⅒ stroke that's the difference between a world-class service company and an also-ran.

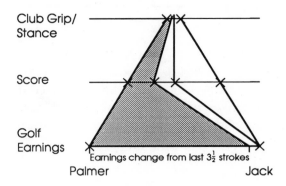

Small Increments, Big Differences

Lots of hotel and motel chains do 90 percent of what Hyatt and Marriott do, but at Hyatt and Marriott a harried traveler doesn't have to wait in line to check in. Essential information—a credit-card number, room preference, and estimated time of arrival—is collected when the reservation is made. When the guest arrives, a packet containing a room key and other information is waiting.

Dairy stores sell milk, eggs, and cheese. Stew Leonard's

sells milk, eggs, and cheese. But at Leonard's, when the checkout lines have more than a couple of people waiting, they open new lines. And if the crowds are such that there are still more than a couple of people in line, they pass out cookies to those waiting.

Randall's Food Markets, a family-run chain of supermarkets in Houston, stocks its shelves with the same products as every other grocery in Houston. But Randall's has also pulled the rest rooms out of the storage areas and placed them in front for customer convenience. Target Stores has done the same thing. So have other service leaders. Small changes in behavior? Sure. But just as the small differences between Arnold Palmer and Billy Jack yield a big difference in earnings, these are small differences that yield a big difference in customer satisfaction. These extra efforts set companies apart. Sustaining Knock Your Socks Off Service means being constantly on the lookout for that little change that will produce a big change in your customer's perception of your service quality.

10
Pinpointing High-Impact Behavior

Service quality is a judgment your customers make as they do business with you. Your knock their socks off when you deliver the product or service the customer expects (outcome result) *and* your service system and the behavior of your people are impressive beyond the customer's experience (process result). Every company has some days when the customer walks away saying "Wow! They did a great job!" The difference between "every company" and Knock Your Socks Off Service companies is consistency. Companies with a reputation for outstanding service take the time to plan and manage relationships with their customers. They know which encounters with customers are deal makers and which are deal breakers.

The key to delivering consistent Knock Your Socks Off Service is identifying the high-impact organizational and personal behaviors that give you that 1/10 of a stroke advantage over the competition. The three basic steps in that identification are:

1. Focusing on the most sensitive customer transactions—those encounters that generate the most praise from and/or problems raised by customer
2. Capturing the key points of customer contact during each of those transactions
3. Separating those contact points, or Moments of Truth, into high-impact and hardly-noticeable events

In 1986, we formalized these activities into a process we call the Moment of Truth Impact Assessment (MOTIA).

MOTIA and the Cycle of Service

As illustrated in Figure 10-1, every service follows a cycle. The cycle begins when a customer has a need for your product or service. It ends when the service or product is safely and correctly delivered or executed. This cycle is composed of Moments of Truth—key encounters between the customer and your organization.

Because the customer is the only reliable arbiter of what is and is not a Moment of Truth, you need an unusually detailed understanding of customer expectations and to be aware of the points in the service cycle where perfect execution is critical.

Figure 10-1. Cycle of service.

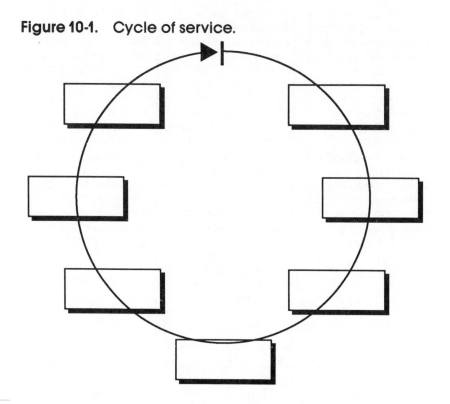

Creating this map of customer-sensitive Moments of Truth requires intensive listening. Customer focus groups, one-on-one interviews, complaint analysis, advisory councils, surveys, and so forth, are the primary tools for understanding customer concerns.

Figure 10-2 is part of an assessment of Moments of Truth

Figure 10-2. Moment of Truth: impact analysis.
Customer Calls To Repair Answering Center

Experience Detractors	Standard Expectations	Experience Enhancers
•I couldn't understand the operator's words. •I had to call more than once to get through. •While I was on hold, I got silence, which made me wonder if I was disconnected. •The operator sounded like he/she was following a form/stock or routine questions. •I thought the operator rushed me. •The operator told me to go to the Phone Mart to have my phone tested. •I had to call an 800 number.	•I will only have to call one number. •I will call a local number. •I will be treated fairly. •The operator will speak clearly. •The phone will not be busy. •The operator will answer within a reasonable time. •The operator will listen to my problems in a manner that lets me know he/she understands my problems. •The operator will seem competent, helpful, and understanding. •The operator will promise me a solution with a reasonable deadline.	•The operator had a melodious voice. •The operator communicated a sense of urgency about my problem. •The operator apologized sincerely. •The operator asked me about medical emergencies or other special situations that may warrant sooner service. •The operator made some comment that let me know that he/she was aware of my area (i.e., sounded like a neighbor). •The operator offered to have work done at my convenience.

completed by a major midwestern telephone company. The "Customer Calls Repair Answering Center" is one Moment of Truth in the cycle of service, Residential Telephone Repair. Once identified as a Moment of Truth, the attributes or component parts of the activity were put into one of three categories.

1. In the center column are the customers' Standard Expectations. The telephone company must meet these expectations to get a passing grade from customers.
2. In the left-hand column are the Experience Detractors, customer experiences that have left a less-than-positive assessment of the phone company. These are *examples* of events or behaviors that have upset or annoyed customers, not a definitive listing. That's an important distinction. Employees should understand that the examples represent a *type* of behavior to be avoided as well as *specific* behaviors customers find detracting.
3. In the right-hand column are the Experience Enhancers, or events and behaviors that customers said distinguished the telephone company favorably—positive actions that customers said exceeded their expectations. Again, it is a list of behaviors that is illustrative, not all-inclusive.

Using this analysis, the telephone company knows what it must do without fail, what it must avoid at all costs, and where it can add value at the moment of truth "Customer Calls Repair Answering Center."

The Five-Factor Alternative

If the MOTIA approach seems like a lot of work, you're right—it is. There is no substitute for a detailed MOTIA. However, there are times when a MOTIA is not possible. For those cases, we have an alternative way of identifying the performance details of high-impact Moments of Truth. The process starts with the cycle of service and understanding which Moments of

Truth are most important to your customers. To speed the process, you use the five service-quality factors developed by researchers Berry, Parasuraman, and Zeithaml, as discussed in Chapter 7.

Potentially every transaction with a customer involves some aspect of the five factors—reliability, responsiveness, assurance, empathy, tangibles. That is also true of almost every Moment of Truth. Figure 10-3 illustrates how the five service-quality factors and a single Moment of Truth are combined to create a matrix for "dry labbing," or synthesizing high-impact details.

Using the grid in Figure 10-3, a cross-sectional group of experienced, customer-savvy employees can identify enhancing, detracting, and standard expectations for a given Moment of Truth—in this case, when a customer calls the office. The group should be composed of employees from different areas or departments who share a familiarity with customer complaints and compliments, as well as customers' historical preferences and problems with your organization. Beginning with

Figure 10-3. Moment of Truth: customer telephones the office.

	Experience Detractors	Standard Expectations	Experience Enhancers
1. Reliability			
2. Responsiveness			
3. Assurance			
4. Empathy			
5. Tangibles			

Figure 10-4. Moment of Truth: impact assessment—first client meeting.

	Detractors	Standard Expectations	Enhancers
1. Reliability	"The fund had fees that my planner didn't tell me about."	"My planner keeps his/her appointments and shows up on time." "My planner calls to confirm appointments."	"My planner sent a self-assessment package one week before the meeting."
2. Responsiveness	"My planner is very slow at returning my calls."	"My planner showed me a way to begin saving for the future while still saving to buy the things I want now."	"My planner called to tell me about a new option that fit me exactly."
3. Assurance	"My planner acts uncomfortable when I ask challenging questions."	"My planner explains options in ways I understand."	"My planner sent me a thank-you note after I recommended him to a friend."
4. Empathy	"My planner kidded me about my conservative investing."	"My planner knows how I feel about high-risk investing."	"My planner sent newsclips about the school my son is considering."
5. Tangibles	"I couldn't make sense of my statement."	"My tax information statements arrive during the first week of January."	"My planner put a personal note with my statement explaining a change in the statement."

reliability, they brainstorm ways each factor is likely to come into play during the Moment of Truth.

The matrix in Figure 10-4 illustrates the results of a MOTIA project conducted by a financial planning company. Customers in this study were individuals planning for children's college funds or for their own retirement. Through discussions with customers, the company identified a Moment of Truth called

First Client Meeting, which not surprisingly had an extremely high impact on customer perceptions. The assessment team filled in the details based on its own successes and failures with customers and its observations of other planners' behaviors.

Although every service-quality factor plays a role, one or two tend to dominate a particular moment of truth. Before the brainstorming exercise, the company had assumed that reliability and responsiveness were the dominant factors. It believed that clients were most impressed when they were directed to the best financial products to meet their individual situation and goals.

What the company didn't realize, however, was that reliability and responsiveness weren't the high-leverage behaviors. Customers assumed that reliability and responsiveness were standard behaviors for financial planners. Just as no one would say to a golfer, "Hey Jan. You brought your clubs and golf balls. Wow! Really impressive!" customers weren't overly excited about behaviors showing reliability and responsiveness, although they did notice their absence (which would be like trying to play golf without clubs or golf balls).

The service-quality factor that provided the ¹⁄₁₀ of a stroke difference turned out to be empathy. The high-impact behaviors were "showed understanding of my life by talking about his/her own family" and "always gave me 100 percent attention during the meeting; held all calls and arranged a private meeting location."

This financial planning company's experience is not unusual. The dominant service-quality factor in customers' eyes is frequently not what an organization believes it to be. So you see that either the MOTIA or the five-factor analysis is useful in multiple ways. Its application to training and coaching is obvious. With these details, new employees—even seasoned employees—can quickly comprehend what customers expect from them in behavioral specifics, not generalities. The assessment can easily be used to audit customer surveys, feedback systems, even some aspects of recognition and reward systems. And of course, the assessment is a giant step toward setting customer-focused performance standards.

11

Training for Lasting Service Quality

Identifying high-impact behaviors that deliver Knock Your Socks Off Service is critical to a service-improvement effort. But knowing what those behaviors are isn't enough. You have to continually revisit them and ensure that they are being converted into on-the-job action.

A Never-Ending Process

Customer expectations change. Moments of Truth change. Behavior that is perceived by the customer as superior service today may be mediocre service tomorrow. Moreover, people come and go. Additions to your staff—replacements or new hires to meet expansion needs—change the complexion of your service system. Unless you continually expand your organization's behavioral repertoire, you will lose the critical mass of behavior necessary to sustain Knock Your Socks Off Service.

In service-successful organizations, training and development of employees is a never-ending process. It starts on an employee's first day on the job and continues until the gold watch is presented. It includes formal and on-the-job training, guided experience, effective coaching, targeted performance review, and strong support for learning from the organization as a whole. It's not piecemeal; not on again, off again; not maybe or maybe not. Learning is an integral part of the service system. A company must be unrelenting in development of its human assets; anything less, and employees will be ill prepared to deliver at ever-increasing levels of service quality.

People learn critical service behaviors in three ways: (1) they see a model; (2) they get on-the-job-training; (3) they receive formal classroom training. Learning takes place regardless of whether you consciously choose to train, manage, and monitor the service behaviors of your people. So train, manage, and monitor those service behaviors.

A Systems Approach to Developing Service Behavior

Most people adopt the behavior of those around them. Without systematic expectations of behavior, employees may not choose the models you would like. In the absence of any guidelines, they will emulate *some* behavior pattern. Whether or not you formalize on-the-job-training, people will get it. It may be the old-timer telling the new kid in distribution, "It's close enough for government work." It may simply be the new kid watching. Worst, it may be the new person with no other guidance than what he or she did on the last job because it seemed to work okay. Without systematic training for service quality, that's the risk you run.

You can help employees learn systematically those behaviors you want them to learn. Companies that sustain Knock Your Socks Off Service develop high-impact service behaviors by creating proper service role models, providing on-the-job training, and using formal education. You don't need a massive, highly sophisticated training organization to develop these behaviors. If you do have a training function, and it's a good one, that's a plus, but don't expect it to carry the full load. That's not knocking training organizations. It's simply the realization that training is so much more than what goes on in the classroom.

The Disney Example

Without a doubt, one of the best examples of "hire-to-retire" learning is that of the Disney organization. It begins in the selection interview, during which prospective "cast members" (Disneyspeak for employees) are given a realistic view of working at the Magic Kingdom. That's apparent and obvious. What is somewhat more subtle but equally important is that the personnel building is labeled "Casting." That sign sends a very powerful message. *All* new cast members at Disney parks, hotels, and resorts—regardless of level—begin with a two-day orientation seminar called "Traditions." The purpose of the seminar is twofold. First, it provides cast members with a firm understanding of the Disney corporation's traditions and values, and inculcates the Disney lore, language, and culture. Second, it provides generic skills essential to job performance.

When we examine the Disney approach to training—and there are variations of this theme in all organizations that sustain Knock Your Socks Off Service—we see a process with three characteristics.

1. The process involves more than just skills training.
2. The process includes mechanisms for ensuring that formal training carries over to the job. It provides an environment that is supportive of Knock Your Socks Off Service.
3. The process starts with the employee's first day on the job.

More Than Just Skills Training

At the department level, custodial cast members at Disney take part in extended training that combines videotapes and classroom training, produced by the custodial department and featuring members of its cast. These are not generic videos. They do instruct in basic skills, but in true Disney fashion they go way beyond and view custodial work from the customer's perspective: How do you clean a rest room *while it is still open to the public?* How do you remove trash *safely and efficiently when the park is still operating?* One of the first videos shown is *24 Hours of Custodial*, a day in the life of the department distilled to about fifteen minutes. Other videos carry titles like *How to Dump Trash* and *How to Clean Rest Rooms*. Videos are nine to fifteen minutes long, breaking the training process into manageable pieces.

In addition to basic job skills, cast members are introduced to simple social graces—concepts like saying "please" and "thank you." This is another example of Disney's dedication to thoroughness and its commitment to managing behavior. Management does not leave to chance or assume that common courtesy is the norm. Through its training, Disney instills traditional values, teaches common courtesy, and helps cast members learn how to communicate with guests.

The characteristic that distinguishes companies like Disney isn't found in the bits and pieces of what it does, but in the thoroughness of what it does. Don't confuse quantity with quality when it comes to training. Relevance counts as much—maybe more—than minutes. To be effective, training should support serving customers better, working smarter, and creating better outcome for the organization.

Necessary Skills

There are four kinds of skills people need to do their jobs well: technical skills, interpersonal skills, product and service knowledge, and customer knowledge. *All* are critical to success. *All* need to be addressed throughout an individual's work career with your organization.

1. **Technical skills.** Employees need to understand your systems and all the equipment that makes them work. This doesn't mean a cashier in a grocery store has to be a computer science major to operate a scanning cash register, but he or she should understand error messages that may pop up on the screen. The cashier should know what procedures to follow when the system goes down. The same is true of other office equipment. Handling paperwork is also a technical skill, an often overlooked one. Employees should understand the purpose and flow of paper in most organizations. Anytime paper affects the speed, reliability, and personal attention provided

to customers, employees need to know the proper forms and procedures.

2. **Interpersonal skills.** We hope you've hired people who are customer-focused, who can listen, understand, communicate with, and relate to customers as well as demonstrate technical knowledge of your products and services. But no matter how good their specific skills, the more practice, the more training, the more knowledge, the more experience you can give, the stronger those skills will become.

At Air Atlanta, management works hard to instill specific customer-focused values in the in-flight attendants, but it also recognizes that it takes a lot of discussion and dialogue to make those values living ideas, not clichés. For instance, anyone can give passengers a lecture on checking a bag that's too large to fit under the seat in front of them. It takes a lot of *skill* to make that a positive—to position the need to do something else with a bag in a way that doesn't offend or embarrass the customer.

3. **Product and service knowledge.** Product and service knowledge encompass three basic areas. First, employees should know the technical aspects of products and services; customers expect service people to know more about the organization's products than they do. Second, employees should know something about the competition—not fluff and hype, but factual material relevant to customers. Third, employees should know what questions are most frequently asked by customers and how to answer them. Training can help them think about and anticipate a customer need or expectation.

4. **Customer knowledge.** Service people can never know too much about the customers. What most organizations overlook is that people are transitory; customer knowledge must be permanent. People may leave your organization, they may transfer to another job within the company, or they may retire. Customers expect they will *not* have to reeducate a new service person every time there is a change in personnel. Companies that sustain Knock Your Socks Off Service treat customer knowledge as a corporate asset. Information about key customers or customer trends is maintained in a repository to which all employees have access. Training should address the collec-

tion, recording, accessing, and general use of customer information and its role in service delivery.

Making Sure the Training Takes

Instructing employees in the classroom on high-impact behaviors is an important undertaking, but it is only part of sustaining Knock Your Socks Off Service. Ensuring that those newly acquired skills are used back on the job is the thing. Without active support and involvement by the supervisor, an employee stops applying the skills acquired in the classroom. But with supervisor support and involvement, these skills are not only locked in but continue to be applied and grow. This concept is illustrated in Figure 11-1.

An excellent example of skills reinforcement is Xerox Corporation. Known as LUTI, for Learn, Use, Teach, Inspect, the training process is a cascading one. With the aid of professional trainers, training is facilitated by supervisors within the organization. The supervisors first *learn* the desired behavior. They then are expected to *use* the behavior. Initial trainers *inspect* that the behavior is, indeed, being used. The Inspect phase reinforces the skills that the supervisor has absorbed and

Figure 11-1. Support and nonsupport of training.

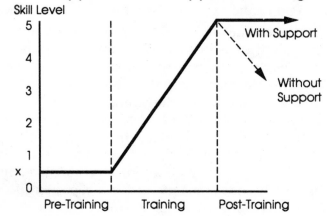

makes sure they are properly applied. The follow-up itself communicates to the supervisor that the behavior is important to the success of the organization. Once the supervisor had learned and used the technique, he or she is expected to *teach* the technique in the organization, then *inspect* and reinforce use of the behavior among those people he or she has trained (see Figure 11-2).

What makes the Xerox method successful, what makes the efforts at Disney and other Knock Your Socks Off Service companies effective, is that employees returning from training are given an immediate opportunity to practice what was preached. Training is just-in-time. There is no lag time between training and the opportunity to use the new skills.

At St. Paul Companies, a large insurance underwriter, while employees are in class taking software training, the information systems organization is exchanging the terminals at their desks or installing new software packages. When the employees return, they sit down in front of the same equipment and software as just learned in class. The St. Paul Com-

Figure 11-2. Training cascade.

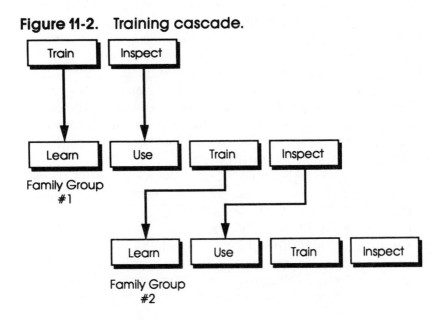

panies found that any delay between training and implementing significantly reduced the amount of information retained from the class.

So, to make an effective training transfer from classroom to job, make the training have a mission. Present it as a highly visible event. Create a little hoopla. Explain why the training is important and what the benefits will be. Create expectations among those who are to be trained. Specifically discuss:

- What the training will cover
- Why the individual is attending
- Why the training is important to the organization
- Your personal assessment of the training's strengths and weaknesses
- How you will help people apply the new skill or knowledge when they return

Involve the employee in pre-training activities. Have them bring to class work experiences relevant to the training topic. For example, if the training covers handling unhappy customers, they might bring along examples of customer conflicts they have faced recently.

Ensure that the training takes by providing an environment that encourages people to use their new skills. In analyzing the failure of well-conceived and well-designed training programs, we note a common pattern: Employees return from a training session with new skills that they quickly put to use, but inevitably they find the skills do not work as slickly as they did during training. Within a relatively short time, employees regress to old behaviors, which may not work either, but at least they are comfortable with them.

One retail establishment found this out the hard way. Over a period of about a year, it put together a well-designed, carefully thought out multimedia training package intended to teach sales clerks all the skills necessary to practice great sales and service. Among other things, sales clerks were taught how to fill out forms correctly, make sure merchandise was arranged in the most eye-appealing manner, determine customer needs, deal with different types of customers, select clothing for customers designed to meet both articulated and unarticulated needs, help customers choose between one piece of merchandise and another, overcome objections, sell related merchandise, and close a sale. Bursting with energy and confidence, the sales clerks graduated from the course and were placed on the selling floor. In a matter of months, however, their skills began to fall by the wayside. The clerks discovered that filling out forms was not as easy on the job as it was in class. The forms were poorly designed, and it was much easier and less time-consuming to fill them out improperly—and, of course, customer complaints about billing errors went up.

The pure selling skills of identifying needs, asking for the order, and selling related merchandise also proved much easier in the classroom than on the job. In the classroom, the instructor was there to help; not so on the sales floor. Moreover, because of the role-play situation in the classroom, the sales clerks experienced a one-to-one success ratio. In other words, just about every time a student tried something, it worked one way or another. However, on the job they were shooting "real bullets." The success ratio in selling related merchandise, for example, fell to about one in nine—each employee had one success in nine tries. While a ratio of one in nine is something an experienced clerk might deal with, these new clerks were devastated. Some of those failures were difficult. Customers became upset when the clerks tried to sell related merchandise, and not all customers responded to the ways prescribed to handle upset or difficult customers.

Overall, the clerks got very little reinforcement for behaving as the training organization had suggested. The department head never gave the clerks feedback on how they were making the transition from training to actual job. In fact, very little was ever said to them except when they made a particularly blatant error. Within a few short weeks, the clerks were back at their pre-training skills level and the service-oriented approach to sales began to taper off. Line management lambasted the training department for designing "another expensive training package that didn't work." The fact is, there was nothing wrong with the training package. The problem was that both line management and the training department had failed to take into account the factors present in the job situation.

To help smooth the transition from classroom to the job:

1. Debrief people when they return from training. Show interest in what was learned to reinforce the notion that the training was important. Talk about what was learned to reinforce the training in the employee's mind.
2. Provide an opportunity for people to teach others. This doesn't have to be a formal presentation, but preparing to teach others means the employee will have to organize his or her thinking about the subject.
3. Provide reinforcement when you see the new behaviors being used. Go out of your way to find positive examples. Set expectations for use. Ask employees for specific examples. If the use didn't get the desired results, find out why. In short, praise success and put failure in perspective.

Starting on the First Day

There is perhaps no other more annoying breach of the covenant between vendor and customer than to have someone say "Gee, I'm new here. I don't know." Granted, there is a first time for everything, and in many ways a customer can empathize with a new employee. But that doesn't change the basic situation: A customer seeks service, and no matter how politely or easily the lack of service is rationalized, the customer doesn't receive the level of service he or she was expecting.

Companies that consistently deliver Knock Your Socks Off Service make sure that new people brought into the service function—or, for that matter, anywhere else in the company—are inculcated in "the way we do things around here." They understand that to operate any other way inevitably leads to a decline in service quality. They make sure that people coming on board share their level of customer commitment, excitement about what they are doing, and knowledge of what it takes to deliver quality service. The best time to start that orientation is day 1—the employee's first day on the job. Marcia J. Hyatt, director of employee development for Minnegasco, a Minneapolis-based natural gas distribution firm, said it well: "If we believe employees treat customers the way they themselves are treated, then isn't it critical that we are as careful about the first impression we make on new employees as we expect them to be of the first impression they make on customers?"

Orientation training is the joint responsibility of the training staff and the line supervisor. Specifically, the training staff should communicate information relevant to all new employees. Supervisors should concentrate on issues unique to the employee's immediate workplace and job. A study at a computer company demonstrated that the time for new people to reach full productivity shrank from five to three months for employees who had been carefully oriented to the company in general and to their job and department in particular. A study by Corning Glass shows that a well-structured, supervisor-led orientation process can lead to a double-digit reduction in new employee turnover. That reduces hiring and training costs, but it also boosts retention of experienced people who have a broader and deeper understanding of customer expectations.

It is helpful to present new employees with a schematic drawing, on which you show customer expectations for product and service quality. "Here is what we mean by product quality. Here is what we mean by service quality. Here is how we deliver on those promises. And here is where your job fits. These are the behaviors that will help you meet the goals of your job." There is an old saying, "Well begun is half done." When it comes to orienting new employees to Knock Your Socks Off Service, well begun is a lot more than half done. It may well be the most important first impression you ever make.

12

The Importance of Informational Feedback

Feedback completes the informational loop, so if you don't have a good feedback mechanism from your customers, you don't have a complete service system. And a partial service system won't consistently deliver Knock Your Socks Off Service. To see how feedback fits into the system, see Figure 12-1, which repeats the scheme presented in Chapter 5.

Motivation and Learning

What's feedback and how does it work? Here's a good example. You've decided to take up bowling. You sign up for lessons at your local Gold Pin Bowling Center. You're assigned a coach. He hands you a ball and says "Okay, go ahead and give it a roll." You set up and roll the ball down the alley, but there are no pins at the other end. The ball simply rolls the length of the alley and disappears. You roll the ball several times, and each time it simply falls off the end of the alley . . . thud! Meanwhile, your coach sits silently, nodding occasionally while he watches you "bowl." How motivated do you think you'll be to continue the lesson? Not very. The goal in bowling is to knock down pins. Without a goal there is no motivation, no focal point for behavior. Without a goal, there's nothing to give feedback on.

Okay, let's add some pins to the scenario. You line up

Figure 12-1.   Service quality as a system.

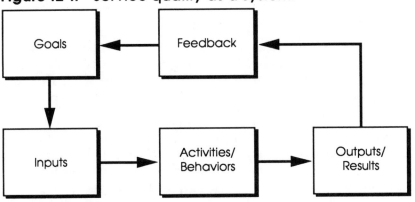

again, hoping for a strike. A few quick steps the way you were taught, and you roll the ball. As soon as the ball leaves your hand all the lights in the building go off. You hear a loud crash as your ball strikes the pins, but when the lights come back on, the pins have been reset. You bowl again. Lights go off. You hear a crash. Lights come on. Pins are reset. Once more, it's likely your motivation is slackening. "Look," you tell the coach, "I need a little feedback on how I'm doing."

"Okay," says the coach, "I'll give you a little feedback." So you roll the ball once more. Lights go out. You hear a crash. Lights come on. Pins are reset.

"How did I do?" you demand.

"Not bad," says the coach. "We'll give you the details at the end of your ten weeks of lessons." How motivated are you to continue now?

"Look," you say, "this is not working. I need to know how I'm doing *right now*, not in two months." You get ready to bowl one more time. A few quick steps. Release the ball. Lights go off. Pins fall. Lights come on. Pins are reset.

"Good," says the coach, "You got four down."

"Which four?" you ask.

"Don't worry about the details," says the coach. "Just keep trying." At that point, you've probably had it with bowling, and you're off to find another activity.

This "bowling lesson from hell" certainly *seems* ridiculous, but it parallels the poor feedback feature of a lot of service systems.

• **No pins.** Far too many service systems operate without goals. People just keep rolling along with no idea of customer perceptions of the level of service, no idea of what they are doing right, and no idea about where they need to improve.

• **Results in ten weeks.** For many employees, feedback in ten weeks would be vast improvement over the more common annual feedback. For many employees the annual performance appraisal is the only time they get any comprehensive feedback on how they are doing. Fortunately, timeliness in a service system can be addressed by shortening the feedback loop, as shown in Figure 12-2.

• **"You got four down."** Timely feedback is only half the story. The feedback must also be specific. You can't improve what you can't measure, and specificity implies measurement.

Information, Not Data

The bowling coach, when he did provide feedback, supplied only data—"You knocked down four." He didn't communicate any information—which four? Without the missing information, you haven't any idea how to change your performance.

Figure 12-2.   Feedback on goals and on behaviors.

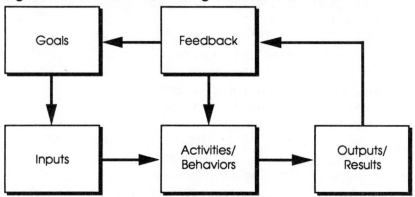

A lot has been written about the distinction between data and information, but the story of a hot-air balloonist lost in the fog is one of our favorite examples. The balloonist had no idea where she was. The wind pushed her first in one direction, then the other. She'd been in the air for hours and could have been just about anywhere. Finally she found a break in the clouds and slowly descended, landing in a vacant lot. She grabbed the first person she saw. "Where am I?" she asked.

"Why, you're at 304 South Maple Avenue," replied the passerby.

"You must be a statistician," said the balloonist.

"Why, yes, how did you know?"

"You just gave me a very precise piece of data that is of absolutely no value to me whatsoever."

We think that statistics and averages are important. They can be useful, but they don't *necessarily* represent good feedback. A well-designed service-delivery system has actionable feedback—information that can be used to confirm or correct performance of the system.

For feedback to be of use, it must *inform, enlighten,* and *clearly suggest* if improvement is needed. Tell hotel housekeeping that "63.7 percent of the guests think their rooms are unacceptably messy after cleaning," and all that's been communicated is "try harder and do better." The housekeepers know there's a problem, but they have little idea of what to do better. Instead, tell them that "yesterday, 63.7 percent of the guests thought their rooms were unacceptably messy after cleaning" *and* that wastebaskets weren't emptied on floors 5 through 11, used towels weren't replaced in rooms 410 through 421, and complaints about missing bath soap came from the fourth floor. Now the steps to correct the problem are clearer.

A word of caution about numbers and feedback. Percentages, averages, and proportions can make small numbers of problems seem like small potatoes due to "the law of unreported angst." Yet even small deviations from customer expectations can have a substantial impact on customer satisfaction and retention. In the hotel, for example, the guests in rooms 410 through 421 who complained about towels may seem like small potatoes. They are not. To these people in those eleven rooms, the towels are a *very* large problem. John Goodman of Technical and Research Program reports that only *half* of all unhappy customers complain. So if your company is averaging seventeen complaints a week, assume at least thirty-four problems out there, unless you have evidence to the contrary.

Exceeding Customer Expectations

There is the potential for an unwarranted assumption in our last comment. If you make sure that wastebaskets are emptied, towels are replaced, and everybody gets soap, then you'll wow the guests. We doubt it. We'll wager that no one ever said to you, "Stay at the Broadmoor the next time you're in Colorado Springs—they always empty the wastebaskets and always replace used towels." Emptying wastebaskets and replacing towels are minimum or nominal expectations. Forget them and the customer is annoyed; do them right and you'll be rated as "no worse than anybody else."

Knock Your Socks Off Service is about meeting minimal customer expectations and most important, exceeding them in a way that leaves customers saying, "Wow! These people are really something special." To consistently have people say "wow," you must continuously revisit the alignment between customer expectations and your goals. You must make sure that achievement of your goals means that customers are getting their socks knocked off. To do that, you need a good feedback system.

The Key Principles of Informational Feedback

Continuous feedback is critical to all aspects of the service system. It is critical to evaluating your goals in terms of customer perceptions. It is critical to ensuring that you spend your resources in the right places. It is critical to ensuring that your employees engage in the right behaviors and improve the right activities. It is just plain critical.

A feedback system that sustains high-quality service is based on six key principles:

The Six Key Principles of Feedback

1. Feedback is tied to service goals.
2. Feedback is both quantitative and qualitative.
3. Feedback is immediate.
4. Feedback goes to the person performing the job or task.
5. Relevant feedback goes to all levels of the organization.
6. Feedback is graphically represented.

Let's take a closer look at each of these basic principles.

1. **Feedback is tied to service goals.** Virtually all human behavior is goal-directed. We are always moving toward some sort of goal. If a feedback system relates to the goals we are striving for, we can identify those behaviors that lead to Knock Your Socks Off Service and those that do not.

Feedback on the job is analogous to yard-line markers on a football field. Just as the markers wouldn't make much sense without a goal line, feedback that doesn't relate to some goal doesn't make much sense, either. Every well-implemented service strategy has measurable promises in it. A well-thought-out feedback system relates to those promises.

2. **Feedback is both quantitative and qualitative.** Numbers and percentages are useful, but some of the best feedback comes from answers to questions like "Do you have any problems or concerns?" "What are your suggestions for improved service?" "Were any of our associates especially courteous or helpful?"

Sound familiar? They might. They're straight off one version of Marriott's guest comment card. The answers provide Marriott with valuable information they couldn't get any other way. Marriott combines this qualitative information with quantitative information they get from another type of card—one with a comprehensive list of questions concerning everything from check-in to room service. They just don't use both cards in all rooms, all the time, at all properties.

Which card is the right one to use? They both are. In a well-designed service system, feedback comes in two forms—quantitative and qualitative. *Quantitative* feedback tells us how much and how many. *Qualitative* feedback tells us how good, bad, or indifferent.

And just as Marriott combines both qualitative feedback and quantitative feedback to sustain Knock Your Socks Off Service, so should you.

3. **Feedback is immediate.** As children, we played some variation on the game "Hot and Cold." An object was hidden in the room. When the person chosen as "IT" moved away from the object, friends yelled "Cold. Colder. Colder. . . ." As the searcher moved closer, everyone yelled, "Hot. Hot. Hotter. Hotter . . ." until he or she finally identified the object. Finding the hidden object was the goal. Moving around the room was the activity. And all the shouting was the feedback. The searcher got immediate information that he or she was heading in the right or wrong direction. That's what made the game fun. But how much fun would it have been if the person looking for the object got feedback only every thirty seconds or so? How long would the person have been motivated to look for the hidden object if, after thirty seconds, someone just said "Cold"? After moving across the room and waiting, again all "IT" heard was "Cold"? Not much of a fun game.

Rapid-fire feedback keeps people motivated. It allows them to make quick adjustments before the problem gets out of hand. You should shorten the feedback cycle wherever you can within the natural context of the job. The quicker the feedback, the easier to relate specific job behaviors to specific service-quality levels. The more immediately the feedback is administered, the sooner those performance problems can be tackled. In essence, the employee learns that customers regard a particular behavior as "cold," another as "hot."

4. **Feedback goes to the person performing the job or task.** The person performing the job is the person responsible for meeting the service goal. Feedback that goes to someone else first necessarily means a delay. The immediacy is lost, and the impact of the feedback is diminished. The employee feels

less in control of his or her situation. In addition, feedback directly to the individual often initiates self-corrective action, thereby reducing the need for higher management to become involved.

An example of targeted feedback is the checkout survey system employed by Fairfield Inns. When a guest checks out, the person at the desk asks a series of questions about the guest's stay and keyboards the answers into a computer. The guest's answers are correlated with whoever performed the service. This system allows the hotel to track service trends, but also provides specific feedback that individuals can use to improve service performance.

The County Fair theme park uses a large board to track guest satisfaction. Service performance in this environment is difficult to feed back to individuals, so it is fed to teams. Which should you use—individual or team feedback? Either. Or both. It depends on what you're providing. If you can provide feedback to Karen as an individual, it helps Karen know exactly how she is doing. If you can provide feedback to Karen, Troy, and Bronc, it helps them know how they're doing as a team.

As a general rule, the more feedback, the better. If there's individual performance involved, try to generate individual feedback. If there's team performance, try to generate team feedback. If there are both individual and team performances involved, try to generate both types of feedback.

5. **Relevant feedback goes to all levels of the organization.** A well-designed feedback system measures and reports on behaviors that can be controlled by individuals receiving the feedback. In other words, individuals should receive feedback that helps them change behaviors to provide better customer service. Management should receive feedback that indicates a change is needed to the service system. Employees only become frustrated when supplied feedback about conditions that are beyond their control.

Richard Haworth, CEO of Haworth, Inc., a $600 million manufacturer of office furniture, accomplishes relevant feedback and several other principles of well-designed feedback through what he calls "quality by design" conferences. Eight

Haworth customers, eight dealers, and fifty Haworth employees are periodically brought together to address the question "How can Haworth do a better job in the next five years?" The groups are divided two ways: cross sections of discussion groups; and groups of all customers, all suppliers, and all employees. Through this process each group applies relevant feedback to its area of performance.

6. **Feedback is graphically represented.** Information is always more readily grasped when it can be represented pictorially. Researchers who have studied people's ability to remember things have found that when people both see *and* hear information, they remember substantially more after three days than when they either see *or* hear it. After three days, people remember 10 percent of what they are told and 20 percent of what they are shown. However, if they *both* hear and see something, they remember 65 percent of that information. Obviously, there's more than a bit of truth in the old saying "A picture is worth a thousand words."

Figure 12-3.   Graphic feedback.

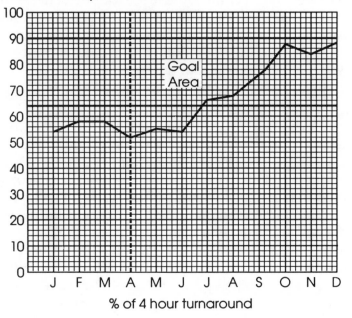

% of 4 hour turnaround

A graph can quickly give both the big picture and the specifics of goal-directed service behaviors. Even if people don't "understand" the numbers, they can understand what a graph is telling them. The goal area (as depicted in Figure 12-3) tells people "Here's where we are, here's where we want to be." As performance is tracked over time, the graph shows people their progress. Unlike reports, which get shuffled and filed (or tossed), a graph can be hung on a department wall to serve as a constant reminder of current and desired performance levels. Graphs can tie together the components of a service-quality program to achieve overall service-quality levels.

For instance, walk into Federal Express, Marriott, and other providers of Knock Your Socks Off Service, and you'll see graphs everywhere. Big, small, individual, team, location, corporate. You name it and they've got it. Follow their example because graphs provide good feedback.

Creating a Learning Organization

Master the six principles of feedback. They will help you create a learning organization that is able to continually improve and grow. If people receive feedback once a year, they have only one opportunity to learn each year. If they receive feedback once a month, they have twelve opportunities to learn each year. If they receive feedback once a week, they have fifty-two opportunities to learn. If they receive feedback once a day, they have some 220 opportunities to learn. Use feedback more frequently and you'll help create a learning organization that can sustain Knock Your Socks Off Service.

13

The ABCs of Knock Your Socks Off Service

The quarterback leans over the center. He glances right, then left and barks out the signals. The ball is snapped. The quarterback hands the ball to the halfback slashing to his right. The halfback cuts back past the block of the trapping guard, breaks a linebacker's tackle, spins to his left, eludes another tackler, picks up a key block downfield and it's a footrace to the end zone . . . the 45-yard line, the 50, the 45, the 40 . . . the defender is gaining . . . the 30, the 15, the 5. The defender makes a desperate leap, but it's too little too late. The halfback drags the would-be tackler the final two yards for the score. A great play. The halfback leaps to his feet, spikes the ball on the artificial turf, and launches into his victory shuffle, but suddenly stops. The stadium is silent. The home fans sit quietly. None of his teammates runs over to congratulate him. He wanders, bewildered, back to the bench. What's wrong with this picture?

Let's look at the halfback's run from a system perspective. He had a goal—literally a goal line—to score a touchdown. He had *resources*: blockers to open a hole in the defensive line. Activities were defined when the coach diagrammed the play on the blackboard at half-time. The halfback received *informational feedback*: clearly marked yard lines told him his progress toward the goal line. And the *result* equated to the goal. Touchdown!

So what's missing?

The applause. The cheers. The positive reinforcement that

comes from doing a good job and having the effort recognized and rewarded.

Feedback as Performance Reinforcement

In Chapter 12 we talked about *informational* feedback—specifics on how far you have progressed toward your goal. Informational feedback is necessary and helps motivation in the short term. But a second type of feedback is the applause aspect, or feedback as performance reinforcement. We call this *motivational feedback*. For the bewildered halfback, fan reaction is one source of such reinforcement.

Although the difference between informational and motivational feedback might seem small, it's very important. Just how important was made clear to us by the regional vice-president of a large distributor. At a regional meeting, he asked his nine branch managers to tell him what he could do, do differently, or stop doing to help them with their jobs. They told him they wanted more feedback. He couldn't believe it. He thought he provided them with feedback. He'd send summaries of customer-satisfaction surveys from other regions. He gave them copies of reports to the company president. They received reports of focus groups. They received copies of how each peer's branch was doing on customer-satisfaction surveys. If anything, he thought he was sending too much feedback.

Then one of the branch managers explained exactly what they wanted. They didn't want more information. They wanted more reinforcement—recognition for their efforts and acknowledgement of jobs well done. They wanted more motivational feedback.

The Behavioral ABCs

The ABCs are the basics in school. A different set of ABCs are the framework for motivational feedback. These ABCs are antecedents, behaviors, and consequences. In particular, consequences are the basis for motivational feedback.

1. *Antecedent*. What happens before the behavior occurs. The antecedent is the trigger or stimulus that starts the behavior. It is often in the form of cues from the environment—a customer's stated expectations, a customer entering a retail shop, information on a computer screen, a dispatcher saying "Take extra care with the Ascott order. Andy is very exacting and they're a really important customer."
2. *Behavior*. What a person does in response to the antecedent. Behaviors include greeting a customer, responding to a customer's complaint, or filling a customer order.
3. *Consequence*. Occurs after the behavior and usually the result of behaving in a certain way. Positive consequences include making a sale to a customer, receiving an award for outstanding performance, being thanked by a customer for taking extra care with an order, and getting a bonus. Negative consequences include being berated by a customer, getting yelled at by someone from another department, having to perform an unpleasant task, and receiving a reduction in pay.

Figure 13-1 presents an example of the interaction of antecedents, behaviors, and consequences and their relationships to behavior. In all four situations, the antecedent is the same, and in all but the fourth, the behavior is the same. But in each case, the consequence is different and leads to a different probable outcome. Thus, the implication for a service-quality effort is:

- Antecedents start behavior.
- Antecedents do not sustain behavior.
- Consequences determine whether or not a behavior will be sustained.

It is critical to understand the importance of consequences for a successful service-improvement effort. Consequences tell you the degree of motivation and commitment people will have over the long haul. Tell someone what to do and that will start behavior. It may even continue it for a short time. But unless

Figure 13-1. How consequences affect outcome.

Antecedent	Behavior	Consequence	Probable Outcome
1. Employee is encouraged to keep an accurate record of all customer complaints and their resolution.	Employee meticulously records all customer complaints and their resolution—has average number of complaints.	Supervisor ignores the employee all together.	Employee eventually stops recording complaints unless specifically reminded. Corrective actions and recovery probably aren't done or are done poorly.
2. Employee is encouraged to keep an accurate record of all customer complaints and their resolution.	Employee meticulously records all customer complaints and their resolution—has average number of complaints.	Supervisor chews out employee for complaints.	Employee becomes "creative" in defining what is, and is not, a "real" complaint.
3. Employee is encouraged to keep an accurate record of all customer complaints and their resolution.	Employee meticulously records all customer complaints and their resolution—has average number of complaints.	Supervisor compliments employee on the detail in the reports and notes reductions in types of complaints and the quality of recovery.	Employee continues to record information accurately and works to reduce the causes of complaints and improve the quality of recovery.
4. Employee is encouraged to keep an accurate record of all customer complaints and their resolution.	Employee meticulously records all customer complaints and their resolution—has a *higher-than-average* number of complaints.	Supervisor compliments employee on the detail in the reports and makes suggestions for reducing complaints.	Employee continues to report accurately and seeks ways of reducing complaints.

there are positive consequences for the behavior, it will diminish or cease.

The Three Types of Consequences

Reinforcement is nothing more than a consequence that the individual perceives as positive. It might be a kind word, a smile, a trip to a conference, a night out on the town, a bonus, a trophy, or any number of things that people perceive as positive. But feedback isn't always positive reinforcement. There's also *punishment*, as when something negative happens as the consequence of a behavior. That's getting yelled at, having to carry heavy boxes, or being caught in a traffic jam because you had to work late.

And then there's something psychologists call *extinction*, which is no feedback. Nothing. No smiles. No frowns. Neither a positive nor a negative experience. There is simply no response at all.

If you tell a joke at the office party, and everybody laughs, that's positive reinforcement. Tell a joke, everybody groans, and one person tells you the joke was inappropriate, that's punishment. But if the joke is met with stone silence, that's extinction. Curiously, extinction is usually more punishing than punishment. Yet "nothing" is too often the response to someone delivering Knock Your Socks Off Service. The three types of consequences are shown in Figure 13-2.

Reinforcement is the positive experience of receiving good attention. Positive reinforcement of desired behaviors enhances superior service behaviors. If a behavior leads to a positive consequence, it will continue; if a behavior leads to a negative consequence, the behavior will diminish or cease. In case 3 of Figure 13-1, the supervisor complimented the employee on the details in her reports, and noted any reductions in the complaints she was receiving and the quality of her recovery with the customer. As a result, the employee not only continues to file detailed reports, she works to reduce complaints and improve the quality of recovery.

Contrast that outcome with the new behavior of an em-

Figure 13-2. **Behavior and its consequences.**

Consequence	Usually Happens	Should Happen
Reinforcement = positive = good attention	—	When someone does something right
Punishment = negative = bad attention	When someone does something wrong	When someone does something really wrong
Extinction = 0 = no attention	When someone does something right	When someone does something a little wrong

ployee who submits detailed complaint reports, but who is "chewed out" by his supervisor because there are complaints (case 2 of Figure 13-1). This negative experience results in bad attention or punishment. To avoid being punished for a required behavior, the employee becomes very creative in defining what is and is not a real complaint. Complaints suddenly get reclassified as questions. Perhaps a process is adopted that complaints aren't recorded until someone is assigned to resolve them; if no one is assigned, there is no problem.

To sustain the behavior that produces Knock Your Socks Off Service, you should reinforce positive behavior and minimize the amount of attention paid to poor behavior. Unfortunately, usually the opposite occurs. When people do something wrong or poorly, they get attention. It might be negative attention, but they *do* receive attention. And either consciously or unconsciously, just about everybody likes attention.

That's why extinction is such a service-quality killer. When a company initiates a service-improvement effort, people start engaging in all kinds of new behaviors. There's a lot of enthusiasm and excitement. But in a couple of weeks, the excitement dies down. People are still engaging in the new behaviors, but unlike the early days, no one is reinforcing those behaviors. Without reinforcement, the behavior is extinguished. The process is like putting out a candle.

You could pour a bucket of cold water on a candle flame. Overkill, perhaps, but effective nonetheless. However, equally effective (and far less messy) is simply turning a glass jar upside down over the flame. Take away the oxygen and the flame is extinguished. Take away people's reinforcement, and the behavior that sustains Knock Your Socks Off Service is extinguished.

A Word About Punishment

In the very short run, punishment has a role in shaping employee behavior. It can stop a person from doing the wrong thing, but it doesn't necessarily follow that he or she will then do the right thing. Over the long haul, punishment is an ineffective way of changing behavior.

If you yell "Don't ever do that again!" the recipient probably won't do it again—at least while you're around. If you pound the table and say "I don't want more than three complaints a day," there might be a lot more than three, but you'll never see them. That's what happened in Detroit during the 1980s. A lot of top auto executives' bonuses were based in part on number of complaints. The easiest way to cut down on complaints was not to deal with them. But cutting off complaints cut off valuable informational feedback. The root causes of the complaints weren't addressed, and the problems just kept occurring.

Punishment almost never works in the long run. It fools us. It backfires. People go underground or come up fighting. They retire, but stay on the payroll. They perform well when you're around, but slack off when you're not there. Punishment also leads to escape and avoidance behavior patterns. If employees are punished for asking dumb questions, they stop asking all questions. If they are punished for providing service outside the boundaries of their job, they stop taking risks. They take refuge in policies and procedures—"Don't blame me if the customer's mad. I just followed the procedure."

Feedback, Follow-Up, and Reinforcement

Sustaining superior service is what you're after. You want a consistent level of Knock Your Socks Off Service over an extended period of time, not spikes of superior service interrupted by dips of poor service. In the short run, you can get the behavior you *expect*, but in the long run, you'll get the behavior you *"inspect."* If you expect people to carry out a task, they will do it satisfactorily in the short term; but unless the tasks are "inspected"—if people receive feedback, follow-up, and reinforcement—the behaviors won't be sustained. Without reinforcement, performance will inevitably decline.

Comments like, "People aren't motivated anymore," "People don't seem to want to work hard anymore," or "The training isn't taking" are the net result of behavior that is not positively reinforced. People know what tasks are expected of them. They know how to perform the tasks. They know when they should perform the tasks. They do not execute them because:

- The right behavior is not being reinforced.
- The right behavior is being punished.
- The wrong behavior is being reinforced.

The solution is to make sure the right behavior is reinforced, make sure it is not punished, and make sure the wrong behavior isn't being reinforced. All three points are important, but making sure the right behavior is reinforced is most critical to sustaining Knock Your Socks Off Service.

14

Stacking Up the Positives

It should be clear by now that ignoring your employees (even inadvertently) when they are doing a good job is no way to sustain Knock Your Socks Off Service. But how much positive reinforcement is required to sustain high-impact service behavior? And how best to implement that reinforcement? This chapter explores the ways and means of reinforcing the behaviors that sustain superior-quality service.

Reinforcement Ratios

There are three ratios that help determine how much reinforcement is needed. If an employee encounters one negative consequence for every positive consequence of a new behavior—a 1-to-1 ratio—the employee will perceive the behavior/consequence relationship as negative. If the ratio is 2-to-1—two positive experiences for every negative experience—then the employee will perceive the relationship as neutral. It's not until a 3-to-1 positive-to-negative ratio is achieved that the employee perceives the behavior/consequence relationship as positive.

And it is not until the 3-to-1 relationship is reached that you stand a chance of sustaining Knock Your Socks Off Service. A 1-to-1 ratio will probably eliminate the behavior and a 2-to-1 will just barely maintain it. You need at least 3-to-1. A 4-to-1 ratio is better. And a 5-to-1 ratio is better yet.

How does this translate to everyday work experience? The nature of service jobs is such that achieving a 3-to-1 positive-to-negative ratio is unlikely to happen by chance. In fact, given that customers have more propensity to complain than to compliment, it's likely that negatives will outweigh positives. (How many people drop in to the airline baggage manager's office to say thanks for not losing my luggage?) That doesn't mean that you can't sustain those behaviors that lead customers to judge your service as superior. It does mean that you can't leave reinforcement of those behaviors to chance.

Here is a simple exercise to give a feel for the positive-to-negative ratios in your organization. We call it the 10-Dime Approach. Take ten dimes, a dime being the smallest and lightest coin, and put them in one pocket in the morning. When you see people practicing Knock Your Socks Off Service, let them know about it. "I saw the way you handled that last customer, Sue. I think we'll be seeing a lot more of her." Move one dime to another pocket. "John, your suggestions on re-sequencing the orders is really going to help reduce cycle time. Keep those ideas coming." Move another dime to the other pocket.

Every time you reinforce a positive behavior, move a dime. If you see someone demonstrating improved behavior, even if it's not quite Knock Your Socks Off, let them know you noticed. "The complaint rate on damaged shipments is really dropping. The extra care the three of you are taking in packing the category 4 items is really paying off. Keep up the good work." Move another dime. Set a goal to move all ten dimes by noon. Then try to move them back in the afternoon.

Do this for one week, and you will probably learn two things. First, there are many more opportunities to positively reinforce the behavior of employees than you likely were aware of. Second, how seldom those opportunities for a word of encouragement are exploited. You might also learn how you personally can make a difference. Continue using the 10-Dime Approach for two more weeks or until you no longer need the dimes to trigger reinforcement. Repeat the exercise once a quarter or so as a check on yourself—are you still taking advantage of all the opportunities at your disposal? If a 3-to-1, 4-to-1, or 5-to-1 ratio feels like a lot of reinforcement, remember that for the vast majority of recipients it does not feel like a lot. It feels *good*.

"Positive" Is Relative

Like beauty, reinforcement is in the eyes of the beholder or—in this case—the recipient. A good example comes from Todd, a colleague who tells the story about a vice-president of sales he once worked for. Along with the rest of the executive staff of the company, the vice-president went through a course in developing people skills that obviously included a section on reinforcement.

> I was walking down the hallway when I saw the vice-president of sales coming my way. Now generally everybody tried to avoid Ed. It didn't matter what you did, Ed would find something to complain about. He'd have criticized Einstein for his haircut. Unfortunately he spotted me and made a beeline in my direction. Well, he came up alongside me, put his hand on my shoulder, looked me square in the eye, and said, "Todd, I just want to say you did a helluva job today. You didn't screw up once."

No doubt Ed intended that remark to be reinforcing, but it was anything but from Todd's perspective. The remark set Todd to thinking just what kind of screw-up Ed thought he narrowly missed. Although a positive experience was intended, it certainly didn't work out that way. So keep in mind that the recipient determines whether or not something is positive.

You may perceive writing a report on how to deal with difficult customers as positive, but the person you assign that task to may well view it as negative. Or you may perceive it as negative and your employee may see it as positive. Use positive, but make sure it's positive from the recipient's point of view.

The Best Reinforcers

The most important aspect of a positive reinforcement is that it be of value to the employee. *Value* doesn't necessarily translate to money. Many actions have value. For example, the Network Products Division of NCR has what it calls "Waytogo Notes." They're preprinted 5½- by 8½-inch cards that say "Waytogo" in big letters and have a place for a note describing a person's accomplishment. Every employee has a supply to be used spontaneously to say thanks to another employee for just about anything—providing good internal service, taking some action beyond the call of duty, or just being pleasant to work with. Walk through the facility and you'll see Waytogo Notes tacked up on work-area walls. People certainly don't put them up because they're expensive or flashy. They post them because they are proud of the recognition.

In addition to having high value for the recipient, the ideal reinforcer should meet certain other criteria. It should be under the deliverer's direct control (often the manager, but just as frequently could be coworkers, other departments, or internal customers). It should be immediate, be reusable, and be of low cost to the organization. The common feature is it be able to be used promptly and frequently. Frequent and inexpensive positive reinforcement is far more effective than infrequent and expensive reinforcement.

Although there is no *one* ideal reinforcer, Figure 14-1 evaluates the four most common categories of high-impact positive reinforcement.

1. **Economic monetary reinforcers.** Just what the name implies—monetary awards such as a salary increase, merit increase, bonus, or some fringe benefit. We enjoy money and presume you do also. The people who work for you no doubt feel the same. Too many companies give perfunctory raises. If you're going to sustain Knock Your Socks Off Service, you need to tie dollars to service behavior and service results.

2. **Economic nonmonetary reinforcers.** Generally two types—a substantial economic cost that the recipient might not otherwise be able to easily afford and a symbolic value that

Figure 14-1.   Types of high-impact positive reinforcement.

	Value to the Individual	Under Deliverer's Control	Immediately Available	Reusable	Cost to the Organization
Econnomic Monetary Reinforcers	High	Perhaps	Usually not	Yes	High
Econnomic Non-Monetary Reinforcers	High	Perhaps	Sometimes	Yes	Usually high
Non-Economic Tangible Reinforcers	High	Usually	Sometimes	Yes	Medium
Non-Economic Intangible Reinforcers	High	Yes	Yes	Almost always	Very low

differentiates it from other compensation. Examples are incentive trips to exotic locations, dinner for two at a five-star restaurant, "pick-a-gift" awards. Again, the value of this type of reinforcement in sustaining Knock Your Socks Off Service depends on how closely the award is tied to the behavior you are trying to reinforce. Awards should be tied to specific criteria that everyone understands. If Joe wins a trip to Bermuda, everyone should know he won it "for re-engineering the order entry process enabling us to deliver print jobs to customers two weeks earlier than before," and not for "doing a good job last year."

3. **Noneconomic tangibles.** Often reinforcers that enhance the status of an individual. It may be giving a person personalized stationery, a larger work area, special parking privileges. Plaques, awards, hats, jackets, and certificates are all noneconomic tangibles. These items derive their significance from what they represent. At some dollar value point, noneconomic tangibles merge with economic nonmonetary reinforcers.

4. **Noneconomic intangibles.** Frequently simple social

reinforcers. Almost any type of open praise—a smile, an invitation to lunch, using and acknowledging an employee's ideas in a larger program, letters of commendation, writing up achievements in a company publication, or private recognition between a supervisor and subordinate. This type of social reinforcement is valuable because it can be given quickly. Immediate feedback is more powerful than long-term reinforcement. That's why the 3-to-1, 4-to-1, or 5-to-1 ratios on a daily basis do a lot to sustain the behaviors you want, while annual performance reviews seldom sustain behavior change beyond a short period.

A System for Rewards and Reinforcements

Throughout this book we've stressed using a systems approach to sustaining Knock Your Socks Off Service. So it should come as no surprise that we believe you need a systems approach to combine all four categories of reinforcers.

People are not one-dimensional. They are most highly motivated when both financial and psychological needs are met. A high salary is certainly important (which is why consultants who give advice on why money isn't important to people charge $5,000 a day), but when a person is having a "hard day at the office," a simple pat on the back can make him or her feel like a million. People need psychological income as well as financial income. And an organization needs to provide both in order to sustain Knock Your Socks Off Service.

Although most people and literature lump reward and recognition together as near synonymous terms, we find it both useful and important to distinguish between them. *Recognition* is primarily psychological; *reward* is primarily economic. However, this is not a black-and-white distinction. Economic reinforcement may primarily be a reward, but it can have significant recognition value as well. Noneconomic reinforcement is primarily recognition, but it can have some economic value. The important point is that for the most effective reinforcement system, you need to mix equal parts reward (economic monetary and economic non-monetary) and recognition (non-economic tangible and non-economic intangible).

Figure 14-2. Types of reinforcers.

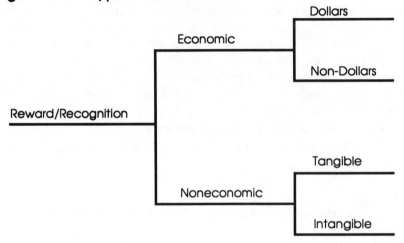

We can learn a great deal about good techniques for reinforcing behaviors by studying the organizations that do it well. In the following chapters, we take a look at some effective uses of the four types of reinforcement. Figure 14-2 provides the road map for our journey through Chapters 15, 16, 17, and 18.

15

Economic Monetary Reinforcers

Money isn't everything, although many people contend that it's way ahead of whatever is in second place. The fact of the matter is that people don't work just for the fun of it. They also work for the money they need to buy the necessities and luxuries of life. Money is a powerful motivator—and a generalized one. It can be the means to vast ends and make possible the fulfillment of many dreams.

Be that as it may, is monetary reward the best and only motivator for Knock Your Socks Off Service? The next two chapters address that question. In this chapter, we follow the path of economic rewards (Figure 15-1), through a discussion of specific monetary rewards and their value in sustaining Knock Your Socks Off Service. In Chapter 16, we choose the second branch of the economic rewards path, and look at high-value noncash incentives.

Trading Risk for Higher Compensation

You can talk about improving service in your organization until the proverbial prodigal comes home, but until you reward employees for their service-related performance, service performance isn't likely to change much. Xerox Corporation, a Baldridge Award recipient and a company on the cutting edge of the quality movement, learned that lesson in 1987.

Citing poor service as a factor in diminishing market share, the company decided to abandon the practice of rewarding

Figure 15-1. Economic rewards—monetary.

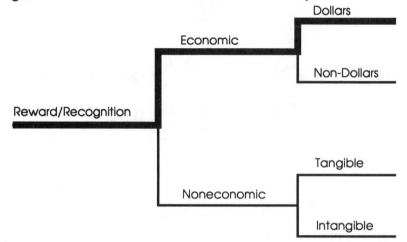

managers only for meeting traditional sales and profit quotas. Today, Xerox managers—even those in areas that rarely deal directly with customers—can increase their pay up to 40 percent by meeting customer-satisfaction targets or lose up to 20 percent if service problems mount. At Xerox, the philosophy is WHEN YOU PAY ON CUSTOMER SATISFACTION RESULTS, THE WORDS "CUSTOMER OBSESSION" TAKE ON A WHOLE NEW MEANING.

In the survey work we've done, we found that Knock Your Socks Off Service organizations tend to pay front-line service people above-average wages for their respective industries. In most organizations, where service seldom surpasses mediocrity, you can count on service pay being at the low end of the scale, and certainly not performance-dependent.

Among the companies breaking the low-paying mold for service is Saturn, where, because of the economic value of customer satisfaction and customer retention, sales assistants are paid handsomely. In one dealership we know, "handsomely" is in the neighborhood of $60,000 per year. Of course, there is a string attached: this "customer service specialist" is expected to bring in twice his or her salary in add-on sales—and does.

In Philadelphia, Fidelity Bank raised by 58 percent the average annual salary of its 100 customer-service representatives. A survey taken after Fidelity made that change and centralized its customer service operation found that over 90 percent of its customers would recommend the bank to a friend—up from 65 percent previously.

And it's not only on the front line where economic rewards for Knock Your Socks Off Service are showing up. Compensation programs with a service focus are in place at IBM for both salespeople and executives. Pay for salespeople and executive bonuses in many organizations are now based in part on customer satisfaction.

Along with the increase in economic reward for service performance, however, is likely to come increased risk and accountability. Increased risk means that a person's compensation can increase depending upon new measures of service performance. It also means a person can lose income. If a manager's base pay is $40,000, and she can earn an additional $10,000 bonus if the department surpasses its service performance measures, then a fifth of the manager's salary is at risk—and the percentage can go even higher. At Steelcase, a premier manufacturer of office furniture, 60 percent of management compensation is made up of quality-related bonuses.

According to the *Journal for Quality and Production*, this trend of exchanging risk for a high potential salary will be applied more and more in the areas of quality and customer satisfaction—not just at the managerial level but across the organization. At Carl Sewell's Village Cadillac in Dallas, virtually all employees are paid based on performance, not salary. Sewell believes employees paid as partners are more likely to provide good customer service and perform quality work. They have a vested interest in the company.

Such an approach makes even more sense when you consider the logic: If financial incentives work for salespeople, they can also work for senior executives. So why won't they be effective for front-line employees as well? In Tom Peters's *Thriving on Chaos*, the suggestions for economic incentive are simple: (1) very low base pay compared to very high incentive pay; (2) reward based on what you want to have happen.

Aligning Compensation With the Service System

Monetary rewards should be part and parcel of your service system. They should emphasize legitimate customer satisfaction. They should be clearly tied to service goals, as reflected by your service strategy and vision.

If you evaluate monetary rewards in terms of their value as motivators, what do you find? To help answer that question, here is a portion of the table we used in Chapter 14 to evaluate high-impact positive reinforcement.

	Value to the Individual	Under Deliverer's Control	Immediately Available	Reusable	Cost to the Organization
Economic Monetary Reinforcers	High	Perhaps	Usually not	Yes	High

Monetary reward is of high value to most people. In a recent survey conducted by the Society of Incentive Travel Executives (SITE) Foundation, 95 percent of the respondents ranked a cash bonus as a meaningful incentive. However, that finding should be tempered with the notion that the motivational value of monetary reward is higher for some groups than it is for others. Compensation and monetary motivators tend to be far more important to younger employees, those earning lower salaries, and those further down the organizational structure. That's a pretty good description of front-line service people in most companies.

A major factor that determines the power of reinforcement is its immediacy to the behavior to be reinforced. The stronger the link between performance and reward, the stronger the effect. First Union National Bank of Charlotte, North Carolina, "shops" its branch offices up to three times a quarter and instantly pays as much as $200 in bonus to any employee who scores a perfect 6 on the evaluation. But generally speaking, most economic rewards are only marginally under such control and are not available to employees with such immediacy.

Monetary reward is "reusable" in the sense that there is no limit to the number of bonus rewards or salary increases a company may give, other than limitations placed on the program by its high cost.

Although monetary reward is not the only, or even always the best, way to reinforce specific service behaviors, attaching economic incentives to service goals and performance sends a signal that the culture is changing and that service is important. Thus, economic rewards for service performance lead to Knock Your Socks Off Service.

Paying for Knock Your Socks Off Service

If an organization is serious about delivering Knock Your Socks Off Service, it probably needs to change its compensation system. It isn't hard to find companies that give out awards like T-shirts, plaques, and Service Person of the Month awards. But companies that build rewards into their basic compensation structures are more rare.

A company may say it wants Knock Your Socks Off Service, but when it really means it wants Knock Your Socks Off Service *that doesn't interfere with management's focus on this quarter's P&L statement*, employees are pulled in conflicting directions. The SITE survey referenced earlier found that 89 percent of American workers think their companies would perform better if employees were given meaningful incentives to improve quality and productivity. Only 40 percent of those surveyed believe that such is currently the case.

Employees at a major telecommunications company are a case in point. After conducting an employee survey, the company was upset to find that most customer-service representatives thought speed came before customers. To change this impression, the company held a weekend seminar and paid employees overtime to attend. The message of the seminar: When you pick up the phone, you own the problem. This was all well and good—except when employees returned to work on Monday. They still faced company policies, procedures, and evaluation systems that emphasized speed in handling calls, including timing how long employees talk to each caller.

Blending service quality and traditional objectives like productivity and efficiency isn't easy, but it's necessary to sustain Knock Your Socks Off Service. Service improvement, to be taken seriously, ought to be part of employee compensation.

Using Team-Based Compensation

One of the most discussed monetary-reward issues today is whether to reward on a team or on an individual basis. One of the most effective approaches to group performance-based compensation is *gainsharing*. Some of the best-known users of gainsharing are Herman Miller Co., an office furniture manufacturer, Lincoln Electric, and Donnelley Mirrors, but companies as large as General Electric, Motorola, and 3M have installed gainsharing in specific units.

Around for over forty years, gainsharing is the sharing of improved financial performance with the employees who made it happen. In gainsharing, a baseline period is established—usually a given year—and employees are promised a share of the profits *in excess of* the profits for the base year. Generally, half of the money in the bonus or excess pool is paid out to employees in the organization or gainsharing unit. Each employee's bonus is based on a percentage of his or her base pay. The other half of the bonus pool remains with the company. And of course if there is no gain, there is no sharing.

University of Southern California management professor Edward Lawler notes that gainsharing programs are most successful when they cover fewer than 1,000 employees. In units of 1,000 or fewer, contends Lawler, employees see a clear relationship between what they do and their pay and thus the gainsharing bonus. He writes, "gainsharing may prove to be more effective in service organizations than in manufacturing organizations because . . . performance is so easily controlled by the people doing the work."*

*Edward E. Lawler III, *Strategic Pay: Aligning Organizational Strategies & Pay Systems* (San Francisco: Jossey-Bass, 1990), p. 153.

Other performance-based compensation plans include straight profitsharing and employee ownership (stock option plans, employee stock ownership plans, and the like). Regardless of what plan you choose, tying monetary rewards to employee performance can, and does, increase motivation. Such plans are not always easy to implement, however; as we observed in Chapter 14, they lack some of the pizzazz of short-term, noncash programs.

In short, look at your compensation plan. If you're saying you want service quality, but your goals take your people in one direction and your compensation plan takes them in another, you'll never be able to knock the socks off your customers over any extended period of time. You must align your compensation plan with Knock Your Socks Off Service.

16

Economic Nonmonetary Reinforcers

As reported in *The Wall Street Journal*, many companies, in their quest for higher-quality service, are experimenting with creative incentives for employees who satisfy customers. The cost of individual awards can range from almost nil to five figures. Group awards can cost an organization well into six figures. Cash is a popular incentive, but according to a survey by the Society of Incentive Travel Executives (SITE) Foundation, so are training, stock options, a trip to a desirable destination with spouse or guest, recognition at a company meeting, and merchandise. In this chapter, we look at economic nonmonetary awards—specifically travel and merchandise incentives—and how they can impact a service-quality effort and where they fit in a motivational mix. Nonmonetary economic awards are of substantial economic value, but when properly used, they also carry significant recognition value. See Figure 16-1 for where these nonmonetary reinforcers are on our rewards chart.

What Merchandise Incentives Are

As an incentive, merchandise awards are given to employees for achieving specific service-related objectives. Merchandise is either selected to fit the profile of the audience or each participant is given a catalog from which to choose an item. In the

Figure 16-1. Economic rewards—nonmonetary.

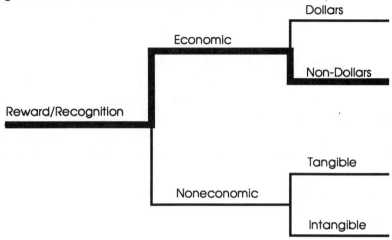

latter case, employees generally are awarded points for defined accomplishments. They then redeem these points as they choose. They may accumulate them toward some grand prize, or redeem them for smaller items. To classify as an incentive, merchandise must be of significant value—generally about 2 percent of an individual's total salary.

Travel incentives can be made available to individuals, families, or groups from the organization. They can be strictly for pleasure or combine business and pleasure, such as a trip to a conference or seminar that includes an extended stay and travel accommodations for a spouse or guest. Trips can range from simple travel vouchers to elaborate affairs like the American Express "Great Performers" trip to New York.

While most companies keep cash performance bonuses hush-hush to avoid interorganizational jealousy, incentive awards don't seem to generate the same jealousy, and incentive efforts are promoted to the hilt, often culminating in elaborate recognition celebrations. Travel and merchandise awards are more easily promoted than cash. It is easier and more effective to promote the excitement of a vacation trip or stimulate the desire for a merchandise award than its cash equivalent. There is an excitement and recognition factor inherent in nonmonetary awards that is not present with cash. It's also more in line with the wants of a life-style generation.

Reasons for Using Incentive Awards

Travel and merchandise awards are of sufficient value and attractiveness to motivate people to improve service-related performance. Not everyone receives an award, but most try and at least improve performance over the norm. Based on research done by Martiz, Inc., of St. Louis, we have four reasons for using nonmonetary awards.

Four Reasons for Offering Nonmonetary Awards

1. **To supplement existing compensation plans.** When people understand your compensation system, and they are satisfied with the way they are paid, it isn't necessary to alter your entire compensation system to improve a specific aspect of service quality. Incentive awards target specific service-related behaviors over a finite duration. They are not a substitute for a poorly understood or implemented compensation plan.

Because incentive awards clearly are not cash, they cannot be confused with the compensation plan. There is little or no entitlement. Using incentive awards to motivate Knock Your Socks Off Service allows the organization to fine-tune or experiment with service measurements and objectives (within reason) without confusing people or raising doubts about their basic salary structure.

2. **To call attention to an immediate and specific problem.** The special attention and focus that incentive awards create helps employees easily differentiate between the level of service an organization is providing and the level of service it *should be* providing. Incentive awards raise the level of awareness of service behaviors that need changing immediately— more so than does cash. Cash compensation is generally associated with "doing the job." A trip to an exotic location or an

expensive merchandise item signals that something about the job has changed.

Of course, this argument can be turned around. Knock Your Socks Off Service *is* part of the job. Why should it be rewarded outside of normal compensation? Many consultants and quality specialists contend that an incentive strategy sends the wrong message. People get the idea that Knock Your Socks Off Service is above and beyond the call of duty, not something they need to do every day. Although it is less than wise to throw incentives at every service problem, it is equally unwise to assume they have no place in the motivational mix.

If you apply incentives to reinforce a focus on the right results—that is, those results that reflect Knock Your Socks Off Service—eventually the behaviors that produced those results will be repeated because they work. Reinforcement will flow naturally from the job—from compliments from customers, from fewer hassles, and the like. Incentives can stimulate behavior and can initially reinforce results, but sustaining Knock Your Socks Off Service requires choosing the right behavior to target in the first place.

3. **To recognize outstanding performance.** Unlike a cash award, nonmonetary awards carry a recognition value that lasts. When was the last time you went to someone's home to see slides of his bonus check? But no doubt you've seen slides of someone's trip to Hawaii, Caribbean cruise, or Mexican holiday. We don't know anyone (and we probably don't want to know anyone) who hangs a facsimile of her paycheck on the wall of her office. But people will point with pride to the stereo they received for providing outstanding customer service. This is the "trophy value" of incentive awards. Every time a person notices the stereo, TV, or VCR, or sees the snapshots from the trip to Hawaii, it motivates that person to continue the behavior that resulted in the award and serves as a reminder that knocking the socks off customers is important.

4. **To appeal to most employee populations.** "Different strokes for different folks," as the saying goes, is another reason to consider nonmonetary incentives as part of the motivational mix for your service effort. For example, surveys

have found that travel incentives appeal most to employees in the 24- to 34-year-old age group, least in the 55- to 64-year-old age group. By varying the incentive, you can tailor a service-quality improvement program specifically at the interests of different target audiences. Pick-a-gift catalog merchandise programs, in which employees earn points redeemable for items of their choice, is about as up close and personal as an incentive gets.

A word of warning here: The wrong recognition for a group may be worse than none at all. Awards must pass the "snicker test." If employees regard the awards as juvenile or see little value in the merchandise, or aren't widely excited about the travel destination, their opinion will show and the program is bound to fail. A reward is considered a reward *only* when the recipient perceives it as such.

Do It SMART

Not all incentive programs work. Some fail to achieve their objectives. Other unwittingly set the wrong targets or place them out of reach. Still others go disastrously wrong. Writing in *Corporate Meetings and Incentives*, John Halbrooks notes that companies considering an incentive program evaluate their plan against the five SMART criteria—Specific, Measurable, Achievable, Results-oriented, Timely.

1. **Be specific.** Incentive programs are a special game. Like any good game, the rules should be specific, clearly stated, and easily understandable. Employees should know what they have to do to win.

2. **Make it measurable.** If the rules for the incentive game are specific, clearly stated, and easy to understand, the players know where they stand. But it's just as important that the company know where it stands. It must be able to measure achievement. Don't base an incentive program on service performance that can't be measured or attempt to use measurements that either aren't clear to all or don't have clear connections to superior customer satisfaction.

3. **Make it achievable.** All or nothing one-winner-takes-all goals seldom motivate more than a few people—namely, those who are already top performers. Once people are out of the running, the program ceases to have any motivational impact for them. One of the best ways to make the award widely achievable is to have more smaller awards rather than one gigantic award. If you insist on offering the "mother of all incentives," be sure to incorporate interim awards that have broader applicability.

4. **Be results-oriented.** Make sure you are rewarding what you think you're rewarding. An incentive program necessarily changes the focus of your people. If you reward them for handling calls efficiently, what impact will that have on the time they take to really understand and solve customer problems?

One solution is to establish "gate" criteria. For example, you might reward individuals for handling an increased number of calls, provided they achieve a minimum level of customer satisfaction. If the customer satisfaction number isn't achieved, then the individual can't qualify for the award, regardless of how many calls he or she has handled. Or send the big producers on a trip as long as their customer satisfaction ratings are above 96 percent—with the added incentive that anyone above 98 percent customer satisfaction flies first class. (The obvious assumption is that you have an effective way to measure both elements—calls handled and customer satisfaction in the first example and sales and customer satisfaction in the second example.)

Many of our clients already have incentive awards in place based on sales. We're recommending to them that they continue those trips, but that they start using customer satisfaction as one of the criteria that determine who gets to go on the trip. We'd recommend that you do the same. If you have such awards in place, keep them. But modify the criteria to include customer satisfaction.

5. **Be timely.** Before putting an incentive program in place, make sure you understand the nature of the business cycles involved. Year-end closing is probably a bad time to

focus your financial organization on developing more user-friendly invoice systems. You probably don't want to have your top salespeople on a cruise ship when your major competition launches a new product. And you don't want to be tied to a long-term incentive program that prevents you from adapting to changes in your customer's needs.

It's interesting to note that studies on incentives have found that it takes 5 to 8 percent of an employee's salary to change behavior if the reward is given in cash. If a noncash reward is given, a value approximating 4 percent of the employee's salary will motivate a change.

Economic nonmonetary rewards are reusable because almost anyone would take another trip to someplace warm in March or add a stereo to the big-screen TV he or she received last year. In fact, successful incentive programs often are repeated for a number of years.

Incentive programs are best suited to stimulate specific service-related behaviors over a finite period of time. They send a signal to employers about specific behaviors that need to be changed, and provide initial reinforcement for those that make the change and achieve results. An incentive program is more results- than behavior-oriented. Incentive programs provide booster shots to your service-improvement efforts, helping to sustain Knock Your Socks Off Service.

17

Noneconomic Tangible Reinforcers

Noneconomic awards also oil the wheels of cooperation and dedication to the job. Recognition, as opposed to compensation, is something given to an employee for taking a little extra time with a customer, for going a step beyond nominal expectations, for caring enough about what he or she is doing to look for ways to do it better, faster, smarter. Recognition says "I care that you care enough to do the little extras that can mean so much to customers." Figure 17-1 highlights this other path through reinforcement choices. In this chapter we look at ways tangible noneconomic reinforcement can help sustain Knock Your Socks Off Service.

Active Symbolism

If you want to give service employees T-shirts to show them how important they are but you haven't addressed the fact that they are poorly paid, consider imprinting the T-shirts with the slogan MY COMPANY MADE $15 BILLION AND ALL I GOT WAS THIS STUPID T-SHIRT. That's what your employees may well be reading no matter what the lettering on the shirtfront says. First and foremost, symbolic items will be positively viewed by employees if workers are basically satisfied with the compensation system. It's Psychology 101, Maslow's Hierarchy of Needs: If their basic needs are not satisfied, people have less interest in nonnecessities like recognition. Symbolic awards are an important part of the Knock Your Socks Off Service motiva-

Figure 17-1. Tangible noneconomic recognition.

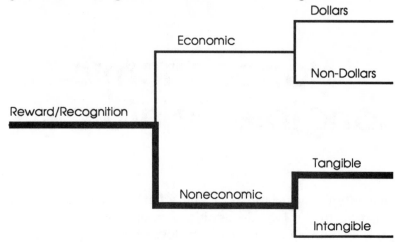

tional mix, but they won't work without other forms of compensation and reward.

Dual-Purpose Symbols

Noneconomic tangible awards are symbolic. They have more "meaning" than they do financial value. Plaques, rings, jackets, desk sets, reserved parking places, a larger work area, a new job title, or membership on a select committee are all examples of noneconomic reinforcers. And they are all as appropriate to sustaining Knock Your Socks Off Service as are significant merchandise and travel incentives or even major changes to a compensation plan—if they are used in the right way.

Symbolic awards are tactics common to service leaders such as First Federal/Osceola, Lenscrafters, Citicorp, and Federal Express. At Citicorp Retail Services in Denver, good suggestions for new and better ways to serve customers warrant a "Bright Ideas" coffee mug or similar keepsake. The employee who submits the month's best idea wins a circulating trophy—a three-foot-high light bulb.

Items like coffee mugs can play a dual role in the effort to sustain Knock Your Socks Off Service: ongoing awareness and recognition. *Awareness* is acknowledging the importance of customers. Organizations have program themes such as WE LOVE CUSTOMERS! printed on selected items and distribute them to all members of the organization, *regardless of their performance*. Warning: This type of generalized awareness does have a place in sustaining superior service quality, but awareness items are communication tools; they are not feedback. They are reminders of the company's focus on Knock Your Socks Off Service, not symbols of achievement.

Recognition is the second use of symbolic items. Recognizing outstanding service performance with a T-shirt or coffee mug is an inexpensive way of maintaining a focus on superior service. Such an award is insignificant in financial terms; certainly the intrinsic value is not enough to motivate people to improve service performance. The power of the award comes from what it represents.

The significance of an award, however, doesn't just happen. It has to be created. A lot depends on how the organization positions the award in the mind of employees. If the employee sees (1) no special significance to his or her award, (2) no connection with company goals, or (3) no connection between his or her performance and the award, then there is no symbolism. Symbolic awards need to be presented with a little pizzazz.

As an executive from Mary Kay Cosmetics puts it, "If an actor received an Academy Award through the mail, would it have the same impact?" At Mary Kay—and at many other organizations that realize the value of symbolism—the belief is that the greatest impact comes from "a nickel's worth of award presented with a dollar's worth of recognition."

One of our favorite symbolic presentations is conducted by Precision Lenscrafters. They celebrate the end of a store-level sales contest in a truly unique fashion. The awards meeting starts in a traditional enough fashion: Performance awards are passed out, customer compliment letters are read out loud, and the individual employee of the period is saluted by the regional sales manager. At this point, the anticipation starts to build. The salesperson with the best record closes the meeting by serving a cream pie—whammo, no ducking allowed—into the face of the regional sales manager. Don't ask. Some organizational traditions and symbols aren't meant to be understood by outsiders. That's part of their power.

Catch Somebody Doing Something Right

CATCH SOMEBODY DOING SOMETHING RIGHT is a motto that succinctly captures years of managerial wisdom and a ton of behavioral science research. It has special meaning and import for the service-management effort: If you want to reward people in your organization for thinking and acting in customer-oriented ways, seek ways to catch them doing just that. But there's a basic implementation problem: *How* do you catch people doing things right?

In the modern corporation, most managers seldom see more than a small sample of employees and therefore have fewer opportunities to personally see employees, particularly front-line employees, doing anything—good, bad, or ugly. So despite the fact that a manager is a powerful influence on employee performance, the improbability of being within reach when the "reinforceable moments" occur negates much of that powerful reinforcement potential. This problem of managing employees seen only sparingly—and seldom, if ever, in the presence of customers—is not a trivial one, especially in light of industry trends to downsize management. It makes everything from performance reviews to assessment of promotion potential tough to do as well. And it can make "catching someone doing something right for the customer" darned difficult.

Difficult, but not impossible. A few progressive organizations use customers to reward and recognize superior employee performance. The approach has great potential for applying symbolic recognition as immediate feedback for behavior that sustains Knock Your Socks Off Service.

Several years ago we worked with a theme park researching various ways to put feedback and recognition into the workday life of employees—and improve customer satisfaction.

We knew we'd have to provide special support to keep guest relations at a high level. We borrowed the term *Warm Fuzzy* from transactional analysis and turned it into a symbol. Every fortieth guest entering the park received two small gold-colored cards identified as a Nice Going Award. The guests were asked to give the cards to theme park employees who made their day more pleasant.

At the same time, supervisors were given blue cards identified as a Fuzzy Award, also to be awarded for good performance. These tickets could be requested by employees to award to someone else on an employee-to-employee basis as well. The Fuzzy Award *could* be awarded for simple acts of niceness, but supervisors were encouraged to award them for specific behaviors that contributed most to guests' enjoyment of the park—friendliness, service, park cleanliness, and show. Employees who received a Nice Going Award or Fuzzy Award jotted the date and reason for the award on the back of the card and later redeemed it for a Fuzzy—a brightly colored fluff ball, which they fastened to their name tag on their costume. The tickets also earned the employees points toward prizes.

We encountered only one problem with the system. Hoarding. Not by the givers, but by the recipients. Employees were not exchanging their Nice Going and Fuzzy Awards for prizes. An employee focus group told us why—the psychological value of receiving the little cards outweighed the value of the prizes. As one employee put it, "When I'm having a bad day, I take out my stack of Warm Fuzzies and reread the notes on the backs. The nice things people said about me. It makes me feel better. That's more important than any prize I could buy for turning the cards in."

The lesson was an important one. It's awfully easy to lose sight of how powerful these symbolic awards can be. When we stopped to analyze the focus-group results, we realized that receiving the Fuzzy card provided not one, but several reinforcement opportunities:

1. When the Fuzzy card was initially given
2. When the Fuzzy ball earned by the ticket was displayed on the name tag

3. When guests asked about Fuzzies on the name tag
4. When the tickets were redeemed for prizes
5. When things were not going well and employees pulled out the cards to reread the comments

Aligning Incentives with the Service System

Using our systemic approach to sustaining Knock Your Socks Off Service, you need to ask yourself how the characteristics of nonmonetary awards should be incorporated into your service-quality system. Much of what we said in Chapter 15 about changes to a company's compensation system apply to the use of incentives (see below, portion of table from Chapter 14). Effective use of incentives means they must be related to specific service goals, as reflected by your service strategy and vision. They should emphasize legitimate customer satisfaction.

	Value to the Individual	Under Deliverer's Control	Immediately Available	Reusable	Cost to the Organization
Economic Non-Monetary Reinforcers	High	Perhaps	Sometimes	Yes	Usually high

Like economic monetary rewards, nonmonetary incentive awards are of high value to most individuals. Their intrinsic monetary value can be increased with emphasis on their "trophy value." The more an organization chooses to promote the incentive program and celebrate its results, the more the incentive itself is valued. Value is also added by selecting incentives to appeal to targeted groups.

It is possible to tailor incentive programs for immediate reinforcement. Some programs, such as Nordstrom's All Stars, reward employees on a monthly basis. Using a point system whereby points are awarded for outstanding acts of service allows a supervisor to bestow points as immediate reinforcement. Points can be accumulated for a larger award at a later date. In general, however, front-line management does not have immediate control over incentive programs and reinforcement of specific behaviors is delayed. That's a lot of value for a small investment.

Aligning Symbolic Awards With the Service System

In general, noneconomic reinforcement differs from economic reinforcement in three key ways: Economic reinforcement has a relatively high cost, is difficult to bestow immediately, and focuses the individual on service *results;* noneconomic reinforcement is relatively low cost, can be given immediately, and has the potential to focus the individual on service *behavior* as well as service results. These characteristics are reflected below in the partial table from Chapter 14.

	Value to the Individual	Under Deliverer's Control	Immediately Available	Reusable	Cost to the Organization
Non-Economic Tangible Reinforcers	High	Usually	Sometimes	Yes	Medium

The theme park example clearly demonstrates that symbolic awards have high value for individuals. Although the program had to be authorized by park management, once under way, it was really under the control of front-line supervisors. Awards immediately followed behavior when presented by park guests and when employees were "caught" doing something right by a supervisor. Not only were the awards reusable, in the sense that employees could receive unlimited Fuzzy cards, but they were also reusable in the sense that there were five opportunities for the same Fuzzy card to remind the employee of his or her service efforts.

Finally, the program cost was extremely low relative to the value. Prizes ranged from discount pizza coupons to $50 gift certificates at a local clothing store. Not exactly stock options and company cars, yet you wouldn't know it from the expressions on employees' faces when they received the coveted Blue Fuzzy. It wasn't just back to the grind for them. It was back to delivering Knock Your Socks Off Service to their "guests."

18

Noneconomic Intangible Reinforcers

After one of our seminars, a participant cornered us with some rather pointed comments. "My department is responsible for filling customer orders," she said. "That's our job. My people are *paid* for filling orders correctly. Therefore, they should fill orders correctly. Shouldn't a paycheck be reinforcement enough?" she asked, fully convinced that it should be.

"Are they filling orders correctly now?"

"No, not at a satisfactory level. We run in streaks where we're mediocre at best. We certainly don't knock the socks off of anyone with our accuracy."

"Are your people getting paid?"

"Yes."

"Well, it seems to me that from a behavioral point of view, you're paying your people for *not* delivering Knock Your Socks Off Service."

Obviously, no one *intentionally* pays people to do mediocre work, but that's essentially what happens in too many organizations. People are reinforced—paid—for not performing well. Salary is a form of "table stakes"—the price you pay for attendance, attention, and a certain level of effort.

In this chapter we follow the noneconomic reward path begun in Chapter 17, but concentrate on intangibles (see Figure 18-1). These intangibles involve social reinforcement of both results and behaviors. Social reinforcement is almost any type of open praise. It can be as simple as a pat on the back, a written note to an employee, coffee and doughnuts in the morning after people have put in a long night, shared infor-

Figure 18-1.   Intangible noneconomic recognition.

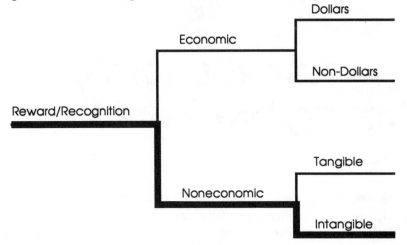

mation, or even a small "gag" gift—giving an employee a bag of mixed nuts for "putting up with nutty phone calls all week."

Simple actions? Sure. Powerful motivators? You bet! P. T. Barnum (in somewhat less delicate terms) once advised a young man trying to run a scam on him "Never try to kid a kidder." This piece of advice has kept managers from using simple social reinforcements to motivate the hardened, the seasoned, the sadder but wiser, the seen it all and done it all—the old salts of every industry.

We agree that insincere adulation and pro forma thanks go nowhere, particularly with employees who have been around the block a few times. At the same time, dozens of industrial sales managers, technical service executives, and health-care professionals combine feedback, incentives, and generous personal attention and thanks—social reinforcement—to increase results as much as 18 percent over base.

Through sincere, well-placed, well-timed praise and recognition, commission salespeople have changed from low producers to high producers and from high producers to even higher producers. Service technicians who had been curt with customers have become paragons of positive customer relations. MRI technicians who seemed more empathetic with their equipment than with their patients have turned into role models of care and concern. The same magnitude of results has been produced in other service organizations. Why?

The Value of Psychological Income

In Chapter 14 we identified two types of income people receive from their jobs. Economic income is the monetary reinforcement; psychological income is the good feeling they get about themselves, their competence, their self-worth, their confidence.

Obviously, people work for economic gain. But people work for recognition as well. Once basic economic requirements are met, the recognition—the psychological income—often becomes more important. We saw that in Chapter 17, with theme park employees. Both economic income and psychological income are important to sustaining Knock Your Socks Off Service. You must have both in your motivational mix.

There are many methods to deliver psychological income. Whenever possible, reinforce people face-to-face. It helps build a one-on-one relationship. Compare, for example, receiving a plaque for good service through the company mail to having someone come to your office and congratulate you for retaining a large customer through your prompt action on a complaint.

Another very effective reinforcement, especially if you are separated from the recipient by geographical distance, is a printed letter with a personal, handwritten note taped at the bottom. The printed quality gives the letter a formal aura while the handwritten note adds the personal touch.

A short telephone call is often the most appropriate way to reinforce behavior, especially when you're trying to bring immediacy to the reinforcement. Acknowledge an employee achievement with a comment like "Nolan, I just read your memo on reducing the time it takes to dispatch repair people. Excellent work. I'm routing it around headquarters."

And in the large corporation, add voice mail messaging,

faxes, and computer mail to the list of ways to deliver praise. Each has appropriate uses, but perhaps more important than the method is the way the employee perceives the reinforcement. If the recipient does not feel the reinforcement is positive—such as our friend Todd in Chapter 14, who was told he had a good day because "he didn't mess up"—then you've probably done more harm than good to your service effort. Praise that embarrasses or isn't perceived as praise is not reinforcing; indeed, it can have a negative effect on future performance.

Empathy With Employees

Each individual responsible for reinforcing behavior must adapt the technique to his or her personal style. Praise that appears insincere turns people off. The key word is *appears*. It's not as important to *be* sincere as it is to *appear* sincere. We don't like that particular fact of life, but it's true. There are two saving graces, however. First, there is a much greater possibility of reinforcement appearing sincere if it really is sincere. Second, if someone practices reinforcement even without 100 percent commitment, and finds that it works, he or she will use the technique more and get better at it.

Take the woman who felt that because her employees were paid to fill customer orders correctly, she shouldn't have to make a special effort to reinforce their behavior. Chances are that anything we might say at a seminar wouldn't change her attitude overnight. At best, we hope that she'd return to her department and experiment with some simple reinforcement. If her reinforcement efforts appear sincere and are correctly targeted at behaviors that improve order fulfillment, there will be an increase in the accuracy of orders. This will happen even though her heart may not be 100 percent in her actions. As time passes, the woman's behavior of providing reinforcement is itself reinforced by the improved service performance of her employees. Her reinforcement activities become more natural, less forced, and more sincere. She is experimenting, learning, and being reinforced by her success at reinforcing others. A well-done feedback and reinforcement system reinforces the efforts of everyone in the system.

The flip side is also true—heartfelt compliments that appear insincere don't work. Many people are uncomfortable complimenting others, just as some people are uncomfortable being complimented. A person responsible for reinforcing others must take both cases into consideration. If you are more comfortable with written notes than face-to-face encounters, then by all means write. If you know an elaborate awards ceremony would likely embarrass a person, take time to personally and quietly let that person know he or she is delivering Knock Your Socks Off Service.

The most heartfelt example is "The Case of Jane," to keep the parties unknown. Jane is a young customer-service rep for a major pharmaceutical company. Two years ago, she did an amazing job and saved the business of one of the largest HMOs in the country. She did *such* a good job that the head of pharmacy for the HMO raved about her to everyone who would listen. Finally, the president of Jane's firm heard about her outstanding job. He was so impressed that he wanted to show his appreciation and invited her to lunch in the executive dining room the following Wednesday. Jane spent the weekend before the big lunch shopping for "just the right outfit," and spent Monday and Tuesday in a panic, gulping aspirin by the handful, trying to figure out just what she was going to say to Mr. Big. She later swore to us that if "I had known what I was going to be subjected to, I would have thought twice about doing such a good job."

Empathy needs to be applied to employees as well as customers. Remember Jane the next time you're "absolutely sure" about the best way to reinforce someone.

Social Reinforcement Through Celebration

Sustaining Knock Your Socks Off Service is a continuous, systematic effort, but even the most effective service organization is going to require a little boost in enthusiasm every now and then. One way to do this *and* provide social reinforcement is with a celebration.

Celebrating the success of your service efforts is more than just an excuse for a party. It puts energy back into your service efforts. It's an important demonstration of faith and commitment. It reminds everyone in the organization of the purpose and mission of delivering Knock Your Socks Off Service. And more important, the celebration is social reinforcement. It is a way for the organization to loosen up and say to everyone— from the front line to mahogany row—"Thanks for delivering Knock Your Socks Off Service." Celebration should be an integral part of the way you reward and recognize your employees.

- When Bill Daiger, president of Maryland National Bank, wanted his front-line people to know that he and the bank needed and appreciated their efforts to make MNB number one in customer service, he hired a hall, sent formal invitations, and threw a magnificent party—a gala for all employees. The affair was such a hit, the bank regularly takes time to throw a party and celebrate its "stars."
- At South Memorial Hospital in Oklahoma City, management found a unique and memorable way to celebrate the hard work and dedication of the hospital staff. It created a musical comedy, in part a send-up of themselves and their behavior, and performed it for all three shifts of employees. And they served a special dinner—or breakfast or lunch, depending on the shift—as well.
- In one division of Honeywell-Bull, management decided it was past time to recognize the hard work and dedication of the group customer-service staff. Managers and field service people worked the customer-service desks and phone while the

> hard-working customer-service reps were treated
> to a catered luncheon and recognition ceremony.

In addition to serving a reinforcement role, celebration is a way of nourishing the spirit of the organization and creating a time to reflect on what Knock Your Socks Off Service really means. It is more than just contributing to the bottom line. It is bettering the lives of the company's employees. Celebration reaffirms in highly human terms that people are an important part of something that really matters.

Just as people work for more than money, they also work for more than praise. They desire to be part of something important and meaningful. Being part of an organization that sustains Knock Your Socks Off Service, being best in the industry, providing recognizable benefits to customers, and earning customer trust and respect have a power that can make salary increases, bonuses, and Employee of the Month plaques pale by comparison.

Celebration reminds everyone that Knock Your Socks Off Service is exciting, important, and *attainable*. Celebrating success reaffirms to your employees that they are headed in the right direction—that they are on course. Confirming to people of *all* levels in the organization that they are a part of something important, that the Knock Your Socks Off Service they provide is vital to the organization and the customers they serve, may be the highest form of reinforcement.

Aligning Social Reinforcement With the Service System

In Chapter 14, we saw that the ideal behavior reinforcer is of value to the individual, is under deliverer's control, is immediate, is reusable, and is of low cost to the organization. Although some company celebrations are expensive, in general social reinforcement comes closest to the ideal. These characteristics are reflected in the portion of the table from Chapter 14, shown here:

	Value to the Individual	Under Deliverer's Control	Immediately Available	Reusable	Cost to the Organization
Non-Economic Intangible Reinforcers	High	Yes	Yes	Amost always	Very low

Social reinforcement is simply showing employees the most basic human gratitude for their efforts. Business is very good at recognizing major achievements. We throw lavish affairs to honor our most productive. We heap honors on those who go above and beyond the call of duty to satisfy customers. We sing the praises of the Employee of the Month. But how often do we recognize the little behaviors that are completed along the way? How often do we stop to say thank you to the individuals, the teams, the employees who are the backbone of the company's success?

If common sense weren't enough, numerous surveys show that no company can have happy customers without happy employees. *Happy* doesn't mean a herd of giddy people who break out the pretzels and beer and head for the softball field after a hard hour at the office. It means employees who care about and are excited about what they are doing.

Here's the bottom line: You can't deliver Knock Your Socks Off Service to your customers if you aren't knocking the socks off your employees by the way you treat them. You can't do justice to customers if you don't do justice to employees. If your employees don't have a positive image of your company, your customers won't, either. In that light, social reinforcement takes on great importance.

It takes an even greater importance if you consider the possibility that economic reinforcers generally capture the bodies and minds of employees. Knock Your Socks Off Service, however, also requires the *hearts* of your front-line service deliverers. And capturing the heart requires social reinforcement for those extra efforts that dazzle your customers.

19

The Nine Principles of Day-to-Day Reinforcement

Positive reinforcement can be as simple as telling an employee that you noticed how well she defused an angry customer. It can be as complex as setting up an executive bonus program based on customer-satisfaction data collected from divisions around the world. It can be as inexpensive as a three-inch button that says "I done good today." It can be as expensive as a trip for two to Cançun. But regardless of ease, difficulty, or expense, positive reinforcement is a powerful tool for sustaining Knock Your Socks Off Service behavior. And the best opportunity is usually on a day-to-day basis. Here are nine principles that help you recognize opportunities to use day-to-day reinforcement to sustain Knock Your Socks Off Service.

Principle 1:
Once Behavior Is Established, a Relatively Small Amount of Reinforcement Will Maintain That Behavior.

Think of shaping a behavior as pushing a stuck car: It takes a lot of energy to get the car moving, but once it's rolling, it doesn't take as much energy to keep it rolling. It might take a lot of energy to get someone to do something, but once the behavior starts, it can be maintained with a little reinforcement.

To sustain Knock Your Socks Off Service you have to sustain those behaviors that have the greatest impact on customer loyalty and satisfaction. You communicate, through your service vision and service strategy, the importance of those behaviors to the organization's success. The initial push might very well be enough to start people adopting the behaviors, but it will take reinforcement to give those behaviors the force of habit—enough positive reinforcement to overcome any random negative reinforcement that comes from the environment.

Few companies that start a service-quality process escape "hitting the wall." Once the hoopla and energy from the initial phases die down, malaise and even resentment can set in if management takes its eye off the service-improvement ball. Organizations that sustain Knock Your Socks Off Service do so by concentrating reinforcement efforts during the introduction and early adoption of high-impact service behaviors (see "Continuous Reinforcement Develops New Behaviors . . ." on page 156).

Principle 2:
The More Immediate the Reinforcement, the More Powerful It Is.

To be most effective, reinforcement should be as immediate as possible. Reinforcement that takes place a week, a month, six months, or a year after the behavior occurs has only a short-term effect. The closer the connection between behavior and consequence, the more tightly linked the behavior and the reward are in the person's mind. The tighter the link, the more apt the behavior is to be repeated. Don't wait. Put the ten dimes in your pocket and start now.

Stew Leonard, Jr., is a good example of the power of immediate reinforcement. When he sees something done right on one of his numerous walks through his store, he doesn't wait to give a pat on the back. If he notices the fish display looks particularly good, he's on his ever-present walkie-talkie to Nick Milillo, who holds court over all the nondairy fresh foods, including meat, fish, produce, and deli. Once he has Nick on the line, he lets him have it.

"Nick," he says in his energetic fashion, "just wanted to let you know that the fish display looks absolutely great this morning. Keep it up." He repeats his reinforcing message to people in the immediate area, and he's off to the next department. It's constant attention to reinforcement that enables Leonard's to sell over 3,000 pounds of fillets in a week versus maybe 800 pounds in a good neighborhood specialty store.

Principle 3:
It Is Important to Reinforce Both Excellence and Progress.

You don't get to be scratch golfer by subscribing to *Golf Digest*. True enough, the magazine is loaded with tips that will improve your game, but it's going to take some hands-on practice. Developing the behaviors required to sustain superior service quality requires the same kind of effort.

So, just because you've trained your people in high-impact service behavior, it doesn't mean they're all going to go out and knock customers' socks off. They're going to have to practice. And at first, they might not be all that good at the new behaviors. Do you still reinforce people delivering less than Knock Your Socks Off Service? Well, if you do it right, it will help them get to a Knock Your Socks Off level. *Not everyone is great, but everyone can improve.* And they get better if you reinforce progress.

Use statements like, "Mary, you're doing a much better job of defusing upset customers. I really appreciate the effort that's gone into that progress. Keep up the good work!" This motivates Mary to continue her efforts (she got reinforced for efforts), acknowledges the progress she's made (she got reinforced for the progress), and helps her with an important skill (she got reinforced for defusing an upset customer). If you add "I particularly liked the way you were able to empathize with her needs," you also reinforced a specific behavior that Mary can use in the future. This technique is known as *shaping*, and it is very powerful in continuously improving the level of service. Whatever you reinforce, you get more of. Reinforce progress and you get more progress. It's as simple as that.

Many people do a reasonably good job of reinforcing excellent service behavior and excellent service results. Most people could do a better job of reinforcing *improvements* in both service behavior and service results, as the following list shows:

1. *Reinforcing excellent service behavior.*	"Ryan, I really appreciate the extra time you spent helping David and Nicole identify their software needs."
2. *Reinforcing excellent service results.*	"Well, team, a big way-to-go to you for January's results. We came in at a 98 percent on our SQI again. We're the number-one region in the country for the third month in a row."
3. *Reinforcing improvements in service behavior.*	"Jill, I noticed that you're much more at ease on the phone with customers. That work you've been doing on active listening seems to be really paying off."
4. *Reinforcing improved service results and motivating for future performance.*	"Well, team, a big way-to-go for you on the improvement in January's SQI. As you can see, we're at 87, which is an increase of 2 over last year's average and an increase of 1.5 over December. Looks like the momentum is going our way now. [*End of reinforcement.*] Let's see what we can do to keep it going." [*Actions*

to keep the momentum going—
probably up to 98.]

Companies that stand still in today's competitive market-place are going to get passed by. If you want to set the standard for your industry, you need to continuously improve both service behaviors *and* service results. That improvement is best brought about by reinforcing improvement. So continue to reinforce appropriate behaviors and good results, but pay particular attention to reinforcing *improved* service behavior and/or *improved* service results.

Shaping is somewhat analogous to weight training. Few people could walk in off the street and press 210 pounds. If someone did, you'd think it was great. However, if someone came in and only lifted 35 pounds, that would be no big deal. But suppose that person last week was only lifting 25 pounds? Thirty-five pounds still isn't much, but it is a 40 percent improvement in just a week's time. Reinforcing that improvement is how you keep the person coming to the gym.

The same concept applies to raising the level of high-impact service behavior, especially if the behaviors are new to the organization. Not everyone is going to make 100 percent of the goal the first time out. Some people may even fall below the minimum standard. You obviously can't and shouldn't recognize these people in the same way you do the top performers—that would be demoralizing to both groups. Nonetheless, it is possible to reinforce *movement* toward the goal. Remember, reinforcement is strengthening. If you reinforce a *level* of performance, you will get more of that level of performance. If, however, you reward *movement* in the right direction, you'll get more movement. And as you build momentum, you get more momentum.

When you reinforce progress in addition to reinforcing excellence, you're going to get more people making more progress. More people making more progress leads to continuous improvement. And in today's competitive marketplace, continuous improvement is key to both survival and success.

Principle 4:
Continuous Reinforcement Develops New Behaviors, and Intermittent Reinforcement Maintains Those Behaviors. Intermittent Reinforcement Increases Resistance to Extinction.

Our friend Cliff is an avid golfer. Unfortunately, to put it kindly, he's somewhat on the shady side of a double-digit handicap. The first two holes are okay, but on the third hole Cliff steps up to the tee and bang—300-plus yards right down the middle of the fairway. Well, that shot keeps him happy through five more average holes. Then on the ninth hole, Cliff rolls in a chip shot from 30 yards off the green. That holds him until the sixteenth hole, where he drops a 28-foot putt. Another 300-yard drive on the eighteenth, and Cliff's in the clubhouse buying new golf shoes.

That's the power of intermittent reinforcement. There are two primary ways reinforcement can be given: continuous and intermittent. Both are shown in Figure 19-1. *Continuous rein-*

Figure 19-1. Continuous and intermittent reinforcement.

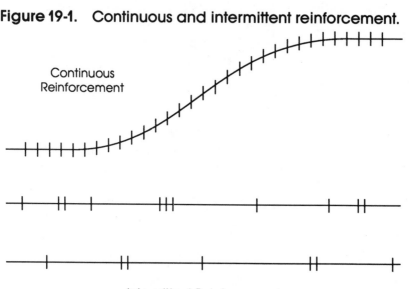

Continuous
Reinforcement

Intermittent Reinforcement

forcement is what the name implies—reinforcing a person every time he or she exhibits the desired behavior or takes a step in the right direction. Continuous reinforcement is most powerful, and probably most necessary, when you first introduce a new service behavior into your organization. It is equivalent to pushing the stuck car. It's the organizational energy required to get the car moving.

Intermittent reinforcement is administered on a random basis. Good golf shots are few and far between for our friend Cliff. And even Cliff doesn't know when they're coming. But he knows that sooner or later he's going to make a good shot, and that's what keep him playing. When service behaviors become ingrained, continuous reinforcement is no longer necessary. Intermittent reinforcement will sustain the effort, as shown in Figure 19-1. You'll still want to keep your 3-to-1, 4-to-1, or 5-to-1 positive-negative ratio. But as individuals become more comfortable with the behavior, and as they get better at it, more of their reinforcement will come from the environment—feedback from customers or, as we'll see, from naturally occurring reinforcers.

Principle 5:
There May Not Be Enough Natural Reinforcement in the Environment to Develop a New Behavior, but There May Be Enough to Maintain the Behavior Once It Has Been Developed.

Naturally occurring reinforcers are things like satisfaction with a job well done, sense of accomplishment, or pride in work. In Knock Your Socks Off Service organizations, a lot of reinforcement comes from people being able to tell themselves "We did great" or "I did great." This self-reinforcement is one reason intermittent reinforcement can replace continuous reinforcement once the behavior has been learned.

However, as beer-loving Norm on the TV program "Cheers" has observed, "It's a dog-eat-dog world out there, and I'm wearing milkbone shorts." In driving for superior service quality, you must be constantly aware of the environment. At times, there may be increased negative feedback from customers, suppliers, or colleagues. When that happens, you'll have to step up reinforcement to keep people motivated.

Principle 6:
Reinforcement of One Behavior in a Category Tends to Increase Other Behaviors in the Same Category.

A real advantage of reinforcement is its ripple effect. If you reinforce Justin for submitting a detailed report on customer complaints, he will probably do a good job on other reports. This makes reinforcement a high-leverage activity. You can identify a class of Knock Your Socks Off Service behavior and increase the frequency of that behavior in a lot of different areas with very little reinforcement.

In service delivery, teamwork is often an important ingredient. If you say to Bob Carothers, "Bob, I really appreciate the help you gave Melissa, Mary, and Avis in getting out that order for Joey Tree. That kind of teamwork is critical to improved customer satisfaction," several things take place. Bob will learn that helping Melissa, Mary, and Avis is important (the specific incident). He will also learn that teamwork is important (the general category of behavior). Thus, when other teamwork opportunities come up, he'll engage in additional teamwork behaviors.

Principle 7:
Reinforcement Should Be Specific, Eliminating "Noise" in the System.

Consider Joan, who is in charge of customer relations for a consumer products company. People who report to her write letters to customers responding to complaints, concerns, questions, and other issues. When Joan finds a letter that is especially well written, she compliments the writer—not in broad terms but specifically. She picks out the exceptional parts of the letter—it gets to the point quickly, it's brief but complete, it's written in the first person, it demonstrates empathy with the customer's concern. Then she writes her specific comments on a copy of the letter, and sends it back to its author.

Joan's practice of using specific reinforcement is the exception, not the rule. Most people tend to be general about what's right, and specific about what's wrong. "Overall, it's a pretty good letter, Bill, but . . . your lead paragraph rambled. You didn't summarize the problem. And you didn't propose a solution." Although this approach certainly tells people where there are opportunities for improvement, it doesn't say where the strengths are. It's all negative, so there is little, if any, motivation to improve.

On the other hand, Joan's specific reinforcement cuts right to the chase. Her people know exactly what Knock Your Socks Off Service means. Her crisp definition of superior letter writing focuses the employees on what needs to be done. The letters coming out of Joan's organization are examples of efficiency, effectiveness, and customer care. They get the job done with minimum effort and convey the image of a professional, yet caring organization.

Principle 8:
Reinforcement Exists Only in the Eyes of the Beholder; Not All Things Are Reinforcing to All People.

The point bears repeating: DO UNTO OTHERS AS OTHERS WOULD BE DONE UNTO. Too many managers attempt to reinforce someone with what they themselves would find reinforcing. Managers who know how to deliver Knock Your Socks Off Service realize the importance of determining what reinforces other people. They put themselves in the other person's shoes.

Principle 9:
It Is Important to Use Reinforcement to Help People Link Service Behavior With Service Results.

Use reinforcement to link Knock Your Socks Off Service behavior to Knock Your Socks Off Service. You'll build a stronger organization of service-oriented people. For example, "Bill, you did a great job solving that problem for Judd and Peg Bell [reinforcing the behavior]. That's the kind of extra effort that improves customer satisfaction [result], and not only keeps them as customers for a long time [result] but often leads to referrals and more new customers" (result). This way Bill not only has a firmer grasp on a particular behavior (problem solving); he has a contextual framework within which to fit that behavior (it leads to customer satisfaction, which affects customer retention and referrals). With this contextual framework, Bill can function with more autonomy and flexibility as he goes about his day-to-day activities. Because he knows that problem solving is the type of behavior that leads to improved customer satisfaction, he'll continue to find situations in which positive behaviors will also improve the customer-satisfaction levels.

20

Developmental Feedback: Addressing Issues of Nonperformance

As we've detailed in previous chapters, you must be specific in defining service goals for your organization and setting up procedures to reach those goals. You must also define behaviors you expect from people in the organization, and provide feedback to them on how they are doing. Chapter 12 discussed informational feedback, which tells you that you are (or are not) knocking the socks off your customers with the quality of your service. It also tells you whether or not the activities of your organization are producing the results you are looking for. Motivational feedback, or reinforcement, was discussed in Chapter 13. You use reinforcement to ensure that the behaviors producing Knock Your Socks Off Service will be repeated.

A third type is *developmental feedback*, the subject of this chapter.

When Corrective Action Is Required

A popular theme of many quality-improvement efforts is continuous improvement. In this book, we have emphasized a systems approach to continuously improving an organization's level of service quality. The necessity of a sound, systematic approach to service can't be overemphasized when it comes to delivering superior-quality service.

However, often overlooked in the quality literature is the role of the individual performer and his or her improvement. "Continuous improvement" applies not only to service systems but to individuals within those systems. Because so much of the service experience is the result of encounters between individuals, continuous improvement of people becomes a key element in sustaining Knock Your Socks Off Service.

Sometimes, individual performance slips and needs corrective action. When that happens, you have to intervene. You have to sit someone down, and discuss ways to get subpar performance up to where it should be. These are times when, despite all your efforts, an employee is not performing to your expectations. Letting such a situation fester only communicates that you are not really serious about service quality. To sustain Knock Your Socks Off Service, you must deal with cases of nonperformance quickly and positively.

Supportive Confrontation of Nonperformance

You use developmental feedback to correct subpar performance and get people moving in the right direction. This is a three-step process consisting of a prediscussion period, an actual discussion, and a follow-up discussion.

Prediscussion

To talk with an employee who is not delivering the level of service you expect, you must first lay a solid foundation. First, you must make sure that goals and action steps, resources, necessary skills, and informational and motivational information are all in place. For example, you may find that some part of the system is blocking that employee from performing up to expectations. Maybe there's not enough time to do every element of the job well. If so, take corrective action. But maybe the person simply isn't performing well; that's when you use developmental feedback.

Next, you must work through how you intend to address the performance discrepancy. This might involve actually scripting how you want the discussion to go. Write down the exact words you will use to define the situation, particularly in the first couple of minutes when the tone is set. Anticipate reactions and be prepared to address them. Above all, know the conclusion you want to reach.

Then, position the discussion properly. Let the employee know specifically what it is you want to discuss, with a focus on the positive. For example, if you want to talk with Brian and his failure to promptly return customer calls, tell him that. Say something like: "Brian, we need to discuss our expectation of promptly returning phone calls to customers. I've noticed that some of the customers in your region report that we're missing our two-hour target. Before the end of the week, I'd like to figure out how we can start hitting that two-hour turn-around on a consistent basis. When are good or bad times for you between now and Friday for us to sit down and discuss that?"

Some key points in positioning are:

- Give the employee time to think about the situation between notification and discussion, but not so much time that the individual can begin to worry. Schedule the discussion for no more than three days after you mention it; even better is later that same day.
- Let the person know the conversation will be a positive exercise in looking for ways to improve, not a "chewing out."
- Be clear that you want to have a focused discussion at a specific time. The problem is real and current. In both positioning and discussing, don't bring up dead issues; that simply communicates to the individual that there is no salvation. Plan to deal specifically with the issue at hand.

Discussion

Immediately set a pleasant tone; put the individual at ease. Until the employee is comfortable, he or she will be using energy to cope with the stress of the meeting rather than focusing on the issue of performance improvement. Although putting an individual at ease should not be artificial and contrived, it can be planned. For example, if you share a common interest, a brief exchange about how the local team did on the weekend, a popular movie that opened, or who was on the "Tonight Show" opens the discussion and helps reduce tension.

Once there is a relaxed atmosphere, describe the performance problem in a factual manner. This is not a time to be judgmental, blaming, or evaluative. That would be perceived as a personal attack and would take the focus off improvement. For example, a statement like "Brian, you're not returning phone calls promptly. Don't you care about customers?" puts Brian on the defensive. Better, a descriptive statement like "I notice from the call log report that sometimes you don't return customer calls for several hours or until the next day"; it defines the problem without attacking the person. The descriptive approach is not designed to let people off the hook. On the contrary, it puts them *on* the hook and makes them account for their performance.

Let the individual know that this is an issue and that you'd like to see performance improve. "I'm concerned about this and want to explore ways we can consistently meet or exceed the two-hour target." Having defined the problem, and expressed your concern over the present level of performance and your desire to see it improve, follow up with a future-oriented neutral question that focuses on improvement. This works better than asking what went wrong in the past or posing questions that can be answered only with a yes or no response. If a person can tell you *how* something can be corrected, he or she has already determined what went wrong in the first place. Once that person acknowledges that he or she is not delivering service up to standards, there's no reason to force a verbal confession.

In fact, whenever the person offers an excuse, use a future-oriented question to get back on track. For example, if Brian says "I could answer all my calls if you want me to do a poorer job with the others," a proper response would be "That's an easy answer, but probably not the best one. We need to keep the level of service high *and* respond in a more timely manner. How can we do that?"

Here are some examples of questions to avoid and others that are effective.

Questions to Avoid

1. Historical questions (going back in time): Why did this drop so much? What caused this problem?
2. Questions that can be answered yes or no: Do you think you could do this? Is it possible to reduce this trend?
3. Questions that build defensiveness (why/who): Why did the drop occur? Who said to do that?

Questions to Use

1. Future oriented (improving service delivery in the future): How could this be corrected? What could we do to reverse this trend?
2. Open-ended (requiring an active response): Which of these solutions are you recommending? How could we get back to our previous average where 95 percent of the customers surveyed were checking "would definitely recommend" in response to question 3?
3. Neutral questions (what, where, when, how, which): How could we get back to two-hour turnaround? What could you do to overcome the impact of that particular perception?

During the discussion be sensitive to positive statements the employee makes. Reinforce those statements either verbally or with some nonverbal reinforcement like nodding your head in agreement or smiling. And be open to any suggestion for improvement, no matter how off-the-wall it might be. Get the ideas down on paper without comment. The objective is to keep the ideas flowing until the two of you arrive at some specific actions.

For example, if you ask Brian "How can we cut down on the time it takes to return phone calls?" Brian might answer that the switchboard operator needs to do a better job routing calls to the customer-service people. By doing so, Brian is generalizing the blame. You need to get the conversation back to specifics. "What do you mean by better?"

"Well," says Brian, "he always routes the calls from the northeast region to me. Those are our largest accounts and it takes more time to handle their requests. That doesn't always leave time to return other calls." Now you've arrived at something specific. You could look at calls on a regional basis and see if Brian is correct. Quite possibly some type of routing priority based on customer location or size may need to be established so one person doesn't take all the complex calls.

Once you've arrived at a tentative solution, get the employee to commit to a target. For example, you might propose to Brian, "Okay, if we start routing some of the northeast region calls to other people, would that help you return all calls within two hours?"

Once you and the employee have reached an agreement, summarize what has been agreed to and express confidence in the employee's ability to handle the situation. You should also set a date to meet again to review progress.

Postdiscussion

It's important that you keep any promises you make. In the conversations with Brian, the promise was made to look into how calls were routed. This should be done, *and the results discussed with Brian*. Your conscientious effort to do what you said you would will help strengthen your employee's resolve to do the same. Also follow up on any milestones. Employees are quick to assume that if there are no checks on what they are doing, no one cares.

Finally, reinforce any signs of improvement. Addressing issues of nonperformance starts a new behavior pattern. A discussion based on the principles in this chapter will lead to an immediate improvement in performance. But it is only a shot in the arm. Without proper follow-up reinforcement, the new behavior will be extinguished and the old behavior will reappear. Say things like "Brian, I see we've made a significant jump toward our goal of returning all calls in two hours. I appreciate the effort that's going into that improvement. Keep up the good work and we'll be at 100 percent turnaround by our target date of March 26." The continuous improvement that comes from that progress leads to sustained Knock Your Socks Off Service.

So make it a point to reinforce the "Brians" for *all* progress they make after one of these discussions. Reinforce early and often. If you do, their momentum will continue to build, and they will soon be doing a knock your socks off job.

21

Bringing It All Together

What we've outlined here is something you keep doing because well-known companies such as Disney and Federal Express, and little-known companies such as Avalon Carpet Care and Ascott Corporation, keep raising the standard for all of us. So here are some ways to expand the application of what we've covered.

One way to ensure that you're continually raising the service standard for your industry is to use the system model introduced earlier (Figure 5-2) to ask the questions that will keep up your forward momentum. Use the following checklist to maximize the impact of your service system.

Goals:

- ☐ Are your overall service-quality outcomes clear?
- ☐ Does every employee understand his or her role in producing those outcomes?
- ☐ Are the desired outcomes realistic?
- ☐ Are your service goals periodically reevaluated to ensure they are consistent with customer expectations?

Inputs/Resources:

- ☐ Do people have enough time to achieve service goals?
- ☐ Are there enough people to provide the level of desired service?
- ☐ Are there sufficient tools, job aids, equipment, and other resources to achieve the desired level of service?

☐ Are your resources being spent in areas important to your customers?

Behavior:

☐ Can the behaviors that lead to service outcomes be performed?
☐ Does something in the system prevent the behavior from occurring?
☐ Are the desired behaviors observable/measurable?
☐ Have you identified high-impact service behaviors?
☐ Do you know the relationship between the desired behavior, its antecedent, and its consequence?
☐ Will the behaviors you are targeting result in outcomes that your customers will perceive as Knock Your Socks Off Service?

Results/Outcomes:

☐ Are both quantitative and qualitative results measured?
☐ Are both outcome and process results measured?
☐ Are results linked back to appropriate individuals and appropriate behaviors?
☐ Are customer satisfaction and customer-focused results measured and reported on with the same sense of urgency as financial and productivity results?

Informational Feedback:

☐ Is the feedback related to a goal?
☐ Is the feedback self-administered?
☐ Is the feedback immediate?
☐ Does the feedback go to the appropriate person?
☐ Does the feedback go to all levels of the organization?
☐ Is the feedback graphically displayed?
☐ Does the feedback indicate how the result is important to the customer?

Motivational Feedback:

☐ Are both results and behavior being reinforced?
☐ Are both improvement and achievement being reinforced?

☐ Is the reinforcement specific?
☐ Is it timely?
☐ Is it tied to a service-quality goal?
☐ Is there a proper mix of monetary and nonmonetary, tangible and intangible rewards?
☐ Are rewards based on outcomes that are important to the customer?

Developmental Feedback:

☐ Is nonperformance quickly and supportively confronted?
☐ Is the discussion carefully thought out?
☐ Are open-ended, future-oriented questions used?
☐ Is the performance issue described factually?
☐ Does feedback and follow-up take place after the discussion?

Building a Customer Focus Into *Every* System

Departments or functions in an organization don't exist in a vacuum. Your service-delivery system is not a single system, but rather a series of systems linked together as illustrated in Figure 21-1. The output of the supplier becomes input to the commissary. And the output of the commissary becomes input to the restaurant.

With feedback built into every step, the elements of the organization constantly improve their way of doing things,

Figure 21-1.   A linked service-delivery system.

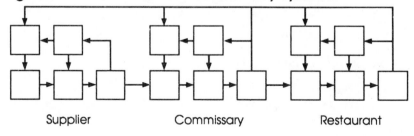

Supplier   Commissary   Restaurant

enabling them to individually and collectively sustain Knock Your Socks Off Service.

Further, within each element or function, there are subsystems. Figure 21-2 breaks the commissary into three subsystems: order entry, cooler, and shipping. The same techniques for sustaining Knock Your Socks Off Service that we've outlined throughout this book apply to individual functions within the organization.

Practice the 10-Dime Approach with your suppliers and "supplier departments." Too many departments are quick to let another know when something wasn't done properly, but slow-to-never in recognizing when something was done well or was improved upon. If you *do* have to confront nonperformance by another department, use the developmental feedback techniques in Chapter 20—especially the "what" and "how" questions with a future orientation.

So look upstream and downstream to see how you can improve your service-delivery system. That way you'll get each subsystem aligned with customer expectations. After all, service quality is really achieved at the subsystem level, where something is received from somebody and then re-created or changed in some fashion and passed along to somebody else. It's one of the paradoxes of service quality: If you don't improve at the subsystem level, you won't improve service quality; likewise, if you only improve at the subsystem level, you won't improve service quality. When you get all the systems aligned with customer expectations, "us" and "them" go away. Instead of thinking in terms of functions or departments, people think of *customer-focused systems*.

Figure 21-2.   Subsystems within one organization.

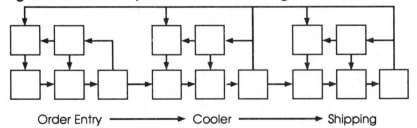

Order Entry ⟶ Cooler ⟶ Shipping

The Hawthorne Effect

The Hawthorne Effect is a revered part of the folklore of behavioral science and management theory. It's based on studies conducted at Western Electric's Hawthorne Works in Chicago by Harvard Business School professor Elton Mayo. Mayo made frequent changes in the working conditions, many of them in the amount of illumination. Curiously, increased productivity accompanied both increases and decreases in illumination. This led to what has commonly been called the "Hawthorne Effect." Quite simply, this piece of folklore says that if you change anything and pay attention to people, performance will improve. The folklore is wrong. We agree that paying attention is important, but it's certainly not enough. In fact, much of what happened in the Hawthorne Studies can be explained by the behavioral principles we have outlined in this book.

Although most people speak of the Hawthorne Effect in connection with a single study on the effect of changes in plant lighting on productivity, in fact seven such studies took place between 1924 and 1932. During those studies, many other factors were changed as well. For example, prior to the experiment the employees had been paid on a complicated piecework system that tied individual reward to departmental performance. Given a department of 100 people, it was difficult to compare individual effort to overall department performance. A worker might have a good day and produce more than the quota, but department performance could be down and individual pay would suffer. He might have a bad day and produce less than the quota, but department performance would go up and the pay would be higher. In essence, the system gave the worker consequences that were not necessarily directly related to individual effort or productivity.

During the Hawthorne experiment, a work group of five women was put in a separate room, and the same basic pay system was maintained. However, because of the reduction in work-unit size, payment was more directly tied to individual effort. Moreover, to collect data on the production, special counters were used to measure the number of relays the employee had assembled. These were clearly visible to the assemblers. Comments made by the assemblers indicate that they were using the counters for performance measurement, feedback, and personal performance targets. For example, the experimental records show that late in the afternoon of April 19, 1929, operator 3 said "I'm 15 relays behind yesterday." Operator 5 said "I made 421 yesterday and I am going to do better today." The change in work-group size is a *systemic* change. It created a system that provided the women with informational feedback. They could look at a counter and see how they were doing, and their rewards were more directly attributable to their effort.

The implications for sustaining Knock Your Socks Off Service? Capitalize on the Hawthorne Effect by doing your version of the changed illumination at the Hawthorne plant: Have posters extol service quality, issue badges that say "I love our customers," and display other visible items of a customer focus. But capitalize on the *real* Hawthorne Effect by changing your systems, measuring service quality, paying for performance, and giving both informational and motivational feedback. Make sure that those elements are in every system that delivers something to your customers. Use the 10-Dime Approach for reinforcement. Have the people in your department do the same. Think, act, and use a systems approach to service quality.

Doing this will enable you to join the Disneys, the Marriotts, the Federal Expresses, the Stew Leonards, and the many other organizations delivering Knock Your Socks Off Service. It will pull you through the frustrating phases that sometimes accompany service-quality improvement and will make Knock Your Socks Off Service your trademark in a crowded marketplace.

About the Authors

Both authors are on the staff of Performance Research Associates.

Performance Research Associates is one of North America's premier training and consulting firms in the related areas of service quality, customer retention, and continuous performance improvement. With offices in Minneapolis, Dallas, and Ann Arbor, the firm provides training and consulting services to client organizations throughout North America and Europe. Among the services are training programs, workshops, keynote presentations, customer surveys, focus groups, and employee surveys.

Ron Zemke is a management consultant, journalist, and behavioral scientist and has become one of the best-known and most widely quoted authorities on the United States' continuing service revolution. As senior editor of *TRAINING Magazine* and editor of *The Service Edge* newsletter, he has covered the emergence and development of the global service economy.

Ron founded Performance Research Associates, his Minneapolis-based consulting group, specializing in needs analysis, service-quality audits, and service-management programs, in 1972 to conduct organizational effectiveness and productivity-improvement studies for business and industry. His clients have included Wachovia Bank and Trust, Citibank, Marquette National Bank, Wells Fargo Bank, First Bank System, GTE-MTO, 3M Company, Ford Motor Company, General Motors–Canada, Air Canada, Western Airlines, Steelcase, General Mills, Deluxe Corporation, the National Safety Council, Pitney-Bowes Corporation, and Union Carbide.

Ron has authored or coauthored eleven books, including *Delivering Knock Your Socks Off Service* (AMACOM), *Managing Knock Your Socks Off Service* (AMACOM), *The Service Edge: 101 Companies That Profit From Customer Care*, and *Service America! Doing Business in the New Economy*.

Tom Connellan manages PRA's Ann Arbor office. He was formerly the CEO of a service company he founded in the health care field. Using the principles of customer focus and continuous improvement, he built the company into a network of 1,200 instructors serving 300 hospitals and most of the Fortune 500 firms. Prior to that, he served as a research associate and program director at what is now the University of Michigan's Executive Education program.

The author or coauthor of five books, Tom includes in his client base such service leaders as Stew Leonard's, Marriott, Radisson, GE, Motorola, IBM–Rochester, and NovaCare. His work with client organizations focuses on the related areas of continuous improvement, customer focus, and customer retention.

Both Ron and Tom, as well as other members of the PRA team, are frequent speakers at company, management, sales, and association meetings. Their presentations give practical how-to's for improving the bottom line by creating lifetime customers.

Readers interested in information about presentations, training programs, consulting, or other PRA services can call the Minneapolis office at (612) 338-8523.

Volunteer Vacations

Volunteer
Vacations

Eighth Edition

Short-Term Adventures
That Will Benefit
You and Others

**Bill McMillon, Doug Cutchins,
and Anne Geissinger**

CHICAGO
REVIEW
PRESS

Library of Congress Cataloging-in-Publication Data

McMillon, Bill, 1942–

    Volunteer vacations : short-term adventures that will benefit you and others / Bill McMillon, Doug Cutchins, and Anne Geissinger.—8th ed.

      p. cm.

    Includes index.

    ISBN 1-55652-461-7

    1. Voluntarism—Directories. 2. Associations, institutions, etc.—Directories. 3. Vacations—Directories. I. Cutchins, Doug. II. Geissinger, Anne. III. Title.

    HN49.V64M35   2003

     302'.14—dc21   2002005846

Cover and interior design: Rattray Design

Cover Photos: © Photo Disc, Inc.

Many of the personal vignettes included in this edition were provided courtesy of the sponsoring organizations and permissions are their responsibility.

The authors have made every effort to ensure that all the listing information is correct and current at the time of publication.

Eighth edition

Published by Chicago Review Press, Incorporated

814 North Franklin Street

Chicago, Illinois 60610

ISBN 1-55652-461-7

Printed in the United States of America

5 4 3 2

To all the volunteers.

Thank you for your efforts.

Together we will change the world!

Contents

Acknowledgments

for Bill McMillon

AFTER 15 YEARS, it's time to move on, and I couldn't have chosen a better time to do so. The first edition of *Volunteer Vacations* was published in 1987, and when Curt Matthews told me then, at the New Orleans meeting of the American Booksellers Association Convention, that the book would be in print for 10 years, I didn't believe him. Obviously he was understating the case, and during the intervening 15 years I have had the good fortune to work with Curt; his wife, Linda; editors Amy Teschner and Cynthia Sherry; publicists Julie Johnson, Kathy Mirkin, and Catherine Bosin; and Mark Suchomel in marketing. All of these, and numerous others at Chicago Review Press, have been instrumental in the long run of the book, and as I have returned to my love of teaching, I am looking forward to this run continuing through the efforts of my new coauthors, Doug Cutchins and Anne Geissinger, who were recruited by Cynthia Sherry to see the book through future editions.

Finally, I completely agree with Doug and Anne that the book would never have been written without the cooperation of two groups, the volunteer organizations who shared their needs and desires with me, and the many volunteers who let me use their experiences, both good and bad, over the past 15 years.

Thank you all, and good luck to you, Doug and Anne.

Acknowledgments

for Doug Cutchins and Anne Geissinger

WE WOULD LIKE to thank Cynthia Sherry and Chicago Review Press for seeking us out and trusting us with this project. Thanks also to Eric and Jennifer for encouraging us to take advantage of this great opportunity.

Thank you to our friends Kathy, Peter, Nancy, and Rob, who encouraged and reassured us that working on this book while caring for a newborn would be "no problem." Luckily for us, they were right! We would also like to acknowledge Emma, our daughter, as a source of inspiration to us.

Also, a very heartfelt thank you to our families for helping to care for Emma, leaving us a little time and space (and sanity) to work on this book. And a thank you to all of our friends (especially Phil, who caught our many typos) for their support this last year as we worked our way through a number of projects including this book.

Last, we would like to acknowledge those at the very heart of this book: the organizations that provide fabulous opportunities all over the world and the volunteers who step into those positions, giving of themselves in the service of others. By working together, you enrich the world through your activities. Thank you!

Foreword

Ed Asner

IT'S BEEN SAID that "man would rather spend himself for a cause than live idly in prosperity." I'm sure upon uttering that axiom in a group, you'd see everyone nodding wisely—agreeing that hard work for a cause is preferable to the good life unfulfilled. It's a noble thought during a philosophical discussion. When everyone's in accord on that point, pull out some airline tickets to Perryville, Arkansas, and ask who's willing to give up their Bermuda vacation in order to work with livestock. Any takers?

It's a hard sell. Public service is an antiquity in today's society. In the thirties the Civilian Conservation Corps instilled in the minds of young men and women the notion that national service is an obligation, indeed, a privilege: putting something back into the country in exchange for all the benefits derived from living in a free and democratic society. It was a wonderful setup and one that should have been perpetuated.

Since that time, however, our country's military bent has made national service an anathema—national service has come to mean the draft, the military, risk of life and limb on some foreign shore. Some states, to supplement low budget allocations, use public service as punishment for misdemeanors. In Oregon, for instance, DWI offenders can be seen picking up highway litter.

In short, the notion of a "volunteer vacation" sounds like a disciplinary measure akin to assigning extra household chores to a balky teenager.

Happily, there are people like Bill McMillon (along with the hundreds of people who have taken volunteer vacations) to set us straight: volunteering for a worthy cause can be fun, fulfilling, and an adventure you'll anticipate year after year. Maybe working with livestock isn't your thing, but there's plenty of variety: go on archaeological expeditions, assist with health care in remote villages, maintain trails in beautiful mountain climes, or build homes for the homeless. Some programs encourage you to bring the kids; some pay part of your expenses.

Best of all, you'll be helping people who need you. These days our local, state, and federal government budgets (and many government budgets around the world) have cut "people programs" in favor of big business and the military. More and more, our nation and our world must look to volunteers to fill the gaps that governments are unwilling or unable to fill—in health care, education, and programs for the disabled and underprivileged.

Read this book . . . try a volunteer vacation. The world will be a better place and so will you.

Preface

WE WERE HARD at work on this book when the events of September 11, 2001, shook the United States and the world. The aftermath of these events led to reactions that had both positive and negative consequences, from an unfortunate rise in hate crimes to a wonderful surge in the recognition of the value of volunteering. Though we were horrified by the events of September 11, we were heartened by many peoples' core reaction: that the best way to fight back against such violence is by reaching out to others, both domestically and internationally. President Bush's call to all Americans to dedicate two years of their lives to service work, as well as his proposal to increase spending on AmeriCorps and the Peace Corps, was a clear manifestation of this new national attitude.

There can be little doubt that the world community is shrinking. As the importance of technology grows, communities and countries that were once geographically isolated are coming into close contact with more developed cities and nations. We recall walking into a village in the remote rainforest of Suriname, commenting on how remote the village was and how little contact it had with the outside world, and then noticing a Nike swoosh shaved into the back of a villager's haircut. That this icon of American corporate culture had made its way to a village that lacked roads, running water, and electricity demonstrated what we already knew but had forgotten: western culture is spreading everywhere.

We would argue that the events of September 11 happened, in part, as a backlash to this process of globalization. Further, we would argue that volunteering is one of the best ways to halt the tide of the nastier effects of globalization, and instead promote the benefits of international understanding and cooperation. By personal, one-on-one exchanges and dialogues, individuals around the world—including people from different communities in the United States—will better understand and appreciate their global neighbors.

Why should you turn a vacation into a volunteer vacation? After researching this book, we're hard-pressed to see why you wouldn't! First, the opportunities presented here are amazing. We challenge you to read this book and not find organizations that make you want to get on the next plane to Nepal, France, or California. Second, your help is desperately needed. The more than 200 organizations mentioned in this book exist for a reason—there is a lot of need in the world, and the skills that you have can be put to tremendously good use in filling that need.

So, we hope that you'll take advantage of the chance that you have to turn a regular vacation into an experience that will truly benefit yourself and others. Almost everyone who undertakes these projects returns home proclaiming that their vacation benefited themselves at least as much as it did the people being served. And when this happens to you, we then hope that you'll take the next step: share the experience. Invite friends over to see pictures of your trip. (They'll be more interested in these pictures than those of your last trip to the beach, we promise!) Talk to a group at your place of worship about what you did. Write a column for the local newspaper. Call an elementary school and ask if you can come speak to a class. The medium isn't crucial; what's most important is that you share the lessons that you learned with a wider audience, because then your understanding of a new community is spread to more people.

Volunteer vacations can change your perspective on the world, teach you new skills, and greatly impact the lives of others. We hope that you are inspired to make an ordinary vacation extraordinary, and to use your talents to better yourself and the world. And keep your mind open—you may even find that a volunteer vacation is so rewarding that you want to take on a longer-term commitment such as the Peace Corps, AmeriCorps, or one of the many faith-based programs in the United States and abroad.

—Doug Cutchins and Anne Geissinger

Introduction

SEE A NEW part of the United States or a completely different country.

Help other people.

Relax.

Make new friends.

Maybe learn a few words in a new language or resurrect the Spanish that you haven't used since high school.

Change your perspective on what it means to be rich or poor, first world or third world, developed or underdeveloped.

How? Take a volunteer vacation.

"A volunteer vacation?" you might say. "Doesn't that imply work? But isn't that why I'm going on vacation, to get away from work?"

Yes and no. If you take advantage of one of the opportunities in this book, you'll certainly work. You'll teach kids how to read, build bridges and blaze trails (both real and metaphorical), take care of injured wildlife, or play with kids in an orphanage. That's work—hard work.

But it's completely different than what most of us do to bring home a paycheck every week.

You'll be in a new place, surrounded by people you don't know. You'll be using parts of your brain and body that haven't gotten a good workout in years. You're likely to experience some kind of paradigm shift, and to look at yourself, your country, or the world in a new way. You'll come home not only refreshed and rejuvenated, as you would after any vacation, but you'll also have the knowledge that you've made a difference in someone's life or in the world.

Sounds good—what's next?

There are really two ways to go about using this guide. The first is to open it up and begin to dream, to allow yourself to exclaim, "That's it, honey—pack your bags for Croatia! I hear it's beautiful this time of year." If you're open to new places to go and things to do, this is the approach for you; start reading and dreaming. Some people, though, need to be a little more intentional in their planning. If you know that you want to go to Europe, for example, or really want to work with kids, or can't spend more than $500, then you need to be more selective in your reading. Make good use of the indexes in the back of this book and check the Web sites of the organizations you're considering frequently, since information can and does change over time.

What This Guide Does and Doesn't Do

This is a resource guide; it is not a review book. We provide basic information about these organizations in order to allow you to begin to make decisions about what organizations are right for you and the experience that you want to have. With more than 200 organizations running thousands of programs in scores of countries, there is no way that we could tell you what kind of housing you'll have, what the experience of the average past volunteer has been (except where we've provided vignettes that, still, only provide a single example of the experience), or which organizations are good or not so good. And in the end, we wouldn't want to try and make that judgment call; what is perfect for some people is horrible for others. Instead, we give you the core information that you need to know about these organizations so that you can begin to make an informed decision. We hope that nobody goes on a volunteer vacation without first talking with the organization and, if at all possible, people who have volunteered with the organization in the past. Research and evaluate organizations the same way you would go about making any other decision about how to use your time and money.

We've given you a valuable tool to start with, though, beyond the basic information. Sprinkled throughout this book you'll find volunteer vignettes, stories written by past volunteers about their experiences with some of these organizations. These more personal glimpses into the daily lives of volunteers will give you a better sense of what your experience might be like.

How Do I Evaluate an Organization to See If It Is Right for Me?

Here are 10 questions you should get answers to before signing on with a volunteer organization.

1. Does the work that they do mesh with what I want to do on my vacation? Does it use or develop skills that are important to me?
2. Will the project take me to a place where I want to go?
3. Do I have the same goals and values as the organization? (This is especially important for organizations that have overt political or religious goals; you don't want to end up promoting a cause, directly or indirectly, that you don't believe in.)
4. What do past volunteers say about their experiences with this organization?
5. What are living conditions at the site like?
6. What will my exact job responsibilities be? How much scut work (cooking, cleaning, filing, and so on) will I be expected to do? Keep in mind that someone has to do this work, and it is often divided among all of the employees and volunteers, from top to bottom.
7. How much does it cost to participate? What exactly is included in a program fee?
8. When does the project take place, how long does it last, and does it fit with my schedule?
9. Will I be working in a group? What is the profile of the average volunteer? Age range? What are the motivations of the other people in the group?
10. What kind of training or orientation is offered? (This is crucial for international organizations, where you might be working in a culture very different from your own.)

Expectations: What Is Reasonable and What Is Unreasonable

Be nice to the organizations that offer these services. Remember that many of them operate on extremely lean budgets with underpaid and overworked staff. Please don't request information from a group unless you are seriously considering volunteering with them. Make ample use of the vast resources of the Internet—almost all of the organizations in this book have Web sites that you can access for basic information. Be polite and understand that your request is one of many that the organization is dealing with at any given time. Act as a partner, not as a consumer. Consider sending a small check along with each request for information, and if the organization is based overseas, send them an International Reply Coupon (available at your local Post Office) to help defray the cost of postage. Remember: the more money these organizations spend on administration, the less they have to spend on what they're working to achieve.

That said, organizations have a responsibility to their volunteers as well. Organizations should live up to their promises and advertising. They should answer your questions fully, honestly, and in a timely manner. To some extent, there is also the aspect that "you get what you pay for." In other words, if you are paying thousands of dollars for an experience, you have a right (within limits) to expect more service than someone whose experience is wholly sponsored by the organization.

Last, don't expect to change the world overnight. Have reasonable expectations of the organization, yourself, and your ability to create long-term change. Recognize that the work you do is important, but is just one piece of the larger puzzle of improving global conditions. Let the process, not the product, be your measure of success.

ACDI/VOCA

50 F Street, NW, Suite 1075
Washington, DC 20001
(800) 929-8622 or (202) 383-4961; Fax (202) 783-7204
E-mail: volunteer@acdivoca.org
Web site: www.volunteeroverseas.com

Project location: Worldwide.
Project type: Technical expertise in areas such as but not limited
   to: accounting, baking, finance, farm management, policy
   reform, and sustainable agriculture. A complete list can be
   found on the organization's Web site.
Project costs: None; ACDI/VOCA pays for airfare, housing, and
   board for qualified volunteers.
Project dates: Year round. Projects are 2 to 12 weeks long.
How to apply: Contact the office listed above.

An American designer from York City volunteers with ACDI/VOCA in Bolivia
to work with artisans and weavers on developing exportable design fashions in
an effort to improve local incomes for the Bolivian people. (Photo courtesy of
ACDI/VOCA)

Special skills or requirements: ACDI/VOCA volunteers are mid-career and senior professionals with 10 to 40 years of experience in their respective fields, who donate 2 to 4 weeks of their time and talent to work side by side with entrepreneurs who are pushing for economic progress and democratic reforms around the world.

Commentary: ACDI/VOCA identifies and opens economic opportunities for farmers and other entrepreneurs worldwide by promoting democratic principles and market liberalization, building international cooperative partnerships, and encouraging the sound management of natural resources. ACDI/VOCA is a private, nonprofit international development organization providing high-quality technical expertise at the request of farmers, agribusinesses, cooperatives, and private and government agencies around the world.

Alaska State Parks

550 W. 7th Ave., Suite 1380
Anchorage, Alaska 99501-3561
(907) 269-8708; Fax (907) 269-8907
E-mail: volunteer@dnr.state.ak.us
Web site: www.alaskastateparks.org

Project location: State parks throughout Alaska.

Project type: Park management and maintenance.

Project costs: Volunteers are responsible for transportation to and from Alaska. Housing or a campsite is provided to volunteers who meet minimum time commitment requirements, along with a small expense allowance. Campground hosts provide their own trailer or RV to live in.

Project dates: Most positions are from May to September for varying periods of time. There are a few winter positions.

How to apply: Contact the Volunteer Coordinator at the above office for a catalog, which contains general information, descriptions of specific positions, and an application. The catalog can also be found on the Web site.

Work done by volunteers: Volunteers assist park staff with some aspect of visitor contact or park maintenance and management—as campground hosts, natural history interpreters, ranger assistants, park caretakers, trail crews, and archaeological assistants.

Special skills or requirements: Varies with position. Must be 18 years old or older and a U.S. citizen. No upper age limit. Some positions require good physical condition; others require some college education in natural resource management. All require some knowledge, skill, and experience in the outdoors. Good communication skills are preferred.

Commentary: Alaska State Parks began its volunteer program in 1986. Park volunteers supplement existing staff and provide programs to the public that would not otherwise be available.

Alliances Abroad

2423 Pennsylvania Avenue NW
Washington, DC 20037
(866) 6ABROAD or (202) 467-9467; Fax (202) 467-9460
E-mail: outbound@alliancesabroad.com
Web site: www.alliancesabroad.com

Project location: China, Costa Rica, and Spain.
Project type: Conservation and education.
Project costs: Varies by program. Please review costs on the Web site.
Project dates: Programs run throughout the year.
How to apply: Download the application from the Web site, call, or e-mail.
Work done by volunteers: Conservation, farm work, social services, hotel, restaurant, administrative, research, program administration, etc.
Special skills or requirements: Varies by program. Volunteers must be at least 18 years old.

Amazon-Africa Aid Organization (3AO)

P.O. Box 7776
Ann Arbor, MI 48107
(734) 769-5778; Fax (734) 769-5779
E-mail: info@amazonafrica.org
Web site: www.amazonafrica.org

Project location: Santarem, Brazil.
Project type: Medical/health and ESL teaching.
Project costs: Volunteers pay own airfare, but all other expenses are covered by the organization.
Project dates: Open.
How to apply: Send cover letter, resume, copy of diploma, and copy of medical, dental, or teaching license.
Work done by volunteers: Dentists and physicians work in a clinic seeing patients. ESL volunteers teach classes for high school, college, and adult students.
Special skills or requirements: Physicians and dentists need a degree in Medicine or Dentistry (residents are accepted, but not medical students). ESL teachers need a degree in teaching or a related field. Unfortunately there are no volunteer placements for nurses.

American Rivers

1025 Vermont Avenue, NW, Suite 720
Washington, DC 20005-3516
(202) 347-7550; Fax (202) 347-9242
E-mail: amrivers@amrivers.org
Web site: www.americanrivers.org

Project location: Seattle, WA, and Washington, DC.

Project type: Conservation, non-profit administration.

Project costs: Participants are responsible for all their living costs.

Project dates: Year-round, although summer positions are the most popular.

How to apply: Send a resume, cover letter, a three to five page writing sample that shows your ability to write, and a list of three references to Anne Hoffert at the above mailing address or via e-mail.

Work done by volunteers: Research, conservation program work, media and communications work, clerical, legal work, correspondence with members, database maintenance, and word processing.

Special skills or requirements: An interest in saving America's rivers and the environment in general, plus basic office skills. Knowledge of legal, political, and environmental issues is helpful.

Commentary: American Rivers is among the nation's leading river conservation organizations. Their mission is to protect and restore America's river systems and to promote a river stewardship ethic.

AmeriSpan Unlimited

P.O. Box 58129
Philadelphia, PA 19102-8129
(800) 879-6640 or (215) 751-1100;
Fax (215) 751-1986
E-mail: info@amerispan.com
Web site: www.amerispan.com

Project location: Throughout Latin America.

Project type: Social work, education, healthcare, environmental work.

Project costs: $350 to $3,500 depending on location and project chosen. Project fee includes language instruction, homestay, full or partial board, travel insurance, and emergency medical service. Volunteers are responsible for airfare.

Project dates: Year round.

How to apply: Request an application package from Amerispan, or you can download application materials from the Web site.

Work done by volunteers: Varies based on position chosen. Some examples are teaching, healthcare, business internship positions, etc.

Special skills or requirements: Some host organizations require Spanish or Portuguese proficiency.

Commentary: You must apply at least 2 months in advance. Amerispan does not accept people under 18 to volunteer, but does have language immersion programs that they can participate in.

Sample projects: National Parks of Costa Rica, orphanages, accounting and engineering firms, schools, nursing homes, rural clinics, and rural hosptials.

Amigos de las Americas

5618 Star Lane
Houston, TX 77057
(800) 231-7796 or (713) 782-5290;
Fax (713) 782-9267
E-mail: info@amigoslink.org
Web site: www.amigoslink.org

Project location: Throughout Latin America.

Project type: Wide variety of public health projects.

Project costs: $3,000 covers training materials, transportation from Houston to the host country, and field supplies. Volunteers are responsible for transportation to and from Houston. The host country provides food and housing.

Project dates: Projects run for four, six, or eight weeks during mid-June to mid-August.

How to apply: Contact Amigos de las Americas at the above address for local chapter locations or information about their correspondence training program for volunteers. There is a March 1 application deadline.

Work done by volunteers: A variety of public health projects, from helping plan and dig public latrines to building stoves to reforestation. All projects are done under the supervision of a field supervisor who lives in the host country and is experienced with volunteers.

Special skills or requirements: Volunteers must speak at least minimal Spanish, be at least 16 years old, and have completed the Amigos training program. Although the majority of volunteers are high school and college students, there is no upper age limit.

Commentary: Amigos began in 1965 as a religious organization but has since dropped all association with any church or religion. It has maintained its benevolent spirit, however, and has placed over ten thousand volunteers in thirteen Latin American countries in the past twenty years. Most of these have been youths who have been given responsibilities far beyond those normally accorded them in the U.S.

Sample projects: Amigos has conducted projects in Costa Rica, the Dominican Republic, Bolivia, Brazil, Honduras, Ecuador, Mexico, and Paraguay. Volunteers have taught dental hygiene, developed community sanitation, initiated family garden projects, improved kitchen sanitation, and promoted general health education.

On Building Stoves in Mexico

❖ by Elizabeth Kistin ❖

Amigos de las Americas Volunteer

Step One: The Base

Choose an appropriate location in the cocina (kitchen) across from an open door or window and begin to build a strong solid base of rock and mud or adobe.

I tossed my backpack down first and then jumped over the side of the faded red pickup truck, disrupting the dirt in a brief puff of smoke where I landed. The driver, Javier, hopped from the front seat and told us he would take us to where we were staying. We first met our host mother, Juana, as she welcomed my partner, Mika, and me into her small adobe home. She sat with us while we unpacked some of our belongings and joyfully asked us about our families and our country. Her broad smile illuminated her beautiful brown face and the entire room. We thanked her for her hospitality and for opening her home to us for the next eight weeks. "They say we are all brothers," she told us as she stared out the window at the corn, "you and I are just fortunate enough to get to live together like family." I smiled and asked about the small photograph in the corner. "My brother," she responded, "And we can only pray he too has found a family in your tierra (country)."

Amigos de las Americas volunteers construct a water trough at a home. Amigos builds water troughs, called "pilas," to provide families with a readily available and clean source of water for cooking, cleaning, and drinking. (Photo courtesy of Amigos de las Americas)

Step Two: The Mold

Adding water, mix 26 buckets of dirt, 9 buckets of dry manure, and three buckets of sand to a desirable consistency. Pour this mixture into the mold to a depth of 40 centimeters within a wood frame on top of the base.

"I am going to teach you how to mix mud." Cecilia, the woman who lived with the big family on top of the hill explained, "because here in Mexico we are experts on mud." I watched intently as she carefully added water to the 38 buckets of material and then, giggling, handed me a pair of her nephew's rubber boots and slipped on her own. "Like this," she told me, as she hurled herself into the dirt and began jumping and prancing about. I jumped in too, but being less experienced I almost fell in nose first and barely managed to save myself by tightly gripping the sleeve of her white T-shirt. We wiggled off balance, but regained our composure and erupted in laughter. It wasn't long before she was teaching me to dance and sing for that is, of course, the secret to perfect mud.

Step Three: The Carving

After the mold has dried for a few days, the carving can begin. Carefully carve the firebox, holes for the pots the family wishes to use, tunnels for the fire and the smoke, and finally the chimney.

I poked my head inside the fence and yelled, *Buenas tardes* to see if anyone was home. Señora Morales was sitting on her front porch in a small wooden chair made for her grandchildren. "Just thinking," she said, "just thinking." She moved her chair into the cocina where the stove was being built and brought in two spoons so we could resume our carving. As we chipped away at the mud to create the tunnels, we moved deeper and deeper into conversation. She asked me what I wanted to do with my life. I shrugged my shoulders and told her I did not know. Surprisingly, however, she looked delighted. I fixed my eyes on her strong silver braid as she explained to me that people waste too much time worrying about the future and forgetting to focus on the present. What matters most, she said is not *adonde van, sino como van*—not where you are going, but rather how you go. What matters most is if you travel joyfully.

Step Four: Aesthetics

After the carving is finished use a small amount of water to smooth the top or the sides of the stove. Some families may also choose to white wash their stove to make it more beautiful.

Mika and I sat comfortably on the hard dirt floor and explained the directions and drawings of the stoves to the *abuelita* (granny) that lived at the bottom of the hill. We helped her remove dry corn kernels from the cob for tomorrow's tortillas and watched as she ran her fingers over the colored-in pictures and the small lettering. *Que bonita* (that's pretty), she told us as she handed the papers back to us. I explained to her that our ultimate goal was not to build four stoves, but rather to teach four families how to create the stoves themselves so they, in turn, could teach others within the pueblo. Upon hearing this, she lit up. She threw her head back, closed her eyes and said *Que bonita* one more time. As I picked up the wheelbarrow and started down the small dirt path to collect manure, I finally realized where I was headed. I was going to make something beautiful.

Amity Institute—Amity Volunteer Teachers Abroad (AVTA) Program

3065 Rosecrans Place, Suite 104
San Diego, CA 92110
(619) 222-7000; Fax (619) 222-7016
E-mail: avta@amity.org
Web site: www.amity.org

Project location: Argentina, Brazil, Dominican Republic, Mexico, Peru, Venezuela, Ghana, Senegal, China, Taiwan.

Project type: Education.

Project costs: $200 to $1,200 depending on location and length of program. Volunteers are responsible for providing round-trip transportation to the host institution and health insurance for the duration of stay (approximately $50 per month). Volunteers are also required to take along at least $150 per month personal spending money.

Project dates: Year-round.

How to apply: Contact Amity at the above e-mail address.

Work done by volunteers: Teaching English and other subjects in English.

Special skills or requirements: Volunteers must be native English-speakers, at least 21 years of age at the time of departure for the assignment. Some teaching or tutoring experience and previous travel abroad is desirable. For those interested in volunteering in a Latin American country, the application process requires a letter of intent in Spanish; complete fluency is not required, although a basic working knowledge of the language is critical. Prospective volunteers will be interviewed via telephone to assess their conversational ability. For an assignment in Brazil, a knowledge of Portuguese is preferred, but a background in Spanish is sufficient. There is no language requirement for assignments in African or Chinese-speaking countries. However, for an assignment in Senegal, a knowledge of French is helpful.

Sample projects: The AVTA Program offers both long and short-term assignments varying in length from several weeks to a full academic year (9 to 10 months). Semester & full-year assignments involve serving as a teacher or teaching assistant in an English language classroom. In immersion and bilingual schools, various other subjects are taught in English. Short-term assignments generally involve the teaching of a workshop series to TEFL (Teachers of English as a Foreign Language) at a participating school.

Amizade, Limited

367 South Graham Street
Pittsburgh, PA 15232
(888) 973-4443; Fax (412) 648-1492
E-mail: volunteer@amizade.org
Web site: www.amizade.org

Project location: Santarém, Brazil; Cochabamba, Bolivia; Hervey Bay, Australia; Nepal; Thailand; Gardiner, Montana; the Navajo Nation, Arizona.

Project type: Community service projects.

Project costs: Varies with program.

Project dates: One- to three-week programs scheduled throughout the year at all sites; long-term opportunities exist in Bolivia. Trips for groups of six or more can be arranged any time of the year.

How to apply: Applications can be obtained by visiting the web site or contacting the office.

Work done by volunteers: Participants work side by side with local volunteers building schools and hospitals, working on historic and environmental preservation, and environmental cleanup.

Special skills or requirements: No special skills needed, just a willingness to help.

Commentary: Amizade programs offer a mix of community service and recreation that provide volunteers with the opportunity to participate first-hand in the culture of the region where they are volunteering.

Sample projects: Current projects include construction of the dining facilities at an orphanage in Bolivia, continuing construction for an organization working with street children in Brazil, and continuing historic preservation at the OTO Ranch near Yellowstone National Park.

Appalachian Mountain Club

Trails Program
P.O. Box 298
Gorham, NH 03581
(603) 466-2721; Fax (603) 466-2822
Web site: www.outdoors.org

Project location: White Mountain National Forest, New Hampshire & Maine; Acadia National Park and Baxter State Park, Maine; the Berkshires, Massachusetts; and other locations in the Appalachian region.

Project type: Trail building and maintenance, many in remote locations.

Project costs: Projects range from $20 to $350. Volunteers are responsible for travel to project sites and all personal gear. Food, cooking and eating equipment, and first aid supplies are furnished by AMC. Camping equipment may be supplied, depending on program.

Project dates: From June through October volunteers can participate in weekend, weeklong, and ten- to twelve-day service projects.

How to apply: Write to the AMC Trails Program at the above address or visit the web site for an application and a program booklet.

Work done by volunteers: Moderate to strenuous manual labor building, maintaining, or repairing trails.

Special skills or requirements: Volunteers should be in good physical condition and have an enthusiastic willingness to work. Some backpacking experience is helpful, as is previous experience in trail building. Training in the use of tools and maintenance techniques is given at each project site. Minimum age is typically 16, but varies depending on program. Specialty crews are available for teens, adults, seniors, and women.

Commentary: AMC is the nation's oldest (founded in 1876) and largest (more than ninety-five thousand members) nonprofit conservation and recreation organization. It has twelve chapters in the Northeast and maintains more than fourteen hundred miles of trail, including 350 miles of the Appalachian Trail. The Trails Program is an extension of their regular activities, and anyone may apply for participation.

Sample projects: Previous projects include construction of new trails in Acadia National Park, Maine; a canoe portage trail in Baxter State Park, Maine; a loop trail to the Appalachian Trail in Grafton Notch, Maine; constuction of bog bridges in the White Mountains, New Hampshire; reconstruction of the Appalachian Trail in the Berkshire region of western Massachusetts; and rock work on alpine trails near the peak of Mount Washington, New Hampshire.

The Cuttings of a Volunteer Trail Crew

❖ by Melanie Rausch ❖

Appalachian Mountain Club

Spending a week in the Acadia National Park on a volunteer trail crew is an experience that I need to share. The Appalachian Mountain Club (AMC) has a wonderful program that enabled me to work at maintaining the beautiful trails on the coast of Maine.

My experience with AMC started with a 7 A.M. bugle call. I left my tent with enthusiasm and made a beeline to a hearty breakfast. Next we met up with a group of Acadia High School students and knowledgeable National Park Maintenance Supervisors who taught me how to maintain the hiking trails that I have traveled along for many years. Our goal is to keep the adventurer on the path, saving the edges from erosion. With rakes, loppers, shovels, and hoes, we cut branches, trimmed trees, cleared out drainage ditches, and lopped off tree roots that could trip up even the most careful hiker. We followed trails around lakes and ponds, through pine-scented forests, and up steep mountains. We were rewarded with incredible views. In addition, families with children stopped to thank us for our efforts and took caution to preserve the trail themselves with every step they took.

Every trail I ever hiked on and took for granted was the result of great planning and a lot of hard work by dedicated people who believe in the nature entrusted to us. As I enjoyed my bountiful packed lunch and swatted a few mosquitoes, I realized that we need to take care of our environment and preserve it with the utmost care. The lesson I learned was to take care of the beauty surrounding us each day. AMC, many thanks for all the inspiration!

Appalachian Trail Conference (ATC)

Trail Crew Program
P.O. Box 10
Newport, VA 24128
(540) 544-7388; Fax (540) 544-6880
E-mail: crews@appalachiantrail.org
Web site: www.appalachiantrail.org

Project location: The length of the Appalachian National Scenic Trail. Crew base camps are located in northern Maine, central Vermont, Pennslyvania, southwestern Virginia, and the Great Smoky Mountains in Tennessee.

Project type: Conservation.

Project costs: Volunteers are responsible for transportation to base camps. Once there, ATC and agency partners provide lodging, food, transportation, tools, and safety equipment. Some basic camping equipment is also available.

Project dates: The Maine Trail Crew operates from June through mid-August. The Vermont Volunteer Long Trail Patrol operates mid-July through mid-September. The Mid-Atlantic Trail Crew works during September and October. The Virginia-based Konnarock Trail Crew operates from mid-May through August. Based in the Great Smoky Mountains, the Rocky Top Volunteer Trail Crew works in September and October. Participants may volunteer for one to six weeks.

How to apply: Contact the above office by phone or e-mail or visit the web site for an application.

Work done by volunteers: Work includes new trail construction, rock work, log work, shelter construction, and other physically demanding tasks. Trail crews of six to eight volunteers work under the supervision of a skilled leader.

Special skills or requirements: Volunteers must be 18 years old; retirees are welcome. Good health, cooperation, community spirit, and enthusiasm are more important than previous trail experience. Base camps provide rustic accommodations; volunteers also camp in tents near their project sites.

Commentary: The Appalachian Trail is the longest continuously marked footpath in the world and America's first national scenic trail. It follows the crest of the Appalachian Mountain chain for more than 2,100 miles along mountain ridges, and through rural farm valleys and rugged high country. The Appalachian Trail Conference is a private, nonprofit, educational organization that coordinates public and private efforts to maintain and protect the Appalachian Trail. The U.S. Forest Service and the National Park Service cosponsor the ATC volunteer trail crews. ATC member clubs are assigned a section of the Appalachian Trail to maintain, and clubs are assisted in their efforts by the volunteer trail crews.

ARCHELON, The Sea Turtle Protection Society of Greece

Solomou 57, 104 32
Athens, Greece
(30) 1-5231342
E-mail: stps@archelon.gr
Web site: www.archelon.gr

Project location: Zakynthos, Peloponnesus, Crete, Rescue Centre (Athens).

Project type: Conservation, rehabilitation.

Project costs: $60. Volunteers must bring own camping gear and stay in free campsites open only to ARCHELON volunteers. Basic sanitary and cooking facilities are provided; volunteers are responsible for providing own food, though living tends to be communal. Volunteers are responsible for own transportation.

Project dates: Nest and turtle protection takes place May through October. The Rescue Centre operates throughout the year.

How to apply: Contact the ARCHELON office.

Work done by volunteers: Nest and turtle protection, public awareness, maintenance and day-to-day duties.

Special skills or requirements: Volunteers must be over 18 years old. ARCHELON operates in English.

Commentary: Volunteers must commit to a minimum of 28 days and must be willing to sleep and live outdoors.

ARFA (Associación de Rescate de Fauna)

Edif. La Vista, Ap. 11-B
Calle Bella Vista, Colina Los Caobos
Caracas 1050, Venezuela
(0058) 212-782-4182
E-mail: valio1@cantv.net

Project location: Venezuela.

Project type: Conservation, education, rescue, and rehabilitation of wildlife.

Project costs: Airfare, personal expenses. Room and board, and transportation to and from the rescue center and the airport are provided.

Project dates: All year. Volunteer projects last one to six months.

How to apply: By e-mail.

Work done by volunteers: Daily maintenance of facilities, feeding and supervision of wildlife.

Special skills or requirements of volunteers: Volunteers must be at least 18 years old and have a high-school diploma. Veterinary students are particularly welcome. All volunteers must have updated yellow fever and tetanus vaccinations, as well as illness and accident insurance.

Sample projects: Rescue, rehabilitation, and release of indigenous species of wildlife, such as fresh water turtles and tortoises, primates, and birds; educational projects with the community of Las Vegas, state of Cojedes and outreach to other parts of the country.

Bardou Project

Bardou
34390 Olargues, France
(4) 67-97-72-43

Project location: The hamlet of Bardou is located in the regional park of Haut Languedoc in the southern Cévennes Mountains, 90 kilometers west of Montpellier, France.

Project type: Restoration and maintenance of sixteenth-century stone peasant houses, gardening, and forest work.

Project costs: Transportation to site and about EUR 50 to EUR 60 per week for food.

Project dates: The minimum length of participation is one month between April 1 and June 30.

How to apply: Send a letter in English to the address listed above. Be sure to give your full name, age, experience, education, and cultural interests.

Work done by volunteers: Assisting builders, painting, maintenance, tending animals, forest clearance, and mountain path repair.

Special skills or requirements: Neither specific skills nor French are required; however, a good cultural education and background are appreciated.

Commentary: Bardou is a meeting place for world travelers and nature lovers. Short-term visitors and study groups, staying a minimum of one week, will be charged an overnight fee, starting at EUR 8 nightly per person.

Sample projects: Restoration and maintenance of houses, helping with building dry-stone walls, arranging paths, and forestry work.

Bike-Aid

c/o Global Exchange
2017 Mission Street, Suite 303
San Francisco, CA 94110
(415) 575-5544 ext. 351 or (800) RIDE-808, ext. 351
E-mail: brooke@globalexchange.org
Web site: www.bikeaid.org

Project location: Bike ride across the United States.

Project type: Education and social justice.

Project cost: Participants must raise $3,600 by obtaining sponsorships of their rides. Riders stay with community hosts in overnight towns, including churches, families, YMCAs, and schools. While riders are responsible for their own food, communities often invite riders to share meals with them.

Project dates: Mid-June through mid-August.

How to apply: Call, e-mail, or apply via the organization's Web site.

Work done by volunteers: Service learning projects in towns along the ride.

Special skills or requirements: Participants should know how to ride a bike. Riders must be at least 17 years old. Parents may not be accompanied by small children in trailers or other attachments to their parent's bike.

Commentary: Bike-Aid is a cross-country bike trip that combines service learning, physical challenge, group living, and political education. The cross-country ride itinerary changes on a yearly basis, but starts and ends in major cities, such as San Francisco and Washington DC.

Biosphere Expeditions

Sprat's Water, near Carlton Colville
The Broads National Park
Suffolk NR33 8BP, United Kingdom
(44) 1502-583085; Fax (44) 1502-587414
E-mail: info@biosphere-expeditions.org
Web site: www.biosphere-expeditions.org

Project location: Worldwide, including the Polish Carpathian Mountains, the Ukrainian Black Sea coast, the Peruvian Amazon, and Namibian savannahs. See the organization's Web site for full details.

Project type: Wildlife conservation expeditions.

Project costs: Around $1,500 for a two-week project, plus airfare and transportation to the assembly point.

Project dates:Year-round. Expeditions average two months in duration and are divided into two-week periods. You can join for two weeks to two months. See the organization's Web site for full details.

How to apply: Apply via the Web site, or at the address listed above.

Work done by volunteers: Various, depending on project. Examples include wolf tracking and radio collaring, bird netting and ringing, cheetah capture and radio collaring, and Amazon wildlife surveying.

Special skills or requirements: None. Projects are as inclusive as possible and encourage participation by disabled people and minorities. Expeditions are open to all; there are no age limits.

Commentary: Biosphere Expeditions is a nonprofit research and conservation organization offering hands-on wildlife conservation and adventures with a purpose for everyone. Their projects place volunteers with no research experience alongside scientists who are at the forefront of conservation work. Volunteers work with local scientists and people in the host country, and at least two thirds of the project cost is spent directly on the project.

Sample projects: **Poland:** Snow- and radio-tracking wolves in an urgent effort to prevent them from being declared legitimate hunting targets and thus being hunted to extinction locally. **Ukraine:** Bird netting, handling, and ringing using nets by the beach and in the country's interior. Participating in the area's first wolf survey through tracking and from nighttime wildlife-viewing blinds. **Peru:** Surveying pristine Amazon rain forest wildlife to aid efforts to declare the area protected and to develop sustainable management strategies. Tracking, counting, and identifying animals in various ways, during both day and night. **Namibia:** Participate in the first concerted monitoring effort of the Namibian cheetah. Covering ground in Land Rovers, counting track and scat frequencies, checking box traps, making behavioral observations, and radio tracking.

Amazonian Medicine Women

❖ by Russell Cobban ❖

Biosphere Expeditions

It's six in the morning. I can tell because our capitão has just switched on the boat engine and is getting ready to leave. We have been moored overnight in some small stream somewhere in the middle of the Amazon basin. Our boat belongs to a guy who calls himself the local mayor. He doesn't talk much, but he has a beautiful double-decker boat with a crew of two, and he is an amazingly good helmsman. Every morning, as I stir in my hammock, we pull out of the little stream that the mayor has chosen as our overnight stop. On either side of the hull there are only a few inches to the windy riverbank, but the boat never even gets close to hitting either side. We glide along, and I can touch the foliage from my vantage point on top of the roof where I have climbed. I share the roof with our resident pet tarantula who is sunning herself in the other corner. Being here is a dream come true. I had always wanted to join a research expedition and do some hands-on conservation work, so when the opportunity arose to investigate medicinal plants in the Amazon, I jumped at the chance.

Our expedition is made up of a bunch of people from all walks of life—students, local researchers, an expedition leader, and us volunteers, all mixed together and bound by a common goal: to find out about medicinal plants in the area. Everyone has heard of the Indians' use of medicinal plants these days. But Brazil harbors another virtually untapped resource of information: the Caboclos. They are people of mixed Indian and European descent (mainly of the

Volunteers head for shore in a low slung native canoe to interview Amazonian medicine women in the backwaters of Brazil. (Photo courtesy Biosphere Expeditions)

early Portuguese settlers) who live in small communities dotted around the Amazon basin.

Our boat-cum-base camp is chugging through the delta, taking us to remote Caboclo communities. When we pull up to a community, the mayor makes the introductions. This is vital, as it will give us a head start in trust and familiarity. We are with the mayor, therefore we must be OK, and people are quite happy and willing to talk to us about their medicinal plants. We then identify the local medicine woman (sometimes a man) and go through the process of conducting our interviews. "Which plant do you use for which ailment?" "How do you prepare it and which part?" "How much do you administer?" "How did you learn about this plant?" "Are there any other plants that have a similar effect?" As some of us conduct the interviews, others gather the plants in question and try to identify them.

Over two short weeks we cover a lot of ground and innumerable communities. Sometimes the rivers get too small for our trusty boat-cum-base camp, and we transfer to dugouts, usually with outboards, or simply walk to the nearest community. On the way we visit some field hospitals, gathering more information. The scenery is amazing. We are surrounded by forest all day and night—no cars, no mobile phones, a gentle pace of life, and extremely hospitable Brazilians everywhere we go. At night we can lie in our hammocks and just listen to the sounds of the forest. During the day we meet interesting people who show us around their community and are happy to explain what they do. We meet brick and roof tile makers (all the brick and tile are made from local river mud and dried in the sun), cattle and poultry farmers, fruit growers, hunters, and gatherers.

On top of all that, I really feel like we are doing something worthwhile for conservation, not just of the natural habitat, but also of the vast knowledge about medicinal plants that exists among these people. Whether all of the plants really work as reported is a question that has to be answered in a follow-up study. But for now, it is clear to me that arguments about the potential benefits of medicinal plants can be used to support rain forest conservation as a whole. If the forest goes, the plants and the knowledge about them will go, too. Therefore, it's a good idea to protect it. That seems pretty easy to understand, really, but it's difficult to get the idea across to some people and corporations.

For me, this volunteer vacation was the experience of a lifetime, a chance to do something active, and to have a holiday with a purpose and a conscience. I had no training in botany and no expedition experience. A layperson straight from the book, I was transformed into Dr. Livingstone for a short while and now am definitely hooked on the experience.

BRIDGES (Building Responsible International Dialogue through Grassroots Exchanges)

1203 Preservation Park, Suite 300
Oakland, CA 94612
(510) 271-8286; Fax (510) 451-2996
E-mail: info@grassrootsbridges.org
Web site: www.grassrootsbridges.org

Project location: Africa, Asia, and Latin America.

Project type: Environmental justice, education, public health, and economic development.

Project Costs: BRIDGES covers all costs, including airfare and room and board.

Project dates: Vary year to year; contact the organization for current information.

How to apply: Via the organization's Web site listed above.

Work done by volunteers: Programs that emphasize community service and empowerment of local communities.

Special skills or requirements: Extensive experience doing community service or organizing in local U.S. communities. Volunteers must have had limited opportunity to travel abroad previously, and no previous international volunteer experience. Volunteers must be at least 18 years old. Volunteers must be low-income.

Sample projects: Using music, art, and dance to work with Afro-Brazilian children in *favelas* (settlements of jerry-built shacks) in Brazil.

Bridges for Education, Inc. (BFE)

94 Lamarck Drive
Buffalo, NY 14226
(716) 839-0180; Fax (716) 839-9493
E-mail: jbc@buffalo.edu
Web site: www.bridges4edu.org

Project location: Eastern and Central Europe.

Project type: Education.

Project costs: Airfare, and administrative costs of $850.

Project dates: Projects take place in the summer and include three weeks of teaching plus one week of travel for teachers. United States and Canadian teachers receive free room and board and travel for one week.

How to apply: Via the organization's Web site.

Work done by volunteers: Teaching conversational English in a team-based camp setting.

Special skills or requirements: BFE prefers certified teachers and college professors. Depending on the needs of the teams, BFE will also accept educated adults, college students, and high school students whose parents or teachers are on the team. There are 100 students and 12 to 15 U.S. and Canadian teachers per camp. Teachers will be trained in basic ESL methods prior to departure in your home area with other volunteer teachers. Teaching participants are provided a handbook and a curriculum guideline. Participants must be flexible, with a sense of humor and a willingness to help others. Details on each camp and a list of frequently asked questions are listed on the organization's Web site.

Commentary: The students in the camps are usually ages 14 to 18, although camps for adults and for students aged 12 to 14 have also been organized. Since 1994, BFE has organized 66 camps in 8 countries, serving 8,500 students from 33 countries. The purpose of BFE is to promote tolerance and understanding, using the English language as a bridge.

Bristol Industrial Museum
Princes Wharf, Wapping Road
Bristol BS1 4RN United Kingdom
(0117) 925 1470; Fax (0117) 929 7318

Project location: At and near the museum.

Project type: Restoration and operation of museum exhibits, most of which are steam-powered.

Project costs: Volunteers are responsible for all travel and living costs.

Project dates: Most weekends throughout the year.

How to apply: Call or send a letter to the address listed above.

Work done by volunteers: Volunteers work as crew for an operating railway and a working steamship. They also do restoration work on trains, ships, steam cars, and motor bikes.

Special skills or requirements: A vague knowledge of engineering principles is useful, but not necessary.

Commentary: This is a small museum with a minimal budget that can use all the volunteers it can get.

Sample projects: In the past, volunteers have served on crews on the Bristol Harbour Railway, a dockside railway run by steam locomotives, or on the steam tug Mayflower, an 1861 steam-powered tug that now carries passengers. Volunteers have also helped maintain an 1878, 35-ton steam crane, served as crews on a 1934 fire-fighting vessel, and restored an electric dockside crane.

British Trust for Conservation Volunteers (BTCV)

36 Saint Mary's Street
Wallingford, Oxfordshire OX10 0EU United Kingdom
(01491) 821600; Fax (01491) 839646
E-mail: Information@btcv.org
Web site: www.btcv.org

Project location: United Kingdom, Europe, North America, Central America, Asia, Africa, and Australia.

Project type: Practical conservation.

Project costs: From £30 to £1500

Project dates: Year-round.

How to apply: Apply via the web site or contact the above address for a brochure (contains an application).

Work done by volunteers: Construction projects, footpath work, habitat management, surveying and monitoring work.

Special skills or requirements: An interest in conservation. Some projects require a certain level of physical fitness.

Commentary: BTCV aims to harness people's energies and talents to protect and improve the environment through practical action. More than 130,000 volunteers participate in BTCV projects each year.

Sample projects: Footpath repair in the Scottish highlands, woodland management in the English Lake District, turtle monitoring in Thailand, coastal conservation in Mexico, and radio tracking wolves in Slovakia.

BTCV Scotland

Balallan House
24 Allan Park
Stirling FK8 2QG United Kingdom
(01786) 479 697

Project location: Throughout Scotland, including Orkney, Shetland, and the Hebrides islands.

Project type: Practical conservation work.

Project costs: About $10 per day. Insurance, tools, training, accommodations, and food are provided. Airfare not included in project costs.

Project dates: Between March and November each year.

How to apply: Contact the office listed above for a program of projects. Include one international reply coupon, available from the post office.

Work done by volunteers: Tree planting, restoration of traditional buildings, pond construction, footpath construction, and habitat management. Volunteers work in groups of 11 with an experienced leader from 9:00 A.M. to 5:00 P.M. each day with breaks. Evenings and one day each week are free. Projects last from seven to fourteen days.

Special skills or requirements: No special skills, just fitness and health. The minimum age is 18; the maximum is 70.

Commentary: BTCV Scotland is a part of the British Trust for Conservation Volunteers, the United Kingdom's largest practical environmental conservation charity.

C.A.I. Pina Palmera A.C.

Apartado Postal 109
C.P. 70900 Pochutla, Oaxaca, Mexico
(52) 958-5843147; Fax (52) 958-5843145
E-mail: pinapalmera@laneta.apc.org or
caippac@yahoo.com.mx
Web site: www.pinapalmera.org

Project location: Playa Zipolite, Puerto Angel, Pochutla, and Oaxaca, Mexico.
Project type: Community-based rehabilitation.
Project cost: Volunteers must provide their own medical insurance and plane tickets.
Project dates: Year-round.
How to apply: Send an e-mail to one of the addresses listed above.
Work done by volunteers: Personal assistance to people with severe disabilities, gardening, carpentry, cooking, rehabilitation, and staff support.
Special skills or requirements: Volunteers must speak Spanish very well and be able to stay for at least six months. A minimum age of 18 is required.
Commentary: Participants are given a bed in shared volunteer quarters and two meals daily.

California Department of Parks and Recreation

P.O. Box 942896

1416 9th Street

Sacramento, CA 94296-0001

(916) 653-9069

Web site: www.parks.ca.gov

Project location: Throughout California. There are 90 parks with camp host programs and more than 250 parks in the state park system, most of which have volunteer opportunities for hosts and interpreters.

Project type: Campground hosts and interpreters.

Project costs: Volunteers furnish their own trailers, campers, or mobile homes. Campsites are free.

Project dates: Year-round. Hosts must commit to work two to five hours per day for a minimum of 30 days, although most parks prefer a three-month stay; the maximum stay at any one park is six months. Opportunities for interpreters are more flexible; contact the organization to make individual arrangements.

How to apply: Call or send a letter to the office listed above.

Work done by volunteers: General campground host duties and specialized interpreter duties, such as living history, environmental studies, and natural science programs. Other work includes horse patrol, archaeology, art, trail maintenance, gardening and museum collection managment.

Special skills or requirements: Volunteers must be at least 18 years old.

Camp AmeriKids

161 Cherry Street
New Canaan, CT 06840
(800) 486-4357
E-mail: camp@americares.org
Web site: www.americares.org/camp

Project location: Lower New York state.

Project type: Special needs residential camp for inner-city children with HIV/AIDS and other life-threatening illnesses.

Project costs: Travel expenses.

Project dates: The month of August. Camp AmeriKids has two 9-day sessions; volunteers may participate in one or both.

How to apply: Call or send an e-mail request to the organization for an application. The application deadline is May 1 each year.

Work done by volunteers: Camp counselors for campers between the ages of 6 and 17; 60 to 75 volunteers are required per camp session. 10 to 12 nurses, as well as 1 to 2 physicians per camp session are needed to help operate a 24-hour infirmary, helping to care for the campers' needs as well as distribute medication.

Special skills or requirements: Volunteers must be open-minded, enthusiastic, and at least 18 years old. Medical staff must have an R.N., N.P., or M.D. license or certification in New York state.

Camphill Special School, Beaver Run

1784 Fairview Road
Glenmoore, PA 19343
(610) 469-1715
E-mail: bvrrn@aol.com
Web site: www.beaverrun.org

Project location: Chester County, Pennsylvania.

Project type: Working with children who have disabilities.

Project costs: None. Room and board are provided to volunteers, but volunteers are responsible for their own transportation costs.

Project dates: Year-round.

How to apply: Write for an application form or download an application from the Web site listed above.

Work done by volunteers: Direct care of children, assisting in homes and schools, managing craft workshops, and other tasks.

Special skills or requirements: An interest in working with children and an interest in community life. Applicants must be at least 20 years of age.

Canary Nature (Project of the Atlantic Whale Foundation)

St. Martins House
59 St. Martins Lane, Covent Garden
London, WC2N 4JS, United Kingdom
(44) 0207 240 6604; Fax (44) 0207 240 5795
E-mail: edb@huron.ac.uk
Web site: www.whalefoundation.f2s.com

Project location: Tenerife and the Islas Canarias, Spain.

Project type: Conservation, education, and research with whales and dolphins.

Project costs: Three programs, with costs from £100 to £800. Housing is provided as part of the program cost, but volunteers are responsible for their own meals.

Project dates: Year-round.

How to apply: Apply via the organization's Web site or e-mail address, or by sending a self-addressed envelope to the address listed above.

Work done by volunteers: Working with the whale watching industry, participating in boat-based dolphin research, participating in workshops, other on-board ship-based research opportunities, and painting wall murals.

Special skills or requirements: An enthusiastic and positive attitude.

Sample projects: Work on the world's largest wall mural of whales and dolphins; complete photo I.D. databases on pilot whales and bottlenose dolphins; track species migration through the Canaries; participate in research on the relationship between bottlenose dolphins and autistic children; work with the Young European Cetaecean Research Project; help with a free poster campaign for tourists.

Cape Tribulation Tropical Research Station

PMB 5
Cape Tribulation
Queensland 4873 Australia
(61) 7 4098 0063; Fax by arrangement (the station relies on
solar power and cannot leave the fax machine on. Call
and ask to send a fax before sending it.)
E-mail: austrop@austrop.org.au
Web site: www.austrop.org.au

Project location: Cape Tribulation, on the Coral Sea coast of
Queensland, Australia, about 120 kilometers north of Cairns.
The area has a variety of habitats, from coastal reefs to a
tropical rain forest.
Project type: Ecology and conservation.
Project costs: Participants pay $15 per day for food and modest
accommodations. Transportation to and from Cape Tribulation is at the volunteer's expense, although every reasonable
attempt will be made to find low-cost transport.
Project dates: Year-round; whether a specific project is available
depends on the weather and the idiosyncrasies of plants, animals, and funding authorities. The normal stay is two to
three weeks, but extensions are available at the discretion of
the director. Long stays may be negotiated after the volunteer arrives.
How to apply: Before applying, potential volunteers should visit
the station's Web site. Vistors may apply as interns, students,
or volunteers and should do so by sending a brief e-mail to
the director describing their interest and likely dates of participation. Include a brief resume. If you must apply by mail,
send an international reply coupon and a self-addressed,
stamped envelope. If there is no response, please contact
them again.
Work done by volunteers: Volunteers assist with research and
station activities, ranging from radio tracking bats to counting figs to constructing station buildings. All volunteers are

expected to actively participate in the household activities of the station. Specifically, projects may include the ecology of flying foxes (fruit bats) and their relatives; development of non-lethal deterrent systems for orchards against flying foxes; productivity and pollination of cluster fig trees; development of techniques for assisted regeneration of rain forests; development of appropriate technology for the wet tropics; rainforest and reef conservation; plus a variety of projects by researchers outside the station.

Special skills or requirements: Volunteers can be of any age, but are preferably more than 20 years old. Couples are especially welcome. Volunteers must have an open and flexible attitude and must not have preconceived notions about their roles at the station. Volunteers should be willing to actively contribute, even to the most mundane activity. The facilities are comfortable, but fairly spartan.

Commentary: The Cape Tribulation Tropical Research Station is a research and conservation organization specializing in lowland tropical ecosystems and appropriate technology for the tropics. It is nonaffiliated and is funded by the not-for-profit AUSTROP Foundation.

Caput Insulae Beli

Beli 4, 51559 Beli
Cres Island, Croatia
(385) 51-840-525
E-mail: caput.insulae@ri.tel.hr
Web site: www.caput-insulae.com

Project location: Beli, Cres Island, Croatia.

Project type: Historic preservation; conservation.

Project costs: One-week projects run from EUR 60 to EUR 122; Two-week projects cost between EUR 100 and EUR 222. Extra days cost EUR 10. The price includes return travel from the town of Cres to the village of Beli, accommodation, training, and supervision. It does not include travel to Cres, personal expenses, insurance, cost of passports or visa, or meals.

Project dates: Mid-January through mid-December. Two weeks' participation is suggested.

How to apply: By e-mail.

Work done by volunteers: Protection of natural and cultural-historical heritage of the island of Cres. The primary purpose is to protect the Eurasian griffons, a dwindling species in Croatia, but there are also educational and eco-tourism programs.

Special skills or requirements: Volunteers should be in good physical condition, able to stand the sub-Mediterranean heat, and able to swim. Volunteers must speak English, be at least 18 years of age, and should be committed to natural conservation. Volunteers should have a positive attitude toward working with people from different cultural backgrounds.

Sample projects: Preparing and placing food in the "vulture restaurant," cleaning and feeding griffons in the bird sanctuary, monitoring griffons on cliffs and in the vulture restaurant and sanctuary; removing garbage from the bird sanctuary; building and restoring dry stone walls; cleaning paths and trails; cleaning ponds of vegetation; and welcoming and guiding visitors.

Caretta Research Project

Savannah Science Museum
P.O. Box 9841
Savannah, GA 31412-9841
(912) 447-8655; Fax (912) 447-8656
E-mail: wassawcrp@aol.com
Web site: members.aol.com/wassawcrp/

Project location: Wassaw Island, one of the barrier islands off the Georgia coast.

Project type: Scientific research of the loggerhead sea turtle population.

Project costs: $550 per week covers food, housing, and transportation to and on the island. Does not include transportation to Georgia.

Project dates: May to September.

How to apply: Write to the project research director at the address listed above.

Work done by volunteers: Tagging adult turtles, recording data, monitoring nests, and working with hatchlings.

Special skills or requirements: Volunteers must be physically able to work at night. Must be at least 16 years old. Exceptions have been made for highly motivated younger students.

Commentary: Days are free for individual activities. Volunteers have come from all fifty states and numerous foreign countries in the 20 years of the project's existence. The project has a high percentage of returning participants.

Caribbean Conservation Corporation

4424 NW 13th Street, Suite A-1
Gainesville, FL 32609
(352) 373-6441 or (800) 678-7853; Fax (352) 375-2449
E-mail: ccc@cccturtle.org
Web site: www.cccturtle.org

Project location: Tortuguero, Costa Rica.

Project type: Marine turtle and migrant and resident bird research.

Project costs: $1,360 to $2,075 (turtle projects) and $1,210 to $1,910 (bird projects) for 9- to 22-day expeditions. Does not include airfare.

Project dates: March through October.

How to apply: Write, e-mail, or call for information or to apply.

Work done by volunteers: Assisting researchers with sea turtle tagging operations, as well as taking measurements and observing nesting habits; assisting bird researchers by making observations and capturing birds in nets along transects and within specific habitats.

Special skills or requirements: Volunteers must be in good physical condition, be able to work with others, and be able to maintain a sense of humor in spite of occasional inclement weather. Volunteers must be at least 18 years of age.

Commentary: This organization was formed in 1959 to support the work of the late Archie Carr, one of the world's foremost sea turtle authorities. Since then, it has blended applied research and conservation projects in efforts to reverse the worldwide decline of sea turtles. It has recently begun bird research.

Caribbean Volunteer Expeditions

P.O. Box 388
Corning, NY 14830
(607) 962 7846
E-mail: ahershcve@aol.com
Web site: www.cvexp.org

Project location: The Caribbean, including the Bahamas, the British Virgin Islands, Trinidad, St. Lucia, Nevis, Antigua, Tobago, Barbados, Guyana, Honduras, and the U.S. Virgin Islands. Some opportunities in Nepal may also exist.

Project type: Surveys of sites such as sugar plantations, measured drawings and photography of buildings, and building inventories.

Project costs: $500 to $1,000 plus airfare.

Project dates: One- to two-week projects year-round.

How to apply: Write to the address listed above.

Work done by volunteers: Historic building surveys, historic site surveys and drawing, recommendations for preservation, historic cemetery inventories, photography, archival work, and restoration construction.

Commentary: Caribbean Volunteer Expeditions (CVE) is a nonprofit organization that recruits volunteers to work on preservation projects in the Caribbean. CVE works with local Caribbean agencies such as national trusts, museums, and historical societies on projects they identify. Group sizes range from 3 to 20, and people of all ages are welcome. Accommodations are in hotels, rental houses, or camp sites.

We Brake for Buildings!

❖ by Karen Alpha ❖

Caribbean Volunteer Expeditions

"WE BRAKE FOR BUILDINGS!" this is the bumper sticker we imagine for Caribbean Volunteer Expeditions (CVE) after two weeks of happily careening around the Caribbean islands of Antigua and Nevis in November. Foregoing the family gatherings and Thanksgiving feasts, we have instead come to these balmy, friendly outposts in the Leeward Islands to document the architectural evidence of their rich colonial past, and at the same time enjoy the delights of their present.

On Antigua, CVE volunteers continued the ongoing windmill survey: measuring, photographing, and systematically documenting the condition of these sturdy remnants of the prosperous sugar cane plantations that dominated the island from the late 1600s well into the 1800s. Not the least of our tasks was first finding these huge structures in the wild and densely overgrown reaches of the more remote corners of the island. In all, we located and documented over 25 more windmills, some of them as approachable as the one used as the gatehouse for the exclusive Mill Reef Club, or the Harmony Hall windmill, converted to a two-story combination cocktail bar and lookout over the nearby Atlantic.

Others were more of a test for our jeep and our map-reading skills. Usually the windmills were located on high ground, and were therefore visible from a distance, but far from a paved road. A winding farm lane would turn into track, then into a cow path, before disappearing into the brush. Some of these cow paths gave us new appreciation for

Volunteers with Caribbean Volunteer Expeditions survey an abandoned windmill on the island of Antigua. (Photo courtesy of Caribbean Volunteer Expeditions)

the virtues of four-wheel drive. Two mills, over on the east side of the island, we never could get to and won't, short of calling in an assault team in an army helicopter.

Each windmill has its own personality. All are individuals of master stone work and design, some signed and dated, one with a beautifully carved plaque of a horse's head set in stone over the doorway; another, gaily striped in runs of natural red and yellow stone. None was more beautiful nor inviting than the westernmost mill we visited, high and alone on a wind-swept bluff overlooking miles of blue Caribbean, looking out straight into the setting sun. We wanted to move in forever.

A typical CVE day involves rising at the first light to make good use of the cool part of the day. We grab a quick breakfast, pack a lunch that includes liter bottles of water frozen overnight, and are off into the countryside toward today's site. The object is to get in a long morning of working outdoors before stopping at one or another perfect empty white beach for a swim, a picnic, and a relaxing afternoon of visiting, browsing, sightseeing, shopping, researching, or driving off for more exploring. Sometimes this actually occurs more or less as scheduled. You can see a powerful amount of an island country in this fashion, more than I have ever done while on a typical sightseeing vacation.

As the evening of our typical day approaches, we shower, mix up a pitcher of icy rum drinks, and retire to our veranda to enjoy the sunset upon the yachts and shimmering waters of Falmouth Harbor. Then, after a short stroll along the road, we choose a dining spot from among the little houses where Antiguan ladies serve delectable spicy plates of West Indian curries and freshly caught seafood at tables on their front porches. We might opt for Jackie's tonight, or maybe Valerie's. Or if we are lucky, we'll be invited to cocktails at the hilltop house where we lounge on the terrace overlooking the harbor and view the dipping sun, past the peaks of Montserrat. However, if it is Thursday or Sunday, we will certainly be obligated to climb the steep hill to Shirley Heights to attend the all-night open-air reggae party held on the stone terrace of the fort. Everyone will be there: locals, boaters, tourists, constructions workers, and us.

There is plenty more work to be done under the host sun of Antigua: at least two more trips are needed to finish the windmill survey. There is also another site at the old town of Parham we have been asked to document. On our way to the airport, we screech to a halt several times to photograph buildings we have admired all week, among them the naturally green stone church of All Saints, incandescent in the morning sun. Another bumper sticker comes to mind: "CVE . . . WORTH EVERY MINUTE."

Casa de Proyecto Libertad, Incorporated

113 North First Street
Harlingen, TX 78550
(956) 425-9552; Fax (956) 425-8249

Project location: South Texas along the Texas–Mexico border.

Project type: Refer legal services to immigrants and refugees. Advocate on behalf of the immigrant and refugee community in the United States.

Project costs: Participants are responsible for all transportation, room, and board. Occasionally, stipends are available.

Project dates: Year-round.

How to apply: Send a resume and cover letter to the address listed above.

Work done by volunteers: Client interviews, case documentation, education, and advocacy.

Special skills or requirements: Volunteers should be bilingual in English and Spanish and able to work in a multicultural setting. Computer skills are helpful. Volunteers must be 18 or older.

Commentary: Volunteers are asked to make a six-month commitment, but shorter commitments are occasionally accepted.

Sample projects: Other than legal and educational projects, there are often fund-raising projects that appeal to special groups for contributions.

Catalina Island Conservancy

P.O. Box 2739
Avalon, CA 90704
(310) 510-2595, ext. 102
E-mail: volunteers@catalinaconservancy.org
Web site: www.catalinaconservancy.org

Project location: Catalina Island, California.

Project type: Habitat restoration.

Project costs: $150. Housing is provided in tents. Volunteers are responsible for transportation to Long Beach, New Port Beach, or Dana Point, but project costs include a round-trip boat ticket from these points to Catalina Island.

Project dates: Seven one-week vacations available in the months of April, May, June, and September.

How to apply: Download an application from the organization's Web site or call and leave a request for a *Volunteer Vacations* application.

Special skills or requirements: Volunteers should be able to conduct physical labor such as removing invasive plants and old fences, building trails, and transplanting plants. Arrive with a willingness to work and a good attitude. Volunteers must be 18, but youth age 12 to 17 may volunteer if accompanied by a parent or guardian.

Commentary: This is a unique way to explore Catalina Island that most people are not able to do. You will work alongside staff that manages each of the restoration projects, and this will allow you to gain an in-depth knowledge of each project and how your work is a vital part of the restoration of Catalina Island. A local volunteer chef cooks evening meals.

Sample projects: Erecting fence enclosures around rare and sensitive plant species unique to Catalina Island, processing and cleaning native seeds, transplanting and monitoring native plants at the James H. Ackerman Native Plant Nursery, and conducting light construction work on the Catalina Island Conservancy's facilities.

Conservation, Education, Diving, Awareness, and Marine Research (CEDAM International)

1 Fox Road
Croton-on-Hudson, NY 10520
(914) 271-5365; Fax (914) 271-4723
E-mail: cedamint@aol.com
Web site: www.cedam.org

Project location: Worldwide.

Project type: Marine conservation and marine research expeditions.

Project costs: $1,000 to $4,500, plus transportation to and from the site. Project cost includes room and board (double occupancy) except in transit.

Project dates: Generally between May and September for one to two weeks, but some expeditions are year-round.

How to apply: Write to the address listed above for complete registration information.

Work done by volunteers: Volunteers—divers and nondivers—participate in marine research projects and help scientists with research activities.

Special skills or requirements: CEDAM prefers volunteers who are certified divers, but others are accepted as needed. Volunteers receive basic on-site training for their projects. There are no age restrictions for certified divers.

Commentary: CEDAM is one of the premier marine research organizations that uses volunteers extensively. CEDAM has been organizing expeditions for 30 years.

Central European Teaching Program

Beloit College
700 College Street
Beloit, WI 53511
(608) 363-2619
E-mail: cetp@beloit.edu.
Web site: www.beloit.edu/~cetp/

Project location: Hungary, Romania, and Poland.

Project type: Education.

Project costs: There is an application fee of $50, and the placement fee runs from $1,700 (not including airfare) to $3,450 (including airfare). Volunteers are also responsible for a refundable contract completion deposit of $200 to $700. Teachers are paid in local currency; pay is comparable to the salaries of native teachers. Salaries are sufficient for covering everyday living expenses and in-country travel. Accommodations are paid for.

Project dates: 10-month projects, beginning in September or October.

How to apply: E-mail the Central European Teaching Program at the address listed above.

Work done by volunteers: English conversation teaching at the elementary, high school, or college level. Some positions for teachers of English/German and English/French are also available, as well as positions at the college level for English for Special Purposes.

Special skills or requirements: A college diploma is required. Volunteers should have classroom teaching experience in English or English as a second or foreign language or demonstrate a commitment to obtaining experience in teaching ESL via training and classroom teaching through an academic or volunteer program before departure.

Commentary: Conversation teachers are responsible for enhancing students' oral fluency via conversation practice, classroom drills, games, audio-visual instruction, and listening comprehension, as well as through working closely with native teachers to emphasize important grammar concepts. Normal teaching hours are from 7:45 A.M. to 2:10 P.M. Teachers will have 18 to 22 class meetings per week, each class lasting 45 minutes. Contingent upon time and interest, conversation teachers may also become involved in extracurricular activities such as sports leagues and drama and musical productions. Most Central European Teaching Program teachers also work tutoring private students or teaching adult groups made up of, for example, business people or factory employees.

Centre for Alternative Technology

Machynlleth
Powys
United Kingdom
SY20 9AZ
(01654) 705 950; Fax (01654) 702 782
E-mail: rick.dance@cat.org.uk
Web site: www.cat.org.uk

Project location: A former slate quarry in the hills of central Wales.

Project type: The Centre is a working demonstration of renewable energy, environmental building, energy efficiency, alternative sewage and water treatment, and organic growing.

Project costs: About £10 per day, plus travel expenses. Costs are £4 to £10 per day depending on income (self-assessed).

Project dates: The short-term volunteer program runs on specified weeks from March to August.

How to apply: Write or call Rick Dance at the office listed above for full details and a booking form.

Work done by volunteers: Gardening, course facilities preparation, site maintenance, landscaping, plus whatever jobs are most urgent at the time.

Commentary: Volunteers come for one or two consecutive weeks, as available. Demand is high—the program was completely booked last year by early spring—so book early. There are no facilities for young children.

Centro de Estudios de Español Pop Wuj

Apartado Postal 68
Quetzaltenango, Guatemala
or
P.O. Box 11127
Santa Rosa, CA 95406
(502) 761-82-86 in Guatemala or
(707) 869-1116 in California
E-mail: pop-wuj@juno.com
Web site: www.pop-wuj.org

Project location: Guatemala.

Project type: Community development programs.

Project costs: $125 to $140 per week.

Project dates: Year-round, for one-week sessions.

Project costs include room and board, but do not include airfare.

How to apply: Contact the Santa Rosa, California, school representative for application information, or apply via the organization's Web site.

Work done by volunteers: This is primarily a language study program, but each student has the opportunity to practice Spanish by working with locals on community service projects, including latrine and stove construction and child day care.

Special skills or requirements: None but an interest in learning Spanish and meeting local people. Volunteers must be at least 18 years old; volunteers under 18 must be accompanied by a parent or guardian.

Chantier de Jeunes

Provence Côte d'Azur
La Ferme Giaume
7, Avenue Pierre de Coubertin
06150 Cannes la Bocca, France
(4) 93-47-89-69; Fax (4) 93-48-12-01
E-mail: CJPCA@club.internet.fr
Web site: www.club-internet.fr/perso/cjpca

Project location: Sainte Marguerite in Annes, France, and various locations in Belgium.
Project type: Work camps.
Project costs: About $200 per week.
Project dates: All holidays in winter and summer.
How to apply: For special information, send a letter in French with a self-addressed, stamped envelope.
Work done by volunteers: Building, environmental protection, and preserving historical monuments. Volunteers work in groups of 14 for 15 days. Work lasts for five hours in the morning; participants are free for the afternoon and night.
Special skills or requirements: Participants must be 14 to 18 years old and speak at least minimal French.
Commentary: Chantier de Jeunes is over thirty years old and offers youth an international living experience.

Chantiers d'Études Medievales

4, Rue du Tonnelet Rouge
67000 Strasbourg, France
Tel/Fax (3) 88-37-17-20

Project location: Châteaux d'Ottrott (Alsace, France).

Project type: Restoration of medieval monuments.

Project costs: EUR 70 to EUR 85 covers insurance, meals, and accommodations. Volunteers are responsible for transportation to sites.

Project dates: 15-day sessions from July 1 to late August.

How to apply: Write to the above address for an application and more information.

Work done by volunteers: Restoration and maintenance of two fortified castles destined for use as cultural and recreational centers. Some work is physically demanding. Volunteers work in teams of 15 or 20 for six hours per day, six days a week.

Special skills or requirements: Volunteers must be at least 18 years old and should speak at least minimal French. Volunteers 16 to 18 years old may come with parental authorization.

Commentary: For the past 15 years, 300 volunteers have participated each year from more than 20 countries. While accommodations are modest, they are sufficient and offer participants an opportunity to experience a true camaraderie with other volunteers.

Cholsey and Wallingford Railway
Hithercroft Road
P.O. Box 16
Wallingford, Oxfordshire OX10 ONF United Kingdom
(01491) 835 067 (weekends only)

Project location: Along two and one-half miles of track running
from Cholsey to Wallingford in England.
Project type: Railway restoration and maintenance.
Project costs: Volunteers are responsible for their room, board,
and transportation.
Project dates: Weekends year-round.
How to apply: Write to the address listed above for information.
Work done by volunteers: General railway restoration and main-
tenance.
Special skills or requirements: None but the ability to do heavy
physical labor.

A Christian Ministry in the National Parks

10 Justin's Way
Freeport, ME 04032
(207) 865-6436; Fax (207) 865-6852
E-mail: info@acmnp.com
Web site: www.coolworks.com/acmnp/default.htm

Project location: Volunteers serve in one of thirty national parks and recreation areas across the country.

Project type: Ministerial services for employees and visitors of the parks.

Project costs: Volunteers pay for their transportation to and from the parks but are provided room, board, and wages from a secular employer.

Project dates: From Memorial Day to Labor Day, with a minimum commitment of 90 days.

How to apply: Write to the address listed above for an application and more information.

Work done by volunteers: Lead worship services and Bible studies, direct choirs, and pursue other ministerial duties.

Special skills or requirements: A commitment to the Christian faith, creativity, maturity, and the ability to work with Christians of all denominations. Volunteers should be lay leaders with special skills in music, Bible study, recreation, drama, or Christian education.

Commentary: This program is for singles and married couples who are at least 18 years old and who wish to spend a full summer working in a national park and ministering to the religious needs of others.

Christian Peacemaker Teams

P.O. Box 6508
Chicago, IL 60680
(312) 455-1199; Fax (312) 432-1213
E-mail: cpt@igc.org
Web site: www.cpt.org

Project location: Chicago and worldwide (includes the Middle East, and North, Central, and South America).

Project type: Human rights documentation and reporting, supporting local peacemakers in conflict situations, and nonviolent direct action.

Project costs: Approximately $1,000 to $2,000 (including airfare), depending on the project location and on-site logistics.

Project dates: Several times per year, depending on location; projects last about two weeks.

How to apply: Contact the office listed above.

Work done by volunteers: Meeting with local peacemakers and populations affected by violent conflict, human rights documentation, and participating in nonviolent direct action. Participants commit to sharing their experiences with a wider audience upon return to their home communities.

Special skills or requirements: Participants share in tasks of writing, photography, speaking, organizing, press work, leading worship, and meal preparation and household chores.

Commentary: Work is always in high-risk conflict situations and is potentially dangerous. Participants should be in good health and able to cope with vigorous physical activity under sometimes extreme or primitive conditions. Volunteers should be prepared to work and live in teams under simple conditions.

Sample projects: Delegations currently go to Vieques, Puerto Rico; Chiapas, Mexico; Colombia; and the occupied Palestinian territories.

Colorado Trail Foundation

710 10th Street #210
Golden, CO 80401-5843
(303) 384-3729, ext.113; Fax (303) 384-3743
E-mail: ctf@coloradotrail.org
Web site: www.coloradotrail.org

Project location: Colorado national forests.

Project type: Trail building and maintenance on the Colorado Trail.

Project costs: $35 registration fee. The foundation sets up base camps for volunteers and provides food. Volunteers provide their own sleeping bags, tents, and personal items.

Project dates: June, July, and August, with both weekend and weeklong projects.

How to apply: Write to the address listed above for a summer trail crew schedule.

Work done by volunteers: Building, maintenance, and signing of trails.

Special skills or requirements: Volunteers should be in good health and willing to work. The foundation provides tools and experienced leaders. Volunteers must be at least 16 years old.

Commentary: The Colorado Trail is a 470-mile trail stretching from Denver to Durango. It was built, and continues to be improved, largely by a massive volunteer effort.

Father and Sons on the Colorado Trail

❖ by T. Brooksher ❖

Colorado Trail Volunteer

Many people choose to work on the Colorado Trail because of the scope and breadth of the project—nearly 500 miles of trail traversing some of the world's most majestic and treacherous mountain ranges, built and maintained solely by volunteers. Others choose to join Colorado Trail volunteer crews to revel in the splendor of the inimitable Rocky Mountains. Still others choose it for relationships and camaraderie that inevitably transforms crew into family. For the Brooksher family, volunteering to maintain the Colorado Trail is an incomparable father and son adventure.

Our experience with the Trail began three years ago. I had heard about this wonder of sweat and enthusiasm for a decade, and about the fact that it had been conceived, initiated, fought for, resurrected, completed, and was being maintained by volunteer workers. But, as the father of two small sons, finding the time to volunteer had to be relegated to the "someday" list. When Andy, our eldest, reached 15, the idea of spending a week together in the beautiful mountains we both loved, working together toward a common goal, seemed a perfect father-son experience . . . at least to the father. So, I sheepishly suggested the possibility. To my delight and relief, Andy said, "Sure." Before he had the chance to think about it I committed us to a week on a Colorado Trail crew. That was the start of a father-son tradition, which has paid wonderful dividends as we've meandered through Andy's teen years.

Andy and I met up with our first crew in the heart of Denver's Summit County ski area. Our crews' assignment was to restore a section of trail that runs above the town of Breckenridge, Colorado. Work included grooming the trail, particularly to facilitate water runoff, and replacing several wooden bridges, which were becoming unsafe due to wear and decomposition. Our crew that year was a rich mixture of retirees, including a group of six who had traveled together from Arkansas, and non-retirees, including a few from most of the decades between adolescence and retirement. Three members of the crew were over 70, including two of the women. The crew bonded quickly while sharing trail work, chores, cooking, and evening campfire time.

On the drive back home after our first week on a trail crew, I asked Andy what the highlight of the experience had been for him. Without hesitation, this quiet, frequently shy teenager answered "the people." We had signed up for the crew thinking it would be an opportunity to build our relationship and give back to the region we love. And, while the experience was rich in both of those respects, we realized it was really about relationships in a larger, family sense. It was about meeting 16 other people for the first time, getting to know them, and becoming a family through a week's experiences together in one of the most beautiful wilderness areas in the world. The following spring I didn't have to feel sheepish when I asked Andy if he wanted to sign on for another Colorado Trail crew, nor did I have any trouble continuing this Brooksher father-son tradition with my younger son, Kyle, a few years later. The experiences we've shared on the Trail and the relationships we've formed will last a lifetime.

Connecticut State Parks Division

79 Elm Street
Hartford, CT 06106-5127
(860) 424-3200; Fax (860) 424-4070

Project location: Campgrounds in various Connecticut state parks and forests.

Project type: Campground hosts.

Project costs: Volunteers are responsible for transportation, room, and board.

Project dates: Memorial Day weekend through Labor Day weekend.

How to apply: Write to the address listed above for an application and a job description.

Work done by volunteers: Volunteers must be available for a minimum of four weeks and will serve as the live-in hosts of a campground. Their primary responsibility is to assist campers by answering questions and explaining campground regulations. Light maintenance work may also be performed. Volunteers are expected to work weekends and holidays, but different hours may be arranged with individual park managers.

Special skills or requirements: Volunteers must be neat, courteous, and willing to meet the public, and must possess a knowledge of state park programs and regulations. Volunteers are encouraged to bring their families.

Conservation Volunteers Australia

P.O. Box 423
Ballarat, Victoria 3353 Australia
(03) 5333 1483; Fax (03) 5333 2166
E-mail: info@conservationvolunteers.com.au
Web site: www.conservationvolunteers.com.au

Project location: Throughout Australia, commencing from the
capital city of any state or territory.
Project type: Conservation projects.
Project costs: The six-week "Conservation Experience" costs
AUD 966 and includes food, accommodations, and project-
related transportation costs during six weeks of practical conservation projects. Project costs do not include airfare.

A team from Conservation Volunteers Australia builds a walking track to
protect fragile ecosystems along Cradle Mountain in Tasmania. (Photo courtesy Conservation Volunteers Australia)

Project dates: The Conservation Experience can begin on any Friday from any Conservation Volunteers Australia (CVA) office (located in all state and territory capitals). Advance booking is essential.

How to apply: Write, fax, or e-mail the organization for further information and an application form.

Work done by volunteers: Conservation projects such as tree planting, weed control, endangered species projects, remote coastal area projects, and habitat restoration.

Special skills or requirements: Volunteers should have a strong interest in practical conservation and should be prepared to live and work as a member of a team. All volunteers should have a reasonable level of physical fitness.

Commentary: Since 1982, CVA has been providing opportunities for volunteers to make a real and lasting contribution to conserving Australia's unique natural environment.

Council on International Educational Exchange

633 Third Avenue, Floor 20
New York, NY 10017
(888) COUNCIL or (212) 822-2600; Fax (212) 822-2872
E-mail: info@councilexchanges.org
Web site: us.councilexchanges.org

Project location: Europe, Asia, North Africa, the Mediterranean, Latin America, and North America.

Project type: Construction, renovation, and social, environmental, and archaeological work.

Project costs: $300 plus transportation, insurance, and spending money.

Project dates: Year-round.

How to apply: Contact the organization for an application and a directory of projects. Projects fill up fast, so apply early.

Work done by volunteers: Manual labor, social work, playground supervision, painting, digging, planting and weeding, visiting disabled people, and more.

Special skills or requirements: Volunteers must desire to work hard in a multicultural setting and have a sense of adventure. There are no more than two people from any one country on any project. Participants must be at least 18 years old.

Commentary: CIEE is one of the major work camp organizers in the United States, offering some 1,100 projects every summer. The organization also offers many other programs for travel and study abroad.

Sample projects: In recent years, volunteers have been involved in turtle conservation in Mexico, restoration of monasteries in Italy and France, working with children in the United Kingdom, and assisting with arts and crafts festivals in Morocco.

Cross-Cultural Solutions

47 Potter Avenue
New Rochelle, NY 10801
(914) 632-0022 or (800) 380-4777; Fax (914) 632-8494
E-mail: info@crossculturalsolutions.org
Web site: www.crossculturalsolutions.org

Project location: Asia, Africa, Latin America, Eastern Europe.

Project type: Short and long-term international volunteering programs including humanitarian initiatives in education, health care, women's empowerment, and rural and community development.

Project costs: Approximately $2,200 for a three-week program, depending on location. Airfare (not included in the price) and program costs are tax deductible.

Project dates: Year-round for varying lengths of time, from three weeks to one year.

How to apply: Call or e-mail the organization for information.

Work done by volunteers: Volunteers work in schools, hospitals, clinics, and orphanages, and with women's groups and small business development programs. Assignment is based on the volunteer's skills and interests. All volunteers receive an orientation before the project starts.

Special skills or requirements: No special skills are necessary. Cross-Cultural Solutions' age policy varies with each program. Most programs have a minimum age of 14 to 18 years old, though children under the minimum may accompany an adult volunteer but may not volunteer themselves. All participants under 18 years of age must have their liability form signed by a parent or legal guardian. Children 13 or younger receive a 50-percent discount on program fees.

A volunteer takes a break from his teaching duties to play soccer with his young students in India. (Photo courtesy Cross-Cultural Solutions)

Working with Mother Teresa

❖ by Anupam Basuray ❖

Cross-Cultural Solutions

I worked at Mother Teresa's Home for the Dying and Destitute. It was a very intense experience. I had a vision of what
it would be like, but when I got there it was a little scary. I
want to be a doctor, so my goal for this experience was to
become comfortable being around people who were very
sick. By the end of my time in the Home, I was.

I speak Bengali and was able to communicate with some
of the people. Some of the patients told stories of growing
up on the street and how Mother Teresa's Home was the
best thing that had ever happened to them. For others who
were more affluent, such as professors, having to come to the
home was the worst thing that had ever happened to them.
When I first got there, the nuns asked if anyone spoke Bengali, and they dragged me over to this one elderly woman.
At first it was difficult to communicate with her and she was
a bit suspicious, but we got to talking. She is from the same
area in India as my grandmother. Her family had abandoned
her. Every day she and I had a conversation. At the end of
my three weeks she was crying. She said I was like a grand-
son to her.

I did rounds with the doctors, assisting by bandaging,
putting away medications, and helping patients eat. I even
did some acupuncture! I don't think that I did anything
(except for talking in Bengali) unique while I was there; any-

one could have done what I did. I learned a lot about the people there, and I connected with them so much more than I had thought possible. I think it was very productive in regard to my personal goals, and it really supported my desire to be a doctor.

Cross-Lines Cooperative Council

736 Shawnee Avenue
Kansas City, KS 66105
(913) 281-3388; Fax (913) 281-2344
Web site: www.cross-lines.org

Project location: Kansas City, Kansas (usually the Armourdale district).

Project type: Home repair for persons living in poverty, usually elderly and/or disabled persons. May also include commodities packing, thrift store sorting and shelving.

Project costs: Varies, but does not exceed a $100 registration fee.

Project dates: April through October, for one to five working days.

How to apply: Contact the work group coordinator at the address listed above.

Work done by volunteers: General home repair, from replacing broken roofs and windows to rebuilding foundations.

Special skills or requirements: General home repair skills are preferred, but not necessary.

Commentary: Cross-Lines will match appropriate projects to a group's skill level, size, average age, and length of time available.

Cultural Destination Nepal (CDN)

GPO Box 11535
Kathmandu, Nepal
(977) 1-426996; Fax (977) 1-426996
E-mail: cdnnepal@wlink.com.np
Web site: www.volunteernepal.org.np

Project location: Nepal.

Project type: Depends on the interest of the volunteer, but projects usually involve education, women's issues, the environment, or working with children.

Project costs: $650, plus airfare, insurance, personal expenses, and visas.

Project dates: Projects commence four times per year in February, April, August, and October. Other dates may be arranged upon request.

How to apply: Contact the organization at the address listed above. Applications must be received two and a half months before the beginning of the program. There is an application fee of $50.

Work done by volunteers: Most volunteers are placed in schools, teaching subjects such as English, social studies, math, science, computer skills, or health and sanitation. The length of the project (one to three months) depends on the volunteer's interest and the needs of the school or organization.

Special skills or requirements: Non-education volunteers must have either special experience or the educational background to qualify them to work with a non-governmental organization. Volunteers must be 18 to 65 years old, have a high school diploma, and should be physically fit, flexible, and willing to immerse themselves in another culture.

Commentary: Cultural Destination Nepal (CDN) offers a two-week orientation phase, which includes a homestay, Nepali language training, a cultural orientation tour, hiking, and four to five lectures. The program fee includes a seven-to-ten-day trek, a "jungle safari," and a rafting trip, all of which occur after the volunteer experience. Throughout the program, housing and two meals per day are provided either by a host family, the volunteer organization, or CDN. There is a maximum of 25 participants per group.

Dakshinayan

F-1169 Ground Floor
Chittaranjan Park
New Delhi 110019, India
(91) 11-6276645
E-mail: sid@linkindia.com
Web site: www.linkindia.com/dax

Project location: India.

Project type: Education, medical work, and orphanage work.

Project costs: $250 per month. Project costs include room and board, but not transportation.

Project dates: New projects begin on the fifth of every month, and last from one to six months.

How to apply: Via the organization's Web site.

Work done by volunteers: Teaching, medical assistance, general community work.

Special skills or requirements: Tolerance and patience. Volunteers must be at least 18 years old. There is no language requirement to participate.

Dane County Parks Adult Conservation Team

3101 Lake Farm Road
Madison, WI 53711
(608) 224-3601
E-mail: goldstein@co.dane.wi.us
Web site: www.co.dane.wi.us/parks/adult/adult.htm

Project location: Campgrounds at Babcock, Brigham, Lake Farm, Mendota, and Token Creek Parks, all in Wisconsin.

Project type: Campground hosting.

Project costs: Volunteers must provide their own camping unit and personal communication device, such as a cell phone.

Project dates: Program runs from May 1 through October 31; however, new hosts are not scheduled in May or after Labor Day, when there is reduced staff.

How to apply: Contact the office at the address listed above; references from past or present employers and/or volunteer supervisors are required, as is a background check, followed by an interview.

Work done by volunteers: Providing hospitality and information to campers, serving as a liaison to staff, some light maintenance, and reporting.

Special skills or requirements: Personable, easygoing, veteran campers who are friendly, and good camping role models are desired. Experience working with the public is a plus.

Commentary: There is a four-week minimum stay. Three campgrounds have full hookups for the host; one has electricity and access to a water spigot, with dumping nearby; one has electricity, with a water spigot and dumping further away.

The Dwelling Place

2824 Dwelling Place Road
Brooksville, MS 39739
(662) 738-5348; Fax (662) 738-5345
E-mail: dwellpl@crawdat.dom
Web site: www.dwellingplace.com

Project location: Mississippi.

Project type: Retreat ministry.

Project costs: There is no project cost, but volunteers are responsible for their own transportation to and from the site. Room and board are provided for volunteers.

Project dates: At the convenience of the volunteer, in collaboration with staff.

How to apply: Request an application form by contacting the organization via mail or e-mail.

Work done by volunteers: Support services, especially yard work.

Special skills or requirements: Good health and a desire to assist where needed. Volunteers must be at least 21 years old.

Sample projects: Creation of a labyrinth, creation of a meditation path, landscape services, gardening, and light maintenance.

Volunteers create beautiful places for everyone to enjoy at The Dwelling Place in Mississippi. (Photo courtesy of The Dwelling Place)

Earthwatch Institute

3 Clock Tower Place
Suite 100, Box 75
Maynard, MA 01754-0075
(978) 461-0081 or (800) 776-0188; Fax (978) 461-2332
E-mail: info@earthwatch.org
Web site: www.earthwatch.org

Project location: Approximately 55 countries worldwide, including the United States.

Project type: One hundred and forty research expeditions in dozens of fields of study, including art and archaeology, public health, marine mammology, ornithology, wildlife management, and ecology.

Project costs: Contributions, which are generally tax deductible, range from $700 to $2,700 for the average two-week project. These donations support the organization's research and cover volunteers' food and lodging expenses. Transportation to and from the site is additional, but is also generally tax deductible. Some financial aid is available to subsidize costs for K–12 teachers and high-school students.

Project dates: Year-round; teams work from one to three weeks.

How to apply: Visit the Earthwatch Institute Web site, call, write, or e-mail for information.

Work done by volunteers: Varies according to project. Activities include animal observations, photographing, excavating, interviewing, monitoring, mapping, and more.

Special skills or requirements: Most expeditions require no special skills, only a willingness to work and learn. When special skills are required, such as scuba certification or photography skills, they are noted in the organization's magazine and expedition briefing. Volunteers who have special skills, such as surveying, birding experience, and nursing training are always welcome.

Commentary: Earthwatch is a nonprofit membership organization with 35,000 members worldwide. Membership is $25 per year. Members receive a biannual magazine that includes first-person articles on expeditions, as well as an annual expedition guide describing projects that volunteers can sign up for. Founded in 1971, Earthwatch Institute offers the public unique opportunities to work side by side with renowned scientists and scholars on a wide range of field research projects. Earthwatch Institute receives more than 1,000 proposals each year from researchers in need of funds and assistance. In 1999, 4,000 people of all ages and backgrounds, from all 50 states and from 46 countries, participated in 720 expedition teams worldwide.

Sample projects: Recently, Earthwatch volunteers examined the effects of rain forest destruction in Los Tuxtlas Biological Preserve, Vera Cruz, Mexico, and looked for fossil evidence of what killed the dinosaurs in Montana. Other previous volunteers measured, tagged, and examined leatherback turtles in the U.S. Virgin Islands and rescued thousands of turtle eggs from erosion. Still other volunteers worked with more than 100 resident dolphins in Sarasota Bay, Florida, netting, marking, and noting dolphins for age, sex, paternity, and social interaction.

Eco-Escuela de Español

c/o ECOMAYA
Calle Centroamérica
Flores, Petén Guatemala
(502) 926-3202; Fax (502) 926-3202
E-mail: ecoescuela@conservation.org

Project location: San Andres and San Jose, Guatemala.

Project type: Spanish language instruction, environmental education, and community development work.

Project costs: $175 per week, including room and board. Project cost does not include airfare.

Project dates: Year-round. Classes begin each Monday.

How to apply: Write or call the office listed above for more information.

Work done by volunteers: Volunteers combine intensive language instruction with work in conservation and community development projects.

Special skills or requirements: None but an interest in learning Spanish and learning about the culture of Guatemala. There is no age requirement for volunteers, but youth under 18 must be accompanied by a parent or guardian.

Ecovolunteer Program

Meijersweg 29, 7553 AX
Netherlands
(31) 74-2508250
E-mail: info@ecovolunteer.org
Web site: www.ecovolunteer.org

Project location: Approximately 30 different locations worldwide
on all continents.

Project type: Wildlife conservation and research.

Project costs: Varies from project to project, starting at about
$150 per week. Project fees include housing, but not airfare.
Most program fees include food, but where inexpensive food
or meals are available nearby, program fees do not include
food.

Project dates: Some projects are year-round, others are for only
part of the year, such as during migratory seasons of specific
species.

How to apply: Via the organization's Web site.

Work done by volunteers: Hands-on assistance with wildlife conservation or wildlife research. Volunteers sometimes also
share the responsibility for household duties.

Commentary: All projects are conducted by local nongovern-
mental organizations, according to local standards. A high
level of adaptability is sometimes required of volunteers.

Sample projects: Humpback whale research in Brazil; conservation of rare breeds of horses, sheep, and livestock-guarding
dogs in Bulgaria; tropical rain forest research in Colombia;
griffon vulture research in Croatia; bonnet macaque and
fruit bat research in India; marine turtle research in Indonesia; bottlenose dolphin research in Italy; howler monkey
research in Mexico; kiwi conservation in New Zealand;
Przewalski horse reintroduction in Mongolia; wolf research
in Poland; research on wolves, brown bears, and lynxes in

Romania; wolf research in Russia; bottlenose dolphin research in Scotland; rhino conservation in Swaziland; gibbon center maintenance in Thailand; African wild dog research in Zimbabwe.

In Africa, a volunteer peeks around a tree at two rhinoceroses taking a mud bath. (Photo courtesy Ecovolunteer Program)

El Porvenir

2508 42nd Street
Sacramento, CA 95817
(916) 736-3663
E-mail: info@elporvenir.org
Web site: www.elporvenir.org

Project location: Nicaragua.
Project type: Village water and sanitation projects, reforestation.
Project costs: $750 plus airfare. Room and board are provided.
Project dates: January, February, and July.
How to apply: Write, call, or e-mail for an information sheet.
Work done by volunteers: Work with local families (who are beneficiaries of the project) constructing a lavandero (community washing facility), finishing a well, building latrines, or planting seedlings. A lavandero has a concrete floor, a zinc roof, no walls, and four to six laundry washing stands plus two to four bath stalls, and is built next to a well or spring. Latrines are traditional pit latrines for which a foundation is built at the top of the hole, a precast floor slab and seat are attached to the foundation, and a little house is constructed to enclose the seat. Reforestation is carried out in hilly areas during the rainy season. Volunteers work with villagers who have produced the seedlings from their village nurseries to reforest the watershed in which they live.
Special skills or requirements: Good health is required. Volunteers must be at least 18 years old. There is no language requirement.
Commentary: A bilingual staff accompanies volunteer groups 24 hours a day. The maximum group size is 10. Work trips through Elderhostel are also offered several times per year.

Eno River State Park

6101 Cole Mill Road
Durham, NC 27705-9275
(919) 383-1686
E-mail: eno.river@ncmail.net
Web site: www.ncsparks.net, select Eno River State Park

Project location: Eno River State Park, which spans more than 2800 acres in North Carolina.

Project type: Natural resource management, education, and maintenance.

Project costs: Volunteers provide their own water and food.

Project dates: Year-round.

How to apply: Contact the park office at the address listed above.

Work done by volunteers: Trail rehabilitation, species inventory, educational hikes, bridge construction, and water quality monitoring.

Special skills or requirements: Volunteers must be responsible, show a willingness to work, and have the ability to follow directions and to interact with the general public in an appropriate manner. Prior experience is useful, but not required.

Explorations in Travel

2458 River Road
Guilford, VT 05301
(802) 257-0152; Fax (802) 257-2784
E-mail: explore@volunteertravel.com
Web site: www.volunteertravel.com

Project location: Sites in Costa Rica, Puerto Rico, Mexico, Ecuador, New Zealand, Australia, Nepal, and the Yukon Territory of Canada.

Project type: Conservation, education, animal rescue, wildlife rehabilitation, and political action.

Project costs: $775 to $975. Project cost does not include airfare. There is an extra charge for room and board, the amount of which varies by country placement.

Project dates: Year-round.

How to apply: Obtain an application form on the organization's Web site or by mail.

Work done by volunteers: Teaching, manual labor, animal care, field research, and more.

Special skills or requirements: Flexibility, motivation, and enthusiasm. Some sites require Spanish language skills.

Sample projects: Wildlife rehabilitation in Costa Rica; assisting at an animal shelter in Puerto Rico; teaching English in Mexico; teaching in Costa Rica; monitoring sea turtles in Costa Rica; and participating in conservation work in Australia, Costa Rica, Ecuador, and Puerto Rico.

Farm Sanctuary

P.O. Box 150
Watkins Glen, NY 14891
(607) 583-2225; (607) 583-2041
E-mail: education@farmsanctuary.org
Web site: www.farmsanctuary.org

Project location: Watkins Glen, New York, and Orland, California.
Project type: Animal rights advocacy and animal care.
Project cost: Volunteers are responsible for all of their own costs.
Project dates: Year-round. Internships begin on the first of every
month and require at least a one-month commitment.
How to apply: To apply for an internship, please contact the
office listed above for an application, or download one from
the organization's Web site.
Work done by volunteers: Interns help with the day-to-day operations of the shelter. Responsibilities may include barn cleaning and farm projects, processing bulk mail and participating
in other office projects, staffing the visitor center, and giving
educational tours.
Special skills or requirements: Interns must be at least 16 years
of age. The most important qualifications are a strong commitment to animal rights and a personal commitment to veg-
etarianism or veganism.

Fellowship of Reconciliation—
Task Force on Latin America and the
Caribbean (Voluntarios Solidarios)

2017 Mission Street, #305
San Francisco, CA 94110
E-mail: forlatam@igc.org
Web site: www.forusa.org

Project location: Puerto Rico; and Latin America, including Mexico, Nicaragua, Panama, Colombia, Ecuador, Peru, Bolivia, Chile, Argentina, and Paraguay. In some cases a volunteer's work will be focused in the capital or another city; in other cases the volunteer may travel to various communities as part of the host group's activities.

Project type: Volunteers work with grassroots peace and justice groups in Latin America and Puerto Rico. The exact work of volunteers will be shaped by the needs of the host organization and worked out in a process of dialogue between the host groups and the volunteers.

Project costs: Volunteers are responsible for their own costs, including travel to and from the region, food and lodging while there, and other personal expenses. A $60 application fee will be charged when an application is submitted. The program sponsors can provide some advice on fundraising methods and resources to explore for financial assistance. In some cases, host organizations can find inexpensive lodging for volunteers. Living costs for volunteers in the region vary widely, from $75 a month to $500 a month. Pre-placement preparation and orientation will be provided. The Fellowship of Reconciliation also works with volunteers upon their return to the United States to help them to share their experience and to undertake appropriate actions in their communities.

Project dates: Year-round. Placements range between three months and two years. Volunteers should apply at least two months before they intend to begin service.

How to apply: Contact the office listed above for an application for a specific program or country of interest. Potential volunteers fill out an application, submit references, and engage in an interview with the sponsoring groups. That process determines volunteers' suitability for placement and with whom they may work. The host organization makes the final decision about the acceptance of the volunteer for work.

Work done by volunteers: Needs expressed by the Latin American groups have included translation of publications and other communications; supporting peace actions; technical assistance in areas ranging from carpentry to computer operation to recycling; collaboration in work with children, peasants, and women; and sharing experiences and methodologies in popular education and conflict resolution.

Special skills or requirements: A commitment to nonviolence is mandatory. Volunteers must be at least 21 years old, in reasonably good health, and able to function in Spanish or Portuguese. Program sponsors can advise volunteers on language-study possibilities in the region.

Commentary: The Fellowship of Reconciliation, an interfaith pacifist organization founded in 1915, is rooted in a recognition of the essential unity of all humanity and a commitment to explore the power of love and truth to resolve human conflict. While it has always been vigorous in its opposition to war, the Fellowship of Reconciliation has insisted that this effort must be based on a commitment to the achieving of a just and peaceful world community, with full dignity and freedom for every human being. The Fellowship of Reconciliation does not run any volunteer programs itself; it acts as a bridge between volunteers and Latin American host organizations.

Sample projects: SERPAJ-Nicaragua: This group is engaged in mediation to overcome the conflicts within the country. The group also works for human rights, peace and nonviolence education, women's rights, and community development. They seek volunteers to work in the human rights program.

Justicia y Paz in Ecuador: This local grassroots group works with street children, assists in a health center, and does pastoral work. Volunteers organize workshops, meet with community activists, translate documents, and share experiences, both in the city and the countryside. Andean Information Network in Bolivia: The Network, formed primarily by volunteers who live or have lived in Bolivia, aims to promote just and effective solutions to the cocaine problem for the peoples of both the Andes and the United States. The group monitors U.S.–backed military activities, documents human rights abuses resulting from the war on drugs, educates the U.S. public about the effect of these policies, and organizes delegations to the coca-growing regions.

Ffestiniog Railway Company

Harbour Station
Porthmadog, Gwynedd LL49 9NF United Kingdom
(01766) 516073; Fax (01766) 516006
E-mail: info@festrail.co.uk
Web site: www.festrail.co.uk

Project location: The mountains of Snowdonia in North Wales.

Project type: A wide variety of projects on a working steam railway.

Project costs: Volunteers are responsible for transportation to the site, as well as room and board. There are several self-catering hostels nearby with reasonable accommodations.

Project dates: Year-round.

How to apply: Write to the volunteer resource manager at the address listed above for an application form and a brochure listing the types of volunteer opportunities available.

Work done by volunteers: Every aspect of railroading is open to volunteers, although some positions, such as locomotive operator, require that the volunteer spend considerable time gaining experience.

Special skills or requirements: Previous experience working on a railroad is always desirable, but a willingness to learn is all that is required.

Commentary: The history of the Ffestiniog Railway goes back to 1836. The railroad reached its peak in the last decades of the nineteenth century and faced a general decline until its closing in 1946. In the early 1950s, a group led by Alan Pegler reopened the line as a nonprofit organization operated with the assistance of a voluntary society. Part of the line reopened in 1955, with other parts opening periodically until the line was completed in 1982. Today it is the busiest independent railway in Britain. It is also run by the oldest independant railway company in the world; it was originally incorporated in 1836 by an Act of Parliament. Most of the steam locomotives and some of the coaches currently in use are more than 100 years old.

Flemish Youth Federation for the Study and Conservation of Nature

Bervoetstraat 33
B-2000 Antwerpen, Belgium
(32) 3-231-26-04; Fax (32) 3-233-64-99
E-mail: n2000@net4all.be, natuur2000@pandora.be, or
natuur2000@pi.be

Project location: Belgium and Holland.
Project type: Nature study and conservation.
Project costs: $100 to $200 per camp.
Project dates: Primarily in July and August, for one or two weeks.
How to apply: Write to the address listed above for information
   and an application, or contact one of the work camp orga-
   nizations in the United States such as Volunteers for Peace,
   Incorporated.
Work done by volunteers: General physical labor connected with
   conservation efforts.
Special skills or requirements: Participants must be between the
   ages of 14 and 25 and be interested in conservation work.

Florida Department of Environmental Protection

Division of Recreation and Parks
3900 Commonwealth Boulevard, MS 535
Tallahassee, FL 32399
(850) 488-8243; Fax (850) 487-3947
E-mail: pwerndli@cep.state.fl.us
Web site: www.dep.state.fl.us/parks

Project location: State parks throughout Florida.

Project type: Campground hosts and general volunteer duties.

Project costs: None. Project costs do not include airfare or food, but volunteers are allowed to use a campsite for free.

Project dates: Vary.

How to apply: Contact the address listed above for names of individual parks and park managers, and apply directly to the park managers.

Work done by volunteers: The primary work is as a campground host, assisting campers in park campgrounds, monitoring activities in the campground, and helping to maintain campground facilities.

Special skills or requirements: A clean appearance and the ability to work with people are required. Volunteers must be at least 16 years old.

Commentary: Campground hosts volunteer for six to twelve weeks, and volunteers must be available in the campground for three hours each day and four nights each week.

Florida Trail Association

5415 SW 13th Street
Gainesville, FL 32608
(352) 378-8823 or (877) HIKE-FLA
E-mail: fta@florida-trail.org
Web site: www.florida-trail.org

Project location: Throughout Florida.

Project type: Build and maintain a continuous hiking trail the length of Florida, as well as side and loop trails for the hiking public.

Project costs: Minimal; mainly travel expenses to work sites. Most participants are FTA members; membership is open to anyone. Annual membership fees are $25 for individuals and $30 for families. Room and board are not provided.

Project dates: Year-round.

How to apply: Membership in the Florida Trail Association (FTA) ensures notification of the organization's work schedule.

Work done by volunteers: Trail building and maintenance activities.

Special skills or requirements: None, but volunteers should be in good physical shape and willing to do manual labor. There is no minimum age for volunteers.

Flying Doctors of America

1235 North Decatur Road
Atlanta, GA 30306
(404) 815-7044; Fax (404) 892-6672
E-mail: fdoamericaperu@mindspring.com
Web site: www.fdoamerica.org

Project location: Worldwide, but focused on Latin America.

Project type: Health care.

Project costs: Varies; all costs are paid by volunteers.

Project dates: Varies, but all are less than two weeks.

How to apply: See the organization's Web site for future projects and information on applying, as well as for stories and photos.

Work done by volunteers: Short-term medical and dental missions to the rural regions of third-world countries.

Special skills or requirements: Volunteers must be licensed physicians, dentists, dental assistants, hygienists, P.A.s, N.P.s, R.N.s, pharmacists, chiropractors, C.M.T.s, or nonmedical support staff.

Food First

Institute for Food and Development Policy
398 60th Street
Oakland, CA 94618
(510) 654-4400; Fax (510) 654-4551
E-mail: foodfirst@foodfirst.org
Web site: www.foodfirst.org

Project location: Oakland, California.

Project type: Varies.

Project costs: Volunteers are responsible for their travel and living costs.

Project dates: Year-round, for varying lengths of time.

How to apply: Contact Marilyn Borchardt at the office listed above.

Work done by volunteers: Volunteers update Food First publications, enter information into the database, and perform clerical work in various departments. Specific volunteer openings are always changing. The Food First Web site lists current volunteer opportunities, with detailed descriptions.

Special skills or requirements: Volunteers should be responsible, self-motivated, organized, and independent. Computer skills are desirable.

Commentary: Food First promotes Third World development that is participatory, equitable, and sustainable.

Foundation for International Education

1145 West 8th Street, Apartment 320
New Richmond, WI 54017
(715) 246-4520; Fax (715) 246-9059
E-mail: kors@frontiernet.net
Web site: www.teachworldwide.org

Project location: Worldwide, primarily in English-speaking counties.

Project type: Elementary or secondary education.

Project costs: About $700, plus accommodations and travel expenses.

Project dates: Primarily during summer months, but occasionally during the winter for three or four weeks.

How to apply: Write to Dr. Korsgaard at the address listed above for more information.

Special skills or requirements: Applicants should be experienced, credentialed teachers.

Commentary: Accommodations are generally inexpensive, as volunteers normally stay in the homes of counterparts. Retired persons are welcome to participate. Graduate credit is also available.

Sample projects: Volunteers have served mainly in Australia, England, India, Ireland, Kenya, New Zealand, Scotland, and Wales. The program was begun in 1972.

Foundation for Sustainable Development
P.O. Box 1446
Arlington, VA 22210
(703) 741-0832
E-mail: fsdmail@yahoo.com
Web site: www.interconnection.org/fsd

Project location: Bolivia, Nicaragua, Peru, South Africa, Tanzania.

Project type: Community development.

Project costs: Vary, beginning at $1,350. Project fee includes room and board, but not airfare.

Project dates: Individual internships are available all year long, but summer internships are set to begin in May or June and run for 9 to 10 weeks.

How to apply: Obtain an application from the organization's Web site.

Work done by volunteers: Community development with a local nonprofit organization, hospital, or school.

Special skills or requirements: Spanish skills are required for the Latin American programs. Volunteers must be at least 18 years old.

Sample projects: Teaching in schools, health education, environmental and conservation, microcredit (small loans to help start income-generating projects), human rights, youth development, women's issues, and business and marketing.

Four Corners School of Outdoor Education

P.O. Box 1029
Monticello, UT 84535
(800) 525-4456 or (435) 587-2156; Fax (435) 587-2193
E-mail: fcs@sanjuan.net
Web site: www.sw-adventures.org

Project location: Arizona, Colorado, New Mexico, and Utah.

Project type: Educational and research programs on the natural and human history of the Colorado plateau region.

Project costs: Projects vary from $595 to $2,195. All programs except research programs include a voluntary $100 tax-deductible contribution to Four Corners School.

Project dates: Year-round.

How to apply: Write to the address listed above for a brochure and an application, or apply via the organizatiion's Web site.

Work done by volunteers: Archaeological documentation, surveying, digging, and endangered species documentation.

Special skills or requirements: No special skills, just an interest in the subject matter.

Commentary: This program has many educational classes that involve volunteers in a number of archaeology and natural history projects. College credit is also available.

Sample projects: In the past years, projects have included an archaeological documentation project of Anasazi rock art along the shores of Lake Powell; archaeological excavations near Dolores, Colorado; and an ongoing peregrine falcon survey of river canyons.

Fourth World Movement/USA

7600 Willow Hill Drive
Landover, MD 20785
(301) 336-9489; Fax (301) 336-0092
E-mail: fourthworld@erols.com
Web site: www.atd-fourthworld.org

Project location: United States, France, England, Germany, Belgium, Spain, Switzerland, and other countries. For current information on activities and countries, see the organization's Web site.

Project type: Three-month internships in the United States for those exploring a two-year commitment to the Fourth World Movement (FWM) Volunteer Corps. Internships involve work camps, street workshops, respite stays, and other activities in European countries.

Project costs: Depends on the country; generally, volunteers pay for the cost of their food and travel.

Project dates: Three-month internships in the United States take place year-round. Activities in Europe take place during the summer and occasionally at other times during the year. For current details, see the organization's Web site.

How to apply: For information on internships and activities in the United States, send a stamped, self-addressed envelope to the address listed above. You may also call or e-mail.

Work done by volunteers: A wide variety of activities, from manual and office work to educational and cultural activities with poor children and families. Volunteer opportunities generally provide some time for discussion on poverty issues, watching informational videos, and other such activities.

Special skills or requirements: Applicants for an internship in the United States must be at least 19 years old. All prospective volunteers should be interested in learning from the poorest families around the world. For details, see the organization's Web site.

Commentary: Fourth World Movement/USA is the U.S. branch of ATD Fourth World, an international nonprofit organization of men and women from different social, religious, and ethnic backgrounds who are dedicated to eradicating persistent poverty. The Movement has three major areas of work: grassroots activities with very poor families and communities (such as educational and cultural projects with children, family centers, literacy, and basic training programs); research on poverty, which is undertaken with poor families; and public information campaigns, advocacy, and forums for representation and dialogue. Through these activities, people in the Fourth World Movement work together toward eradicating poverty and ensuring human and civil rights for all. The FWM Volunteer Corps works in partnership with the poorest of the poor in all activities. Projects in 26 industrialized and developing countries focus on learning from the poorest, building on the strengths of the family, and providing poor families with opportunities to represent their own interests and educate others about the kinds of support needed to eradicate poverty.

Sample projects: Street workshops that encourage artists, craftsmen, professionals, sportsmen, librarians, and others to come and share their skills with children, young people, and their parents in underprivileged neighborhoods in Europe (principally in France). Various workshops, such as painting, crafts, computing, communication via the Internet, sports, and reading take place in the street and last from one to three weeks. These street workshops provide a concrete way to come together with the most underprivileged people and, through a sharing of skills to invent paths leading toward the participation of everybody in tomorrow's world. Respite stays enable poor families to come together for a vacation in order to have a respite from their difficult daily lives. This is a time when families, some split apart by poverty, can reunite for a peaceful time of relaxation, learning together, discovery, and sharing with others.

Fresh Start Surgical Gifts, Inc.

351 Santa Fe Drive, Suite 210
Encinitas, CA 92024
(760) 944-7774; Fax (760) 944-1729
E-mail: freshstart@freshstart.org
Web site: www.freshstart.org

Project location: Worldwide, but chapters are located in San Diego, Tennessee, and India.

Project type: Medical. Fresh Start Surgical Gifts, Inc. provides free reconstructive surgery, primarily to children who suffer from physical deformities caused by birth defects, accidents, abuse, or disease. Its vision is to build a community of volunteers committed to seeing that every child with a physical deformity is given the opportunity to have a positive self-image.

Project costs: Free.

Project dates: Fresh Start holds surgery weekends every six to eight weeks, where children can receive free reconstructive surgeries.

How to apply: Contact Fresh Start Surgical Gifts, Inc. via letter or telephone, or visit the organization's Web site and fill out the on-line "sign-up" questionnaire.

Work done by volunteers: Volunteer work includes donations of medical services, fundraising efforts, patient referral, providing housing accommodation for patients or their families, making or serving meals during surgery weekends, entertaining children while they wait for surgery, and assisting with travel and transportation needs.

Special skills or requirements: The skills required of volunteers are dependent on the type of work being accomplished. Volunteer nurses, doctors, and dentists are needed for medical care; others donate their time and efforts to do various non-medical work. There is no minimum age requirement.

Friends of the Cumbres and Toltec Scenic Railroad

6005 Osuna Road NE
Albuquerque, NM 87109
(505) 880-1311; Fax (505) 856-7543
Web site: www.cumbrestoltec.org

Project location: Southern Colorado and northern New Mexico.

Project type: Historic preservation.

Project costs: Volunteers are responsible for their own transportation, room, and board. The registration fee of $10 to $35 dollars includes five noon meals.

Project dates: Work sessions are conducted between early May and October, Monday through Friday.

How to apply: All volunteers must be members of the Friends organization. All members are notified of work sessions through the organization's newsletter. Information is also available on its Web site. To become a member, write for an information packet at the address listed above, or join via the Web site.

Work done by volunteers: Maintenance of the "finest example of Rocky Mountain narrow gauge steam railroading technology in North America." This work includes stabilization, preservation, and restoration of historic structures, freight cars, work cars, and trees alongside the 64-mile-long right of way. Projects also include interpretation of the site by Friends docents. Volunteers do not engage in the operation of the steam trains, as that is done by paid staff.

Special skills or requirements: General maintenance and mechanical skills are always welcome, but the desire to do historic preservation work at a historic 1920s steam railroad and the ability to work in a cooperative work environment is all you need. Volunteers should be in reasonably good health and able to work at high altitudes, from 7,800 to 10,000 feet above sea level. Volunteers must be at least 13 years old.

Commentary: This railroad is owned jointly by the states of New Mexico and Colorado, who lease the railroad to the Friends' subsidiary operating company, the Rio Grande Railway Preservation Corporation. The RGRPC is charged with the responsibility of carrying tourists on scheduled rides and maintaining the rolling stock and facilities it uses, including the six steam locomotives. The entire railway is a registered National Historic site.

Frontier Volunteer/Society for Environmental Exploration

50–52 Rivington Street
London EC2A 3QP United Kingdom
(44) 0-20-7613-2422; Fax (44) 0-7613-2992
E-mail: info@frontier.ac.uk
Web site: www.frontier.ac.uk

Project location: Madagascar, Tanzania, and Vietnam.

Project type: Conservation of savanna, marine, arid forests, and rain forest wildlife and habitats.

Project costs: Start at £2,250 for 10 weeks (plus airfare and visa).

Project dates: January to March, April to June, July to September, and October to December of each year.

How to apply: Contact the office listed above for an information package, or complete the application found on the organization's Web site.

Work done by volunteers: Collecting information on wildlife and habitats, conducting biodiversity surveys, carrying out mapping of habitats, and learning about the problems of indigenous populations.

Special skills or requirements: Volunteers should speak English and have a good attitude regarding living in very basic conditions. Experience in science is not necessary. Volunteers must be at least 17 years old.

Commentary: All projects are developed and operated in conjunction with a parallel research institution, government department, or university in the host country. Frontier works alongside local scientists and rangers, and it trains local students in the conservation work as well. The data collected by the volunteers is used by these institutions to implement management plans to help protect some of the most endangered areas of the world.

Gap Year in Vietnam

❖ by Joanne Roberts ❖

Frontier Volunteer/Society for Environmental Exploration

My sister took a gap year to teach English in Brazil and came back with some amazing stories, so I knew that I definitely wanted to do something different before attending the university. What caught my eye was the possibility of doing some conservation work in Vietnam with Frontier. I've always liked animals and do my best to reuse plastic bags, so this opportunity seemed the perfect way to actually do something practical for the environment as well as have fun. A mix of people were selected to go, including a few other gappers like myself, some university students, and some older people as well. We all hit it off pretty much straight away.

When we arrived in Hanoi, the first thing that struck us was the heat and humidity. It seemed strange to think that when we left Heathrow it had been overcast and drizzling. Those first few days were spent getting used to the hustle and bustle of Vietnam life, attempting to learn Vietnamese, and adjusting to a different culture.

It took us three days to actually get to our work site up in the north. We started off in a truck, then swapped to a four-wheel drive vehicle once the road deteriorated. The final ten kilometers were spent on the backs of ponies as we climbed into the mountains. It was long, it was tiring, but we all loved it! We really felt like we were to going to the end of the world. Everything else seemed a lifetime away.

Our time in the mountains was amazing. The work we were doing really made a difference. We weren't building fences or other physical stuff. Instead, we were carrying out actual environmental research, looking at the different species that live in the forest, and talking to the local people to find out what problems they faced. It's hoped that in a few years' time, the area will be made into a forest reserve, protecting not just the wildlife, but also the lifestyle of the local people.

The people were incredible; they were so friendly, giving us food when they clearly didn't have enough for themselves, and also offering help. And boy, were they curious! Obviously we were interested in them, but they were just as interested in us and our lives. We were the first westerners they had seen in 20 years. I had some photos of home with me, and they ended up extremely tattered and dog-eared. Eventually I gave them away to some of the kids.

We played two games of soccer with the villagers. During the first game, I was amazed to discover how many people were watching. I was expecting 20 or 30 people at the most, not the whole village! The referee was resplendent in black, and even had an out-of-date copy of the FIFA rulebook. The game itself was the most enjoyable I have ever played. The Vietnamese are crazy about soccer and, despite playing in bare feet, they beat us easily 3–0 in both games. After each goal, about 70 people would run onto the field and celebrate with the team.

Now that I'm back in the United Kingdom and attending a university, my time in Vietnam doesn't seem real. I have so many happy memories of the place, the friends I made, and the work we did. My fondest memory of the whole expedition, though, is of the people. Working as a part of Frontier allowed us to become genuinely close to the local villagers. We weren't travelers spending just a couple of days there.

Instead, we lived and worked with these people and experienced their customs and cultures. I felt extremely privileged that we were welcomed so readily by them.

I certainly changed while I was out there. I am a lot more confident in myself and what I can do. Knowing that I spent months living in the wilds of northern Vietnam makes me feel that I can do anything. The only depressing thing about it is wondering whether I'll ever have a better few months in the rest of my life!

Frontiers Foundation—Operation Beaver

2615 Danforth Avenue, Suite 203
Toronto, Ontario M4C 1L6 Canada
(416) 690-3930; Fax (416) 690-3934
E-mail: frontiersfoundation@on.aibn.com
Web site: www.frontiersfoundation.org

Project location: Northwest Territories, Quebec, Yukon, and Ontario.

Project type: Building and renovating homes and community centers and participating in cold-weather agriculture projects. All projects involve joint community and volunteer efforts. Volunteers are also used in the organization's national and regional offices.

Project costs: Vary by project.

Project dates: Recreation and building projects continue year-round with three-month minimum commitments. The project length varies according to the needs of both the foundation and the volunteer.

How to apply: Write to the address listed above for an information brochure and an application.

Work done by volunteers: A wide variety of construction and recreation work, plus some office and clerical tasks.

Special skills or requirements: Volunteers must have a willingness to work hard in a cross-cultural setting. Previous construction experience is helpful, but is not required.

Commentary: Operation Beaver was begun in 1964 as an ecumenical work camp by the Canadian Council of Churches, and the Frontiers Foundation assumed responsibility for the program in 1968. In its first 29 years, 2,687 volunteers from 70 countries and 17 North American Indian Nations helped build or renovate more than 1,748 homes, 30 community training centers, 3 greenhouses, and a cold-climate agriculture station.

Fundación Jatun Sacha

Eugenio de Santillán N 34 248 y Maurian
Casilla 17 12 867
Quito, Ecuador
(593) 2-243-2173 or (593) 2-243-2246
E-mail: volunteer@jatunsacha.org
Web site: www.jatunsacha.org

Project location: Ecuador.

Project type: Conservation.

Project costs: $30 application fee, and $300 per month. Volunteers are provided lodging and three meals per day. Transportation as well as any tourism expenses are paid by the volunteer.

Project dates: Year-round.

How to apply: Send the following to the office listed above: a letter of application stating why you want to become a volunteer, the type of work you want to do, and dates of availability; two passport-sized photos; a health certificate; certification of health insurance; any police record; and a check for $30 payable to Jatun Sacha.

Work done by volunteers: Reforestation, organic agriculture, crafts projects, personal projects, light construction and maintenance, environmental education, English classes, and assisting at meteorological stations.

Special skills or requirements: A basic knowledge of Spanish is recommended but not required. Volunteers must be enthusiastic and have a desire to contribute to the conservation of the forest. Volunteers under 18 must have written authorization from a parent or guardian.

Genesis II Cloud Forest Preserve and Wildlife Refuge

Apartado 655
7.050 Cartago, Costa Rica
E-mail: info@genesis-two.com
Web site: www.genesis-two.com

Project location: Talamanca Mountains of central Costa Rica.

Project type: Trail construction and maintenance, reforestation project management, and cataloging of flora and fauna.

Project costs: $150 per week, plus transportation to and from the site.

Project dates: Month-long projects are available year-round.

How to apply: E-mail the office listed above.

Work done by volunteers: In addition to trail and reforestation work, projects include T-shirt design, landscaping, pictorial property mapping, cookbook design and scribing, water tank construction, and nursery construction. Projects may also include light housework and gardening.

Special skills or requirements: Participants must be at least 21 years old. Strong environmental or conservation background is preferred.

Commentary: Genesis II is a private reserve and wildlife refuge owned and operated by two Canadians. It is a preserve for the endangered resplendent quetzal, and it has a unique reforestation project in operation.

Georgia State Parks and Historic Sites

2 Martin Luther King Drive SE, Suite 1352
Atlanta, GA 30334
(404) 656-6539
E-mail: ChuckG@mail.dnr.state.ga.us
Web site: www.gastateparks.org

Project location: State parks and historic sites throughout Georgia.

Project type: Conservation, education, interpretation, construction, and campground hosting.

Projects costs: Volunteers are responsible for their own transportation, but are provided with a free campsite and utilities.

Project dates: Year-round.

How to apply: Apply via the organization's e-mail address, phone number, or Web site.

Work done by volunteers: Campground hosting, construction, interpretative and school program assistance, and trail and habitat improvement.

Special skills or requirements: Volunteers may be any age, but those under 18 years old must be accompanied by a parent or guardian.

Gifford Pinchot National Forest

USDA Forest Service, Mount Adams Ranger District
2455 Highway 141
Trout Lake, WA 98650
(509) 395-3354
E-mail: rbluestone@fs.fed.us

Project location: Gifford Pinchot National Forest in Washington state.

Project type: Conservation and education.

Project costs: Bunkhousing may be available to volunteers, and transportation costs from home to the forest may be reimbursable; contact the office for more information.

Project dates: May 1 to October 1.

How to apply: Apply via phone or e-mail.

Work done by volunteers: Trail crew work, campground and facilities maintenance, information reception, and interpretation.

Special skills or requirements: Must be able to work effectively with the public. Physical fitness is a must for trail maintenance. A driver's license required of all applicants. Volunteers must be comfortable working outdoors in the forest. Volunteer placement is based on knowledge, skills, and abilities. Volunteers must be 18 years old, or accompanied by a parent or guardian.

Global Citizens Network (GCN)

130 North Howell Street
St. Paul, MN 55104
(651) 644-0960 or (800) 644-9292; Fax (651) 646-6176
E-mail: info@globalcitizens.org
Web site: www.globalcitizens.org

Project locations: Kenya, Nepal, Guatemala, Arizona, New Mexico, and South Dakota.

Project type: Community development and cultural immersion programs.

Project costs: Between $600 and $1,650, plus transportation to the site. Trip-related expenses are tax deductible.

Project dates: Year-round for one, two, or three weeks.

How to apply: Contact the office listed above for more information and a current project schedule.

Work done by volunteers: Participants stay with local families or at other facilities within the community while working on site-directed development projects. Past projects have included building health clinics, renovating a youth center, teaching in a primary school, and constructing a bridge.

Special skills or requirements: Volunteers only need a willingness to experience and accept a new culture. No special physical or occupational skills are needed. There is no minimum age requirement.

Commentary: GCN was formed in 1992 with the following mission: "Global Citizens Network seeks to create a network of people who are committed to the shared values of peace, justice, tolerance, cross-cultural understanding, and global cooperation; to the preservation of indigenous cultures, traditions, and ecologies; and to the enhancement of the quality of life around the world."

Chasing Elephants in Kenya

❖ by Sean Maurer ❖

Global Citizens Network

While spending last week in the shadow of Kilimanjaro with Global Citizens Network, the thought occurred to me, "Is anywhere still truly remote?" Though we were in the middle of Maasailand and a five-mile walk from the nearest town, Britney Spears still wafted through the air as we worked to lay the foundation for a Maasai health clinic. In short, the town of Rombo, in the far south of Kenya, is both very remote and shockingly global.

Likewise are the other volunteers with whom I am working to bend metal for the clinic's framework. These are Rita from Latvia, Anton from Russia, and Oleysa from Moldova. The group also includes Patty and Katie, a mother and daughter on their second Global Citizens Network (GCN) trip; Sharma, who was celebrating her fiftieth birthday by coming to Africa, and Shari, a Canadian fine art dealer. Rounding out the group are Veronica, a trader on the floor of the New York Stock Exchange, Chris, a freelance photographer known for his J. Crew catalog shoots, and Amelia, who seemed to be either a professional student or volunteer, I couldn't tell which. She was great to have along, especially because she had a book about how to avoid common African dangers such as quicksand and safari ants.

Everyone seemed to share Veronica's feelings at the beginning, which were summed up by the answering machine message she left behind in the States, "If I return from Africa, I'll call you back." But by the middle of the first week, everyone had adjusted to the outside toilets, the lack of electricity, and no running water.

One of the main precepts of GCN is the cross-cultural aspect of volunteering. We weren't merely building a clinic for the Maasi, but were instead helping them build their clinic. They were working side-by-side with us each day, even going as far as to give us our own Maasai names.

My last night with the team was my finest in Africa. Under a nearly full moon, our friend Joseph led us off into the bush. A week ago, elephants from the national park had come through the area looking for food and destroyed an entire farm. Tonight we were going to help the Maasai defend their shambas against the elephants. We charged through the bush, everyone stomping and screaming to frighten the elephants (as much as you can frighten a four-ton animal). We caught up with the three elephants and were close enough that I could have hit them with a rock. Once we (mainly the Maasai, using torches and slings) chased them back into the bush, Joseph made us stop, explaining that in the shambas the elephants were thieves, and they knew it, but in the bush they were at home, and they would charge us if we chased them any further. We returned, triumphant, to the safety of the fire and celebrated with vodka and fresh oranges.

Tip of the week: Volunteer with GCN. It was the most fun I've ever had chasing elephants or bending steel.

Global Routes

1 Short Street
Northampton, MA 01060
(413) 585-8895; Fax (413) 585-8810
E-mail: mail@globalroutes.org
Web site: www.globalroutes.org

Project location: Costa Rica, Ecuador, Ghana, Kenya, India, Thailand, and the Navajo Nation.

Project type: Volunteers live with host families and teach in local schools in rural communities.

Project costs: $3,950 (summer programs) and $4,250 (fall, winter, and spring programs). Airfare is not included in the project fee.

Project dates: Mid-June to mid-August, mid-September to early December, mid-January to mid-April, and mid-March to mid-June.

How to apply: To receive an application, request a registration form by mail, or download it from the organization's Web site. Applications must be received no later than 45 days prior to program start date.

Work done by volunteers: Teaching English, math, and science; coaching sports; and designing and executing a small development project.

Special skills or requirements: The Costa Rica and Ecuador programs require strong conversational Spanish skills. There are no education certification requirements for teachers. For high school programs, students must have completed a certain amount of schooling before undertaking a project: see Web site for details on projects. For college programs, volunteers must be at least 17 years old and a high school graduate, but there is no upper age limit.

Welcome Teacha' James

❖ James (no last name provided) ❖

Global Routes

Dear Mom and Dad,

My first report from Ghana. Where to begin?

I have been placed in a village with a host family. Francis, my host father, teaches primary school and speaks excellent English, which has made my time much easier. Most of the people in my village speak only the native language, Twi. Sandra—my mom—is wonderful and if you can imagine a typical African village mom, she is it: always cooking, cleaning, looking after the kids, breaking up quarrels, while at the same time breastfeeding my five-month-old sister. I have two brothers, Sammy (seven) and Junior (three), and a sister Eunice (five), who is so cute. I play soccer with Sammy, and tickle torture never gets boring for the younger ones.

Things are going well in the family. I have my own room with a fan and screens and they boil water for me. We also have a fridge and a TV (talk about the lap of luxury!), but there is no running water. I have to go collect water a few times a day from the village well, and believe me, I never waste water anymore! The well is far away, and every ounce of water used in that house is brought to the compound in a bucket on someone's head.

Teaching gets better every day, but it's not easy. Teaching styles are really different here, so it's taking time to draw out the students and relate to the teachers. But we grow to understand and like one another more every day. I teach mostly English, but also some math and science classes. The kids are really smart and more outgoing than when I first got here. Teaching isn't as hard as I thought it would be, but I definitely have a lot more respect and appreciation for my teachers and my education.

The village is called Yasse. It is dusty and has a paved road running down the middle. Some of the houses are mud huts with bamboo skeletons, and the rest are cement brick, painted white (skirted in brown from the dust), with a pink and sky-blue fringe. Add to that scene chickens, goats, food stalls, Africans, and 1,000 kids shouting, "Abruni, abruni!" (White person! White person!) as you walk past, and that is my village: no cars, police, hospital, or post office—just a school.

Village life is relaxing and very peaceful. I wake up at 6:00 A.M. and doze for an extra hour, get up and brush my teeth, bathe, eat, and go to school. On my way, everyone greets me with "Akwaaba (welcome) Teacha' James. How are you?" (spoken in either English or Twi). I am in my bed at 10:00 every night. Sometimes I teach only three or four hours on any given day, so there is time to explore or relax. Some of the other interns say they feel restless, but I like settling into the slower pace of things.

I write in my journal every night, almost 10 pages a day! There is so much to write about and so much I want to be sure to remember—not just the stories, but the feelings and thoughts, too. I have promised not to read it until I get home.

Thank you for letting me come here, it has really been a great experience.

Love,
James

Global Service Corps (GSC)

300 Broadway, Suite 28
San Francisco, CA 94133-3312
(415) 788-3666, ext. 128; Fax (415) 788-7324
E-mail: gsc@earthisland.org
Web site: www.globalservicecorps.org

Project location: Tanzania and Thailand.

Project type: Education, agriculture, health, and environment. Short-term, long-term, and college internship service projects that actively contribute to sustainable international development and provide participants a broader global perspective. All projects include village homestays and work with local community organizations.

Project costs: Short-term projects are between $1,800 and $2,000, plus airfare. Long-term programs consist of the short-term program plus extensions (daily fee: $30), plus airfare. Summer and semester internships cost between $2,835 and $3,335, plus airfare. A portion of the cost goes to the ongoing support of the GSC–sponsored community service projects. All costs associated with the projects, including airfare, are normally tax deductible.

Project dates: All programs are available year-round on specific starting dates.

How to apply: Contact the office listed above for an application and more information, or see the organization's Web site.

Work done by volunteers: In Tanzania, volunteers work on rural self-help programs that emphasize HIV/AIDS awareness, sustainable agriculture, women's group activities, and classroom teaching. In Thailand, volunteers teach English, aid in local health care programs, and work on environmental projects.

Special skills or requirements: Volunteers should have the desire and flexibility to live and work in a developing country. They must be in good health, be at least 20 years old, and have at least college sophomore status for the internship program.

Participants are given in-country orientation and training specific to each program.

Commentary: Global Service Corps is a project of the Earth Island Institute, an umbrella organization that works to develop projects for international social justice and for the conservation, preservation, and restoration of the global environment. Global Service Corps is committed to fostering global awareness by providing volunteers international grassroots exposure to global issues through involvement in community service and sustainable development activities. Volunteers are welcome at both the project sites and the home office to assist in GSC's international and environmental goals.

Global Volunteers

375 East Little Canada Road
St. Paul, MN 55117
(800) 487-1074 or (651) 407-6100; Fax (651) 482-0915
E-mail: e-mail@globalvolunteers.org
Web site: www.globalvolunteers.org

Project location: China, the Cook Islands, Costa Rica, Ecuador, Ghana, Greece, India, Indonesia, Ireland, Italy, Jamaica, Mexico, Poland, Romania, Spain, Tanzania, Ukraine, Vietnam, and nine states in the United States.

Project type: Volunteer opportunities include teaching conversational English, nurturing at-risk infants and children, renovating and painting community buildings, assisting with health care, and natural resource projects.

Project costs: The cost of Global Volunteers' programs ranges from $500 to $2,395, excluding transportation to the site. The fee includes all meals as well as lodging and ground transportation in the host community. All costs, including airfare, are tax deductible for U.S. taxpayers.

Project dates: There are more than 150 one-, two-, and three-week projects year-round.

How to apply: Contact the office above for an application.

Work done by volunteers: Tutoring local schoolchildren, teaching conversational English, painting and constructing homes and public buildings, providing dentistry, basic medical care, or nursing expertise, laying pipe for water systems, and assisting with environmental projects. All projects are undertaken in cooperation with the local community.

Special skills or requirements: No special work skills are required at most sites, but a willingness to share, learn, and work alongside others is expected. Projects are especially popular with women, educators, retirees, medical and health care professionals, tradespeople, or anyone wishing to share of themselves and experience a culture in a non-tourist manner.

Commentary: Volunteers of all ages, professions, and backgrounds join together in teams on these projects to live in rural villages or in urban communities in emerging democracies and to help local residents improve their communities. This volunteer service, working only at the invitation and under the direction of a local host, fosters friendships, greater understanding, peace, and justice. Predeparture orientation materials are provided by Global Volunteers.

A college student volunteers over Spring Break to help with school lessons in Metcalfe, Mississippi. (Photo courtesy Global Volunteers)

Global Works

RD2, Box 173-A
Huntingdon, PA 16652
(814) 667-2411; Fax (814) 667-3853
E-mail: info@globalworksinc.com
Web site: www.globalworksinc.com

Project location: British Columbia, Quebec, Ecuador, Ireland, Costa Rica, Spain, Mexico, Peru/Bolivia, the Fiji Islands, Puerto Rico, and France.

Project type: Environmental and construction work.

Project costs: Around $3,000, plus airfare.

Project dates: Three- and four-week trips during the summer.

How to apply: Request an information book and application via the organization's Web site.

Work done by volunteers: Rebuilding habitats; constructing community centers, playgrounds, and water systems; and reforestation.

Special skills or requirements: Open to people aged 14 to 18 years old only.

Commentary: Most trips involve no more than 15 students. Language learning and homestay options are available.

Habitat for Humanity Global Village Work Teams

121 Habitat Street
Americus, GA 31709
(800) 422 4828, ext. 2549 or (912) 924-6935;
Fax (912) 924-0577
E-mail: gv@hfhi.org
Web site: www.habitat.org/gv

Project location: Throughout the United States and in 40 countries around the world.

Project type: House building and community development projects.

Project costs: Volunteers are responsible for all transportation, room, board, and insurance costs. On most work projects, participants make a financial contribution toward home building. International programs cost $1,800 to $3,800, which includes the contribution.

Project dates: Year-round. U.S. projects generally run one to two weeks, and overseas projects run two to three weeks.

How to apply: For an application and information packet describing current projects, call or write to the Global Village Work Team coordinator at the office listed above. Information and applications are also available on the oganization's Web site.

Work done by volunteers: General construction.

Special skills or requirements: At least one member of each overseas group should speak the language of the host country, and all participants should be at least 18 years old.

Commentary: Habitat for Humanity is an ecumenical Christian housing ministry that helps build bridges between people as they help those in need build their own houses through "sweat equity."

Hanging Rock State Park

P.O. Box 278
Danbury, NC 27016
(336) 593-8480
E-mail: hangingrock@mindspring.com
Web site: www.ncsparks.net, select Hanging Rock State Park

Project location: North Carolina.
Project type: Campground host.
Project costs: None. A free campsite with all hookups is available.
Project dates: March through November. Volunteers work a minimum of one month.
How to apply: Contact the volunteer coordinator at the address listed above or via e-mail.
Work done by volunteers: Registering and assisting campers, plus light maintenance work. No law enforcement measures are taken by volunteers.
Special skills or requirements: Volunteers must be cheerful and helpful, and be model campers.

Health Volunteers Overseas (HVO)

c/o Washington Station
P.O. Box 65157
Washington, DC 20035-5157
(202) 296-0928; Fax (202) 296-8018
E-mail: info@hvousa.org
Web site: www.hvousa.org

Project location: Africa, Asia, the Caribbean, and Latin America.

Project type: Training and education of local health care professionals.

Project costs: Average expenses for a one-month assignment are $2,500 for transportation, housing, and living costs.

Project dates: Year-round, usually for one month.

How to apply: Contact the program department at the office listed above for more information and a membership application, or visit the HVO Web site.

Work done by volunteers: Volunteers are involved in a variety of activities including clinical training, teacher training, curriculum development, mentoring students and faculty, and providing continuing education workshops. They lecture, serve as clinical instructors, conduct ward rounds, and demonstrate various techniques in classrooms, clinics, and operating rooms.

Special skills or requirements: All volunteers must be fully trained and licensed health care professionals. Three to five years' professional experience is desirable. There is no language requirement for volunteers.

Commentary: HVO is a private nonprofit organization committed to improving health care in developing countries through training and education. HVO currently solicits fully trained health and medical volunteers to participate in programs in the following specialties: anesthesia, dentistry, hand surgery, internal medicine, nursing, oral and maxillofacial surgery, orthopedics, pediatrics, and physical therapy. Volunteers need to be flexible and creative, and should possess excellent communication skills.

Heifer Project International

Heifer Ranch
P.O. Box 8058
Little Rock, AR 72203
(800) 422-0474 or (501) 889-5124; Fax (501) 889-1574
E-mail: info@heifer.org
Web site: www.heifer.org

Project location: Volunteer positions are at Heifer Ranch 40 miles west of Little Rock, Arkansas, Overlook Farm in Rutland, Massachusetts, and Ceres Center in Ceres, California.

Project type: Sustainable agriculture.

Project costs: Work camps have a fee per group. Individual volunteers who stay for a month or longer receive a small stipend, room, and board. Volunteers are responsible for preparing their own meals.

Project dates: Work camps last one week during the summer months. Individual full-time volunteers have no standard length of stay. Summer staffing is generally from late May to mid-August.

How to apply: Work camp groups may contact the events planner at the telephone number and address listed above. Individual volunteers may contact the volunteer coordinator at the telephone number, address, or e-mail address listed above.

Work done by volunteers: Work camp groups may spend all week on one project, or they may do a variety of jobs. Individual volunteers may work in the following areas: education, maintenance, gardening, administration, and livestock care.

Special skills or requirements: Youth work camp volunteers should be in the ninth grade or above for youth camps, and adult camp volunteers should be at least 19 years old. The minimum age for individual volunteers is 18.

Commentary: All three learning centers are educational campuses that teach about the issues of global hunger and its solutions through the use of livestock and sustainable agriculture. The learning centers support Heifer International's mission to help low-income families around the world become sustainable through training and the use of livestock.

Idaho State Parks and Recreation

5657 Warm Springs Avenue
Boise, ID 83716
(208) 334-4180, ext. 242
E-mail: KHampton@idpr.state.id.us
Web site: www.idahoparks.org

Project location: Throughout Idaho.

Project type: Campground hosting, program hosting, working on conservation projects and special one-time maintenance and construction projects, trail maintenance, bridge building, and yurt building.

Project costs: There is no application fee. Volunteers are provided with a campsite with hookups, but are responsible for their own food and transportation to the worksite.

Project dates: Year-round.

How to apply: Contact the volunteer services coordinator at the office listed above.

Work done by volunteers: Meeting and greeting the public, giving tours, collecting fees, and physical labor.

Special skills or requirements: None; training is provided.

Illinois Department of Natural Resources

524 South 2nd Street, Room 500
Springfield, IL 62701-1787
(217) 785-4963
Web site: dnr.state.il.us/legislation/consrv/constit.htm

Project location: Parks, conservation areas, forests, and recreational areas throughout Illinois.

Project type: Volunteers serve as campground hosts, park interpreters, and park technicians, and assist the department field biologists in the departments of wildlife, forestry, national heritage sites, and fisheries.

Project costs: Volunteers are responsible for all travel and living expenses.

Project dates: Year-round, for varying lengths of time.

How to apply: Write to the Volunteer Network at the address listed above for information and an application.

Work done by volunteers: Campground hosts serve at state park campgrounds for a minimum of four weeks, working approximately thirty-five hours per week, helping other campers check in and providing them information about the park. Park interpreters lead educational programs, workshops, hikes, and other activities that enhance visitors' experiences at the parks. They also conduct some research on the park's natural vegetation, wildlife, and geology. Park technicians help with the maintenance of the parks, including construction, renovation, and general maintenance.

Special skills or requirements: An interest in parks, a willingness to learn on the job, and the ability to follow through are all necessary skills. Campground hosts must be at least 21 years old.

Indiana Department of State Parks and Reservoirs

402 West Washington Street, Room W298
Indianapolis, IN 46204
(317) 232-4124
Web site: www.in.gov/dnr

Project location: State parks throughout Indiana.
Project type: Landscaping, and grounds and trail maintenance.
Project costs: Participants pay camping and entrance fees to the parks.
Project dates: Year-round.
How to apply: First, contact the office listed above for a list of parks currently requesting volunteers, and then contact the parks directly.
Work done by volunteers: Maintenance, gardening, campground hosting, and working in nature centers.
Special skills or requirements: Projects are based on the skills of the volunteers, and volunteers are selected for projects by park managers. There is no minimum age for volunteers but those under 18 must have written parental consent.
Commentary: Projects will be developed according to the length of stay. Camping in parks is limited to 14 days, and projects as short as two days can be arranged.

Insight Nepal

P.O. Box 489, Zero K.M.
Pokhara, Kaski, Nepal
(977) 061-30266
E-mail: Insight@fewanet.com.np
Web site: www.insightnepal.org

Project location: The cities of Kathmandu and Pokhara, in Nepal.
Project type: Language and cross-cultural experiences through various activities.
Project costs: $40 application fee; $800 program fee. Program fee does not include airfare, but does include room and board.
Project dates: Projects last for three months and begin in February, April, August, and October.
How to apply: Request an application form by mail or e-mail.
Work done by volunteers: Participants teach English or other subjects at the primary to high school levels. Placements may also be arranged for those who wish to work on community development projects.
Special skills or requirements: Volunteers should be flexible, physically fit, and willing to immerse themselves in another culture. Volunteers must be 18 to 65 years old, and have a high-school diploma.

International Center for Gibbon Studies (ICGS)

P.O. Box 800249
Santa Clarita, CA 91380
(661) 296-2737; Fax (661) 296-1237
E-mail: gibboncntr@earthlink.net
Web site: www.gibboncenter.org

Project location: Saugus, California (approximately one hour north of the Los Angeles International Airport).

Project type: Captive breeding of several species of rare gibbons and nonintrusive behavioral research.

Project costs: Volunteers are responsible for travel, food, and required health insurance. Housing is provided.

Project dates: Year-round, with a one-month minimum stay. There is a shortage of volunteers from September through April.

How to apply: Request a volunteer application and send a resume and two letters of recommendation to the address listed above.

Work done by volunteers: Depending on the volunteer's skills, work includes feeding and care of captive gibbons, data entry, light maintenance work, observation, library research, and word processing.

Special skills or requirements: A love for animals is required. Word processing, library research, and maintenance skills are preferred. Ova, parasite, and stool cultures, CBC and blood panels, a tuberculosis test, and Hepatitis B and other vaccinations are necessary for admission to the facility. Volunteers must be at least 18 years old.

Commentary: ICGS is a nonprofit organization and the only facility in the world devoted exclusively to the study, preservation, and propagation of gibbons by establishing secure captive gene pools in the event that attempts to preserve species or subspecies in the wild fail. It has the second-largest collection of gibbons in the world, including six of the nine extant species. The comfort and well-being of these primates is the center's primary concern. They are housed in spacious outdoor enclosures ranging from 30 to 60 feet in length and from 12 to 20 feet in height.

International Cultural Adventures

362 Bunganuc Road
Durham, ME 04011-7320
(207) 725-9288 or (888) 339-0460
E-mail: info@icadventures.com
Web site: www.icadventures.com

Project location: Nepal (rural, urban, and semi-urban locations throughout the country); India (Sikkim, Ladakh, Delhi, and various other rural, urban, and semi-urban locations throughout the country); and Peru (rural, urban, and semi-urban locations throughout Cusco and the Sacred Valley).

Project type: Education, agriculture, environmental conservation, health care, construction, women in development, nutrition, small business development, and childcare. ICA attempts to meet the specific needs and desires of volunteers.

Project costs: The Cultural Immersion Experience summer program (six weeks) starts from $1,900; semester-length programs (two to five months) start from $2,500. These costs cover almost all services during the program. Customized programs may be arranged; their costs depend on the services requested.

Project dates: The Cultural Immersion Experience programs run July through August, and semester-length programs start in January and August. Custom programs may be arranged at any time of the year for any length of time, upon request.

How to apply: For more information, contact the program director by e-mail or phone.

Work done by volunteers: Various volunteer service experiences are available, depending on the skills and background of the participants and the availability of the host organization. Every effort is made to match the interests and skills of the participants to the needs of the host organization. Specific responsibilities depend on the project.

A volunteer who taught English at a monastery in the Solukhumbu region of Nepal poses with some of his young students. During his time at the monastery, he learned Tibetan language and studied a bit of the Dharma in addition to his volunteer work. (Photo courtesy of International Cultural Adventures)

Special skills or requirements: Most service project opportunities require no experience or special skills. More options are available for those with specialized skills and training. There are no age limits.

Sample Projects: Teaching English to monks in rural Buddhist monasteries in the Himalayas; assisting local health care providers in remote areas of Ladakh, India; empowering women via small business development in Cusco, Peru; helping to manage a small family-run apple orchard in Nepal; providing basic care, education, and role modeling to destitute children in Sikkim, India; maintaining an indigenous tree nursery and planting trees in the Sacred Valley of Peru; assisting in the management of a specialty travel and trekking company in Kathmandu; renovating a private monastery in the Nepal Himalayas; increasing basic opportunities for education, health, and income generation for women; working with children in various capacities at orphanages; assisting medical staff in various rural and urban health clinics and hospitals; teaching various subjects in private and public schools; educating local people about nutrition and mother-child health; performing various construction projects at a rural school; and participating in environmental conservation and sustainable development projects.

International Jewish College Corps (IJCC)

American Jewish World Service
45 West 36th Street, 10th Floor
New York, NY 10018
(800) 889-7146 or (212) 736-2597
E-mail: ijcc@ajws.org
Web site: www.ajws.org

Project location: Honduras, Ghana, and Israel.

Project type: Construction, informal education, and rehabilitation.

Project costs: $3,500, which includes round-trip airfare to New York City and all international transportation, meals, and accommodations. American Jewish World Service (AJWS) will help students identify ways to defray their portion of the cost of the trip, if necessary.

Project dates: Mid-June to early August.

How to apply: Applications may be requested by e-mail or phone, or downloaded from the organizaton's Web site. The application includes a personal statement, two references, and an interview.

Work done by volunteers: International Jewish College Corps (IJCC) volunteers live and work in rural villages and assist the local communities with development projects.

Special skills or requirements: No special skills are required. Spanish is helpful for Central America placement. Volunteers must be between 18 and 25 years old.

Commentary: IJCC programs begin with an intense, seven-week cultural immersion experience that weaves together in-depth exploration of international development, study of social justice in a Jewish context, and humanitarian service in hands-on volunteer community projects in the developing world and Israel. Following the summer program, participants continue in the IJCC yearlong domestic program that includes educational seminars, retreats, public speaking engagements, article writing, and volunteer service opportunities.

Sample projects: IJCC volunteers assisted the village of Santa Rosita, Honduras, to build a potable water system (dug trenches, laid water pipes, and mixed cement for a cistern). In Jerusalem, volunteers have painted homes and made minor home repairs for families on welfare in an impoverished neighborhood. Volunteers have also worked alongside members of the community of Ziavi-Lume, Ghana, to build a secondary school.

International Volunteer Program (IVP)

210 Post Street #502
San Francisco, CA 94108
(415) 477-3667; Fax (415) 477-3669
E-mail: rjewell@ivpsf.org
Web site: www.ivpsf.org

Project location: Various locations in France, the United Kingdom, and the United States.

Project type: Work with the elderly, the disabled, children, at-risk youth, women in crisis, and homeless people.

Project costs: $1,500, which includes a round-trip ticket from San Francisco or New York to Paris or London (depending on the destination country), transportation from the airport to the site, room, and meals (accommodations include host families, dorms, or on-site lodging; meals include breakfast, lunch, and dinner), and a certificate of completion from La Société Française de Bienfaisance Mutuelle. Volunteers are responsible for their own airfare from their home airport to San Francisco or New York.

Project dates: Programs in the United States run from mid-July to the end of August. European programs run from mid-June to the end of July. Programs are six weeks long.

How to apply: Contact IVP through its Web site, e-mail address, or mailing the address listed above. The application deadline for volunteer work in the United States is April 15; March 15 for European programs.

Work done by volunteers: IVP's host agencies provide volunteers meaningful, full-time (35 to 40 hours a week) work in a variety of fields. Work might include reading the newspaper to the elderly, leading a tour of a thirteenth-century museum, working with the disabled, or being a camp counselor at a children's summer camp.

Special skills or requirements: Volunteers must speak the language of the host country, be at least 18, and carry a valid passport.

Interplast, Incorporated

300 B Pioneer Way
Mountain View, CA 94041-1506
(888) 467-5278 or (650) 962-0123; Fax (650) 962-1619
E-mail: ipnews@interplast.org
Web site: www.interplast.org

Project location: Bangladesh, Brazil, Ecuador, Honduras, India, Myanmar, Nepal, Nicaragua, Peru, the Philippines, and Vietnam.

Project type: Providing free reconstructive surgery for needy children and adults in underdeveloped countries.

Project costs: $325, which is used to partially offset trip expenses. Interplast pays all remaining transportation and accomodation costs, though team members are responsible for their own meals during the trip.

Project dates: Year-round, for two weeks.

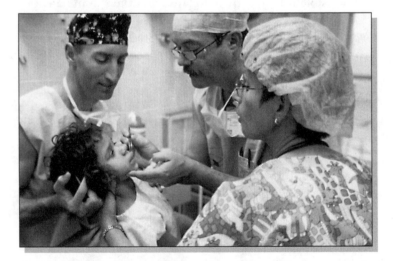

An Interplast volunteer pediatrician examines a Peruvian child prior to surgery. (Photo by Kate Lapides, courtesy Interplast)

How to apply: Contact the Interplast office to request volunteer application information by mail, or visit the "volunteer" page on the organization's Web site.

Work done by volunteers: Reconstructive surgery.

Special skills or requirements: All volunteers must be plastic surgeons, anesthesiologists, pediatricians, or registered nurses (operating and recovery room).

Commentary: This nonprofit organization sends volunteer medical teams to developing nations to provide free reconstructive surgeries, primarily for children born with such correctable facial deformities as cleft lips and cleft palates, or for children who have suffered crippling injuries, generally those associated with severe burns. Medical volunteers also work closely with host-country medical personnel to provide instruction in advanced surgical techniques and related patient care.

Involvement Volunteers of Australia (IVA)

P.O. Box 218
Port Melbourne, Victoria 3207 Australia
(61) 3-9646-5504
E-mail: ivworldwide@volunteering.org.au
Web site: www.volunteering.org.au

Project location: Argentina, Australia, Bangladesh, Belgium, Brazil, China, Denmark, Ecuador, England, Fiji, Finland, Germany, Greece, India, Italy, Japan, Kenya, Korea, Lebanon, Malaysia, Mexico, Mongolia, Nepal, New Zealand, Poland, Russia, Samoa, South Africa, Spain, Thailand, Turkey, Ukraine, United States, Venezuela, and Vietnam.

Project type: Ecologically sustainable development programs and social service projects.

Project costs: AUD$220 registration fee; AUD$255 single placement program fee or AUD$390 multiple placement program fee; and AUD$80 placement fee (per placement). Further fees may be applicable, depending on placement and country.

Project dates: Year-round.

How to apply: Contact the above office for application information.

Work done by volunteers: Generally, volunteers perform manual labor on practical projects. Ecologically sustainable development programs may involve planning, revegetation and maintenance, and endangered species protection and research. Social service projects include providing assistance in refugee situations, village health guidance, assistance in medical centers, orphanages, and homes for elderly or disadvantaged people.

Special skills or requirements: Skills are not necessary but are appreciated and will be utilized on a project whenever possible. Volunteers must understand spoken English (or Spanish in some countries). Volunteers generally communicate in English. Many volunteers with IVA have just finished high school or college, but people of all ages are welcome. IVA has had volunteers as young as 16; however, written parental consent is required if the volunteer is under 18. Certain placements have a lower age limit of 21; see the Web site for further information.

Commentary: Involvement Volunteers of Australia enables people to travel and participate in volunteer activities for the benefit of the natural environment and social support of communities. Volunteers may be placed on projects on an individual basis or in groups.

Jewish National Fund—Canadian American Active Retirees in Israel (CAARI)

42 East 69th Street
New York, NY 10021
(212) 879-9300, ext. 284; Fax (212) 327-0436
or
1980 Sherbrooke Street W, Suite 500
Montreal, Quebec H3H 1E8 Canada
(514) 934-0313; Fax (514) 934-0382
E-mail: travel@jnf.org
Web site: www.jnf.org

Project location: Eliat, Galilee, Jerusalem, Tel Aviv, and Beer Sheba.

Project type: Community and forestry work, as well as volunteer work with the Israel Defense Force.

Project costs: About $5,000, which includes airfare, three kosher meals per day, hotels, tax and tips, a tour guide, medical insurance, and incidental expenses.

Project dates: Late December or early January through late March.

How to apply: Call the Canadian or U.S. office for information.

Work done by volunteers: Volunteers work in a variety of settings, including teaching English to Ethiopian immigrants, spending time with patients in hospitals, trail maintenance in forests, and assembling food packets for the Israel Defense Force. Other placements are available in retirement homes and libraries.

Special skills or requirements: None, except good health, an enthusiastic personality, and a willingness to participate in all activities. There are no age restrictions, but volunteers must be retired, so most are above age 55. Volunteers must be active and fit.

Commentary: In the first ten years since its inception, the number of participants in this program has more than doubled. Many participants have returned over and over because of their love for the country. Volunteers get a complete tour of Israel by professional tour guides, work together as a family, attend seminars in archaeology and ecology, and visit museums and cultural events. For an additional fee, volunteers may participate in a pre-program in Beer Sheba, which includes tours, lectures, and social events.

Jewish Volunteer Corps (JVC)

American Jewish World Service
45 West 36th Street, 10th Floor
New York, NY 10018
(212) 736-2597
E-mail: jvcvol@ajws.org
Web site: www.ajws.org

Project location: Various locations throughout the developing world.

Project type: Jewish Volunteer Corps (JVC) volunteers provide technical assistance and training to local non-governmental organizations. They work in their area of professional expertise, providing direct services and training others to continue the work after the volunteer returns home.

Project costs: JVC pays for the volunteer's round-trip airfare and emergency evacuation insurance. Volunteers must cover their own costs, such as housing, food, and local transportation, while on assignment.

Project dates: Year-round. Placements range in length from one month to one year.

How to apply: The JVC application requires a written questionnaire, a personal statement, three references, and an interview. Please request an application packet by phone or e-mail, or download one from the organization's Web site.

Work done by volunteers: Varies, according to the volunteer's skills and the needs of the partner organization.

Special skills or requirements: All JVC volunteers must be skilled professionals, with a number of years of work experience, who would feel comfortable training others in their areas of expertise.

Commentary: JVC is a project of American Jewish World Service (AJWS), an independent not-for-profit organization founded in 1985 to help alleviate poverty, hunger, and disease among the people of the world regardless of race, religion, or nationality. AJWS works in partnership with local grassroots organizations to support and implement self-sustaining projects that expand basic educational opportunities, nurture civil society initiatives, improve primary medical care and health conditions, promote economic development, and introduce improved methods of ecologically sound agriculture. AJWS is helping people in some of the poorest regions of the world to help themselves.

Sample projects: Recent placements include those of a retired business owner who assisted women living in a squatters' camp in Zimbabwe with entrepreneurial projects; a clinical psychologist who trained the staff of a shelter for abused children in Belize; and a dentist who treated patients in 24 rural villages and trained nurses in a regional dental clinic in Nicaragua.

Joint Assistance Centre (JAC)

P.O. Box 6082
San Pablo, CA 94806-0082
(510) 464-1100
E-mail: jacusa@juno.com
Web site: hometown.aol.com/jacusa/

Project location: Rural locations around India, Bangladesh, and Nepal.

Project type: Short-term work camps involving community welfare, education, rural health, agriculture, and youth development; long-term projects lasting three months or more involving work with children and women and education and community development.

Project costs: Volunteers are responsible for transportation to the project site, insurance costs, a $50 registration fee, and a monthly contribution of approximately $125. There is a $100 fee for long-term placements. Costs are slightly different for programs in Nepal and Bangladesh. No visitors to India, Nepal, and Bangladesh may receive any remuneration for work or study, and volunteers who do work must make a contribution to their sponsor organization and carry a tourist visa only. Program fees do not include airfare to Hawaii.

Project dates: Vary. A schedule of work camp dates is included in the information packet. Long-term projects are arranged on an individual basis.

How to apply: Write to the address listed above for an information packet and application.

Work done by volunteers: Construction work, agriculture, office work, public education, and various social service activities.

Special skills or requirements: No special skills are needed. Volunteers must be flexible and able to adapt to living in a different culture, often in difficult conditions. All volunteers must be at least 18 years old.

Commentary: Joint Assistance Centre (JAC) is a voluntary, non-governmental organization that attempts to improve the disaster preparedness of the people of India. In the work camps there are stringent rules concerning living conditions and activities. Only vegetarian food is served in India; no smoking, drugs, or alcohol are allowed, and living quarters may be without modern amenities such as electricity or a municipal water supply. JAC is also involved in the education of solar therapy and encourages alternative, nontraditional medicine.

Kalani Oceanside Retreat

RR2, Box 4500
Pahoa, HI 96778
(808) 965-7828 or 800-800-6886
E-mail: volunteer@kalani.com
Web site: www.kalani.com

Project location: Hawaiian island's southeast coast, the Aloha State's largest nature preserve.

Project type: Housekeeping, maintenance, gardening, and kitchen work.

Project costs: $900 for three months.

Project dates: Year-round.

How to apply: Complete and send the applications found on the organization's Web site.

Work done by volunteers: 20 to 30 hours per week of assistance in the departments listed above.

Special skills or requirements: Related work and community living experience.

Commentary: One-month and three-month programs are available. Meals, lodging, and educational activities, such as daily yoga, are provided.

Kansas Archeology Training Program Field School

Kansas State Historical Society
6425 SW 6th Avenue
Topeka, KS 66615-1099
(785) 272-8681, ext. 255; Fax (785) 272-8682

Project location: Throughout Kansas.

Project type: Archeological investigations of prehistoric and historic sites.

Project costs: $75 registration fee for non-members; $15 registration fee for members of the Kansas Anthropological Association ($22 per year for individuals, $25 per year for families; $5 for project duration for students) or the Kansas State Historical Society, Inc. ($30 per year basic; $35 per year for families). Participants are responsibile for all transportation, room, and board. Motels and camping are available near the project sites.

Project dates: Early June.

How to apply: Send a letter of interest to the address listed above.

Work done by volunteers: Archeological excavation and survey, laboratory work, specialized processing of artifacts, and formal class instruction.

Special skills or requirements: Volunteers must be at least 10 years old; those between the ages of 10 and 14 must work with a sponsoring adult.

Commentary: The Kansas Archeology Training Program Field School is a cooperative effort of the Kansas State Historical Society and the Kansas Anthropological Association. Since 1975, it has offered volunteers the opportunity to participate in the scientific excavation of archeological sites. The program is structured as an educational experience in which participants may be involved in a wide range of excavation and laboratory functions.

Kibbutz Program Center

633 Third Ave, 21st Floor
New York, NY 10017
(800) 247-7852; Fax (212) 318-6134
E-mail: kibbutzdsk@aol.com, ulpankad@aol.com

Project location: Various kibbutzim throughout Israel.

Project type: The center sponsors programs that range from learning Jewish heritage and studying Hebrew to working on a kibbutz.

Project costs: Costs range from $150 for work programs to over $950 for study programs.

Project dates: Year-round. Projects range from two to six months in length.

How to apply: Contact the office at the address above for current information about the many programs offered.

Work done by volunteers: Varies greatly by program; it is best to obtain information about the various programs and then ask about the specific work each requires.

Special skills or requirements: Different programs have different requirements. Generally, volunteers must be between 18 and 35 years of age.

Kimochi Incorporated

P.O. Box 316
Boulder, Colorado 80306
(303) 494-9542
E-mail: ccambrid@carbon.cudenver.edu
Web site: www.bitahnii.com

Project location: North American and international sites.

Project type: Assisting individuals and indigenous projects. Each work camp is different in design. The work is usually physical and hard.

Project costs: Fees vary for each camp; see the organization's Web site for details. Travel and insurance costs are the responsibility of each volunteer. The work camp provides food, tools, and materials for the duration of the project.

Project dates: Summer and vacation times.

How to apply: Contact the organization at the address listed above.

Work done by volunteers: Construction, earth moving, tree cutting, renovation, assisting in traditional rituals, archeology, landscaping, collecting of building materials, removing materials, cleaning, and painting.

Special skills or requirements: Volunteers must be at least 16 years old. No special skills are required.

Commentary: Volunteers must have a sense of humor and patience. The work camp is a camping situation with primitive facilities. Volunteers are expected to provide their own tents and sleeping bags. See the organization's Web site for camp listings and other information.

Sample projects: Archaeological work in Maui and San Juan Bastista Mission, California; building construction in the Yukon; painting in British Columbia; construction on the Navaho Reservation in New Mexico; wood cutting for sun dance ceremonies in South Dakota.

Landmark Volunteers

P.O. Box 455
Sheffield, MA 01257
(413) 229-0255; Fax (413) 229-2050
E-mail: landmark@volunteers.com
Web site: www.volunteers.com

Project location: Twenty states within the United States.

Project type: Park and path improvement.

Project cost: $735. Project fee includes accommodation and meals, but not transportation.

Project dates: Two-week sessions between mid-June and mid-August.

How to apply: Request a brochure, or download an application from the organization's Web site.

Work done by volunteers: Manual outdoor labor.

Commentary: Landmark Volunteers is primarily for high-school students, but is in the process of beginning a new program for adults aged 25 to 35.

Sample projects: Trail building, footbridge construction, painting, and removal of invasive plant species.

Latin American Language Center (LALC)

PMB 123
7485 Rush River Drive, Suite 710
Sacramento, CA 95831-5260
(916) 447-0938; Fax (916) 428-9542
E-mail: info@enjoylearningspanish.com
Web site: www.enjoylearningspanish.com

Project location: Costa Rica.

Project type: Education, medical work, and social services.

Project costs: $345 per week includes four hours per week of intensive Spanish immersion, with a homestay, three meals per day, a three-hour cultural excursion once a week, laundry service, airport transfer, and Costa Rican cooking and dancing classes. Volunteers are responsible for their own transportation costs.

Project dates: Year-round; volunteers may enter and leave programs at any time.

How to apply: Contact the organization at the address listed above.

Work done by volunteers: Volunteers assist in medical and health clinics, work with public school English and computer teachers, build homes for low-income people, or provide support services to at-risk populations including street children and pregnant minors under the direction of a local nonprofit foundation. Other local projects are in development and are based on the skills and interests of volunteers.

Special skills or requirements: Volunteers must be able to speak some Spanish and be familiar with Costa Rican culture. Enrollment in the organiztion's two-week Spanish program is a prerequisite to placement in a volunteer program. LALC's programs are designed for adult students. However, teens at least 14 years old are welcome if accompanied by their parents, and youth aged 16 to 18 can be accepted by the program director with written consent of their parents or guardians and acceptance by a host family.

Commentary: Upon arrival in Costa Rica, volunteers will be referred to an appropriate program based on the volunteer's background, skills, and interests. There are more volunteer opportunities than there are volunteers.

LEAPNow: Lifelong Education Alternatives and Programs

P.O. Box 1817
Sebastopol, CA 95473
(888) 424-LEAP or (707) 829-1142; Fax (707) 829-1132
E-mail: info@leapnow.org
Web site: www.leapnow.org

Project location: More than 10,000 volunteer projects through-out the world, in 129 countries, on every continent.

Project type: Projects for individuals, families, and groups include agricultural, environmental, and wildlife work; teaching; social service; scientific research; orphanage and child care work; outdoor education and adventure; camp counseling; participation in work camps or equestrian centers; work with artisans and artists, resorts, hotels, and chateaus; botanical, anthropological, and architectural work; historic restoration; business and media-related work; work with living history, disaster relief, sports, zoos, aquariums, political aide situa-tions, ranches, theatrical agents; and more.

Project costs: Variable placement fee to LEAPNow. Volunteers are responsible for transportation to all sites. Volunteer posi-tions range from those that pay a stipend, room, and board to those that have a fee of up to $15 per day.

Project dates: Year-round. Projects last from one week to one year.

How to apply: Download a brochure and application from the organization's Web site. Call for a free phone consultation, which leads to receiving a list of 25 to 75 options tailored to your interests.

Work done by volunteers: Many different kinds of work are available for unskilled to highly skilled volunteers.

Special skills or requirements: Volunteers must be at least 17 years old. There is no upper age limit.

Commentary: LEAPNow has collected a database of over 20,000 volunteer opportunities since 1980. The staff has over 35 years of experience placing volunteers, and each year makes 500 placements and visits myriad volunteer sites throughout the world. A network of LEAPNow representatives in 32 countries can provide special support, orientation, airport pickups, and assistance with information about immunizations, visas, and travel.

Sample projects: Sea-turtle protection work in Costa Rica, teaching positions in over 65 countries, farm placements in 35 countries, construction placements in 70 countries, care for baboons in South Africa, whale watching in Newfoundland, work at a Buddhist retreat center on a Greek island, assisting a Danish furniture maker, working at a ski hotel on a glacier in Austria, taking care of street kids on a island in the Philippines, participating in a Triple A baseball team in Idaho, assisting an archaeologist in Oregon, and much more.

Life Line International

P.O. Box 84361
Greenside, 2034, South Africa
(27) 11-789-7963
E-mail: lifelineinternational@ibi.co.za
Web site: www.lifeline.web.za

Project location: Australia, New Zealand, Korea, Taiwan, Japan, Malaysia, China, Papua New Guinea, Tonga, Fiji, South Africa, Namibia, Botswana, Liberia, United States, Canada.

Project type: Crisis intervention and counseling, mainly by telephone.

Project costs: Varies, depending on the country of service. Applicants are required to participate in training, selection, and ongoing training and supervision. The trainee pays for the training.

Project dates: Year-round.

How to apply: Apply directly to the National Office of the country of choice or to a specific center. See the organization's Web site or contact the International Office listed above for information.

Work done by volunteers: Telephone and face-to-face counseling as well as "hands on" relief work.

Special skills or requirements: Volunteers must have a willingness to be trained and a concern for people in crises.

Sample projects: Peer counseling projects in schools, HIV/AIDS counseling, assisting in shelters for abused women and children, providing relief to flood and earthquake victims around the world, and counseling relief workers in crisis situations (such as the firefighters and others working in New York after the events of September 11, 2001).

Little Children of the World, Incorporated (LCW)

361 County Road 475
Etowah, TN 37331
Tel/Fax (423) 263-2303
E-mail: lcotw@conc.tds.net

Project location: Dumaguete City, Philippines, about 450 miles south of Manila.

Project type: Educational and social services for children who are victims of poverty.

Project costs: Volunteers are responsible for transportation and food. Housing is provided at a cost of $10 per week.

Project dates: Volunteers may negotiate their preferred dates and length of stay, but should stay for at least one month.

How to apply: Write to Little Children of the World (LCW) for information and an application.

Work done by volunteers: Work includes teaching children on an informal basis, tutoring math or English, or working in a community-based health clinic assisting doctors or paramedics.

Special skills or requirements: Volunteers must be at least 18 years old and speak English or Tagalog.

Commentary: The LCW program is not residential. As a rule, children are not housed at LCW, but instead live at home. It is a community-based, holistic program that focuses on the needs of families and children. It is also participatory, training recipients to manage as much of the program as possible. All volunteers work alongside Filipino counterparts.

Loch Arthur Community

Stable Cottage
Beeswing
Dumfries DG2 8JQ Scotland
(01387) 760-618

Project location: Located in the country, six miles from the town of Dumfries, Scotland.

Project type: Working and living in a community with adults who have learning disabilities.

Project costs: No cost except travel. The community provides board, lodging, and pocket money.

Project dates: Year-round, with stays lasting from one month to one year or more.

How to apply: Write to Lana Chanarin at the address listed above. Provide information regarding your age, interests, previous work experience, and dates available.

Work done by volunteers: Gardening, housework, farming, weaving, cheese making, baking, helping in the houses and with care of people, and participating in all aspects of community life.

Special skills or requirements: No special skills are necessary. Volunteers should have a willingness to work and be open to the community way of life. Opportunities for volunteers under age 18 are very limited.

Commentary: Life in the community is demanding—there are no set hours, and volunteers must be willing to participate in all aspects of life. Work is based on the ideas of Rudolf Steiner, and the group celebrates festivals throughout the year. The community prefers to have volunteers join them for six months to one year, but will accept shorter periods in the summer months.

Lolo National Forest

Building 24 A, Fort Missoula
Missoula, MT 59804-7297
(406) 329-3970
E-mail: jkipphut@fs.fed.us
Web site: www.fs.fed.us/r1/lolo

Project location: Various campgrounds in and around Lolo National Forest in Montana.

Type of work: Campground host in a national forest-managed site.

Project costs: Volunteer is responsible for transportation to site, housing, and board.

Project dates: Late May to early September.

How to apply: Send an e-mail to the address listed above expressing your interest and experience.

Work done by volunteers: Providing visitor information, light maintenance, picking up litter, cleaning toilets, and mowing grass.

Special skills or requirements: Volunteers should have good public relations skills and must pass a background check.

Commentary: The host does not handle money. Phone, electric, water, septic, and propane services are provided to volunteers.

Mar de Jade

PMB 078-344
705 Martens Court
Laredo, TX 78041-6010
(322) 222-3524; Tel/Fax (322) 222-1171
E-mail: info@mardejade.com
Web site: www.mardejade.com

Project location: Oceanfront retreat and vacation center on Chacala Beach in Nayarit, one and a half hours north of Puerto Vallarta, Mexico.

Project type: Three-week volunteer program, which may be combined with Spanish classes. Responsible tourism center assists multiple community projects. Volunteers are welcome to apply for longer terms (three to six months).

Project costs: $1,200 for a 21-day program that includes meals and shared accommodations plus 15-percent tax on room rates. There is an additional cost of $80 per week for Spanish instruction, plus $20 for materials. Volunteers are responsible for their own transportation costs.

Project dates: Year-round.

How to apply: Visit the organizations' Web site or fax or telephone for information, an application, and reservations.

Work done by volunteers: Community projects include a primary-care clinic, an after-school program, a community kitchen, a community garden, an adult education program, English classes, and microenterprises such as a sewing cooperative.

Special skills or requirements: Skills must be appropriate to the area of work. Volunteers must be over age 16. Language requirements vary by position; in general, positions with more human interaction, such as in a hospital, require more Spanish ability than positions without as much human interaction, such as organic gardening.

Learning from the Children in Mexico

❖ **by Merilee Baker** ❖

Mar de Jade

Volunteering at Mar de Jade was one of the best experiences of my life. The memories that I have of the people I met, the children I taught, and the places that I visited will forever be cherished.

I volunteered at a time in my life when I wanted to get away from the daily grind. I also felt that I wanted to make a contribution, to help people, and to make a difference. Mar de Jade offered me the chance to volunteer as an English teacher in the community and to take Spanish classes during my free time. Best of all, Mar de Jade is a beautiful resort on the ocean.

I have a background in teaching and child development, so I was really looking forward to teaching English to the local children. It was explained to me that there is no specific format for volunteers to follow, so when I arrived I really didn't know what to expect. I taught class in an open common room at a clinic in Las Varas, a poor farming community. Here, farming and money received from relatives working in the United Sates are the largest sources of income. English gives the children of Las Varas an opportunity to one day work in the tourism industry in Mexico, or to work in the United States if they choose.

On my first day of class I had about 30 children of all ages and levels. Armed with my chalk, I set out with the children on an adventure to learn the English language, and more important, to learn about each other. After the first day, word of the class spread throughout the community and the number of children increased daily. The children and I would sing songs both in English and in Spanish. We would talk and write about our families, our friends, and what we liked to do. My Spanish improved daily, as did their English. Every day after class I would walk down to the square in the center of town. There, a small circle of children would form around me. They would ask me about America, and they allowed me to join in their games. At the end of the three weeks, I felt that I learned as much from the children as I hope they learned from me.

I feel that I have made a difference, however small, in the lives of these children. I saw the joy on their faces when they described, in English, their favorite activity. I felt a swell of pride each and every time a child called me "teacher." I will be forever grateful for the opportunity to know them, to play with them, and to teach them.

Mar de Jade has been a wonderful experience for me. For anyone who would like to make a difference in a small community, to be accepted into that community, and to grow with that community, Mar de Jade is the place for you. Mar de Jade exceeded all my expectations.

MAR—Bulgarian Youth Alliance for Development

5, Triaditza Street
1000 Sofia, Bulgaria
(359) 2-9802037; Fax (359) 2-9802651
E-mail: mail@mar.bg
Web site: www.mar.bg or www.workcamp.ws

Project location: Bulgaria.

Project type: Environmental protection, social action, and restoration and conservation work.

Project costs: There is a participation fee of about EUR120. Volunteers are responsible for their insurance and travel costs to the site. Accommodations and food are provided by the organization. Hosting is usually in schools and community or youth centers. In most Bulgarian work camps, beds are provided, and meals are prepared by a cooking staff. In the very rare cases when sleeping bags are needed, it will be mentioned in the information sheet. Volunteers are expected to help with cleaning and domestic chores.

Project dates: July and August. Projects last for 15 days.

Work done by volunteers: Projects and activities vary from camp to camp. A detailed description of all projects is available on the organization's Web site. Volunteers work four to six hours a day, five days a week.

Special skills or requirements: Volunteers must be 18 to 30 years old. No language or other skills are required.

Sample projects: Program of social activities for orphans.

Marine Environment Awareness Project

Biosphere Foundation
H-1052 Budapest
Semmelweis utca 19, Hungary
(36) 1-483-1989; Fax (36) 1-4831988
E-mail: enquiries@marineaware.org
Web site: www.marineaware.org

Project location: Dahab, Egypt.

Project type: Environmental awareness and conservation.

Project costs: $690. Project fee includes lodging in a bed-and-breakfast. Airfare is not included in the project cost.

Project dates: Two-week projects from April to May.

How to apply: Send an e-mail to the address listed above.

Work done by volunteers: Monitoring of coral reefs and frequently visited dive sites around Dahab.

Special skills or requirements: Participants need to be physically fit and able to swim, and must possess a strong desire for wildlife conservation and contact with people from other cultures. Volunteers must be at least 18 years old.

Commentary: The project incorporates diving, snorkeling, introduction to marine research techniques and conservation issues, and desert adventures. This year's work will include monitoring of some frequently visited dive sites around Dahab by using a video transect method. Participants will explore the coastal ecosystems of the Red Sea, including its coral reefs, mangroves, and sea grass beds. They will also become acquainted with linked ecosystems such as deserts, wadis, dunes, and their inhabitants; learn about Egypt's natural history; and take part in practical conservation work. Curious travelers and family members are also welcome. Family members and others who just want to dive and not participate in volunteer activities are also welcome.

Medical Ministry International (MMI)

P.O. Box 1339
Allen, TX 75013
(972) 727-5864; Fax (972) 727-7810
E-mail: mmitx@mmint.org or mmican@mmint.org
Web site: www.mmint.org

Project location: Worldwide.

Project type: Medical.

Project costs: Participants pay a participation fee plus their airfare. Participation fee for a two-week project is $875; $660 for a one-week project. Room and board are included in the project cost.

Project dates: Year-round.

How to apply: E-mail or call the office at the address listed above and ask for an application.

Work done by volunteers: Both medical and nonmedical volunteers are accepted, including dentists, primary care and specialty physicians, surgeons, optometrists, nurses, health educators, other health professionals, translators, technicians, handy people, and general helpers. Spouses and teens may accompany volunteers. To provide the very best possible care for patients, only qualified professionals participate directly in surgical or dental procedures. Children under 18 years of age will not be allowed in operating rooms.

Special skills or requirements: Participants must be able to travel. Flexibility and a positive attitude will help make each of your projects memorable ones.

Commentary: MMI is a faith-based opportunity to serve by providing spiritual and physical health care. Participants come from a variety of Christian traditions and backgrounds. Volunteers are united by MMI's mission of serving the poor through medicine and evangelism. MMI welcomes those who are not Christian to participate and provide medical care.

Sample projects: Medical and project directors assign each participant a role, matching their skills and training to the needs of the project. The people served are the lowest on the economic scale. The health care MMI offers is usually all that is available to the recipients. Days are full, and volunteers work hard as a team to see as many patients as possible during the week. In the evenings, volunteers enjoy fellowship and relaxation with other team members. Accommodations vary, but are usually in a hostel, dorm, or small hotel setting.

Aerobics for the Soul

❖ by Madonna Yates ❖

Medical Ministry International (MMI)

It's January. I've had to miss volunteering on the Eye Team with Medical Ministry International (MMI) in Jamaica this year. Sitting at home, watching it snow, my heart is with my annual mission team. I, like most of the others, am a repeat volunteer, and the participant list is like my family. Many of us have been doing these "working vacations" for over 30 years. Some scattered medical families hold their reunions while volunteering on MMI projects. Still other volunteers are faithful to specific locations and return year after year to the same country. Statistics keep changing, but MMI plans close to 70 projects annually in 35 countries, bringing general medicine, surgery, and dentistry to remote population centers all over the world. North American affluence and specialized training are brought face to face with the working poor, who are doing their best to obtain medical care for their families. They pay a small fee (less than one dollar), and this dignifies the relationship of the doctor and the patient. We help them, one by one, and as we work, we learn the value of relationships.

The Eye Team will be in Jamaica for two weeks, fitting eyeglasses, doing cataract surgery, treating eye infections and injuries, and even fitting artificial eyes. This is the first time MMI has ever had a complete eye project in Jamaica, although MMI has taken medical, surgical, and dental teams there for years. I know the lines will stretch down the block and around the corner. The people will be seen in the order of their arrival; some need glasses, others need surgery. Word travels quickly when people regain their sight, and the lines will lengthen.

MMI optometrists spend their days refracting folks who need prescription glasses. We search our eyeglass collection by laptop computer. Eighty-five percent of the time we can give the patient a good, usable pair of glasses gathered from North American discards. MMI opticians train the general helpers, and together we mold old eyeglasses to fit a new face. Smiles abound!

Many of our cataract patients are octogenarians or older. Some have been without sight for a decade. The ophthalmologists say that we'll all get cataracts, if we live long enough. But can you imagine the thrill we feel when a grandmother has the bandages removed from her eyes, and calls her children and grandchildren to her side, one by one so she can see what she has only imagined their faces to be? All eyes are wet, even mine as I write. Once, in a morning devotional, a team member called this moment "aerobics for the soul." How desperately our tired world longs to do something really good.

❖ ❖ ❖

Our accommodations vary according to where we go. MMI provides clean food and water, meets each team as it arrives, and gets everyone back on the plane when the project is over. Volunteers all arrive on a Saturday, set up the clinic and surgery on Sunday afternoon, and begin seeing patients on Monday. By Wednesday of the first week, a typical MMI team functions smoothly, knowing what skills and capabilities are represented, and what materials are at hand. We work alongside the local medical system, with many local doctors, nurses, pastors, and health educators who volunteer with us.

I am home watching it snow as I write, but my prayers are in Jamaica. Today is the second Saturday of the project, and the volunteers will be hiking, sight-seeing at the basket market, wandering the beach, enjoying the beauty of the land and its people. When they start work again on Monday, this team may see up to 900 patients, fit 800 pairs of reading and prescription glasses, do 15 to 25 surgeries, and fit 2 or 3 artificial eyes for young people. On a two-week project, they may see 8,000 patients and do more than a hundred life-changing surgeries.

MMI teams work hard, enjoy relaxing, and fit in a bit of sight-seeing. We often go where tourists are rare and patients have no access to care. This is a ministry to both the affluent professional and the patient. We should print a warning label: This experience is both habit forming and contagious! It is aerobics for the soul.

Los Medicos Voladores (LMV)—
The Flying Doctors

P.O. Box 445
Los Gatos, CA 95031
(800) 585-4LMV
E-mail: info@flyingdocs.org
Web site: www.flyingdocs.org

Project location: The Copper Canyon area of northern Mexico and villages in Baja California.

Project type: Providing medical, dental, optometric care, and health education in remote villages and other medically underserved areas.

Project costs: $300 to $400. Volunteers pay for their transportation to San Francisco.

Project dates: Generally the second weekend of each month, plus two days.

How to apply: Visit the organization's Web site and call the trip coordinator regarding the month you want to go.

Work done by volunteers: Patient scheduling and nonskilled assistance (for example, "Hold the flashlight, please."). Medical volunteers are needed in ophthalmology, optometry, and dental care (including dentists, dental assistants, and hygienists). There are also volunteer positions for physicians, PAs, and RNs. All medical volunteers must be board certified. Projects are four-day trips in which volunteers fly in small planes from the San Francisco Bay area to a small town, set up a clinic, and provide optometry, medical, and dental services and education. Saturday night is free, and volunteers return Sunday.

Special skills or requirements: Volunteers must have a sense of humor, adaptability, and "no excess dignity."

Commentary: On Thursday and Friday, volunteers eat and sleep in villages where accommodations are simple; Saturday night is spent in a large town with more comfortable accommodations.

Soaring in Sacrifice

❖ by Adrian Fenderson, D.D.S. ❖

Los Medicos Voladores (LMV)—
The Flying Doctors

I learned about the existence of Los Medicos Voladores (LMV) in 1980 at a dental meeting and I immediately joined. The LMV mission statement rekindled memories of my many volunteer experiences as a dentist stationed in Vietnam. Several days a month, I would join a team of volunteers including nurses, physicians, and Red Cross personnel on missions of mercy. We would take the Med-Evac helicopters to small remote villages and set up primitive clinics in order to aid the orphans and the needy. The teary-eyed thanks and Velcro hugs we received from so many children and appreciative locals gave me highs and warm feelings that became very addictive. When I heard about LMV, it had been eight years since I'd done that kind of volunteer work and experienced those feelings from which I was still suffering withdrawal symptoms. It was time to get my "fix" and renew that incredible sense of intense satisfaction. So, I joined LMV and was off to Mexico just four weeks later. That trip to Mexico was the start of what would average out to be approximately three missions a year for the next 20 years with LMV.

Los Medicos Voladores was founded in 1974 to provide free health services and education to the people of Northern Mexico. This goal is accomplished by flying medical teams that consist of a pilot, an interpreter, a medical professional (usually an M.D., dentist, or optometrist), and sometimes a copilot or general volunteer into remote areas of Mexico. The areas we service are often so underdeveloped that there is no dentist within a day's drive. When I first joined LMV, some towns we served had no telephones. We simply announced our arrival by flying in low circles over the town before landing our small planes on the community's dirt airstrip, then someone would drive around town with a loudspeaker letting everyone know that we were there to help. The next day, before we even opened our clinic, the villagers would be lined up at the door.

On every trip I get hugs and sincere thanks that fill my heart to the brim. On my first trip, the town elementary school teacher came in with a broken front tooth. She was a pretty young lady who, for five years, had been afraid to smile. I repaired the tooth and filled in the gap. After looking in the mirror, she wept with joy. She hugged me, kissed me on the cheek, blessed me with the sign of the cross, and said that I was surely an angel from heaven.

For years my daughter, Tiffany, saw the sparkle in my eye when I returned from these trips and she begged to go. When she turned 14, she took Spanish in high school, learned to assist with dental work, and has come with me once a year for the past seven years. Since dental assisting is not her chosen career, I ask before each trip why she continues to volunteer for these missions. She simply shrugs and says, "I do it for numerous reasons, but—most of all—I just love helping people and seeing their grateful smiles."

One of my favorite stories is from my pilot friend, Don. On one trip, he assisted the team optometrist in fitting a pair of glasses on an elderly lady. During a walk around the village afterward, Don saw her in church, crying. He had an interpreter ask why she was in such distress. The lady told him she was crying for joy, as it had been 20 years since she had been able to read the Bible herself.

We all have our own reasons for serving as volunteers. I do it for the adventure and the challenge. More important, though, I do it for the warm and wonderful feeling of satisfaction and happiness that engulfs me for months after my volunteer trips. I do it because I love it—and I always will!

MERCI (Marion Edwards Recovery Center Initiative)/North Carolina Conference United Methodist Church Disaster Recovery Ministries

676 Community Drive
Goldsboro, NC 27530
(888) 440-9167
E-mail: merci@nccumc.org
Web site: www.merciumc.org

Project location: Eastern North Carolina.

Project type: Repairing Hurricane Floyd—damaged houses, rebuilding destroyed homes, and repairing substandard housing.

Project costs: Volunteers are responsible for travel to and from North Carolina. Housing is provided at a cost of $5 per person per day to offset utilities expenses. Kitchens are provided and volunteers are asked to cook their own meals.

Project dates: Year-round. Teams volunteer for as little as one day or a weekend, or as long as a week.

How to apply: Contact the volunteer coordinator at the office listed above for an orientation packet containing general information and volunteer forms. A 10-minute video is available upon request.

Work done by volunteers: Volunteers do general carpentry, drywall work, finish carpentry, plumbing, roofing, painting, and landscaping. Persons skilled in the building trades are most helpful for all teams. General helpers are also needed.

Special skills or requirements: Volunteers must be at least 16 years old. Youth groups of high school students must have one adult over 18 for every four to five youth volunteers.

Commentary: Building materials are supplied by Disaster Recovery Ministries and are delivered to the sites as needed. A construction coordinator is on hand to advise and assist teams when necessary.

Sample projects: Teams may tear out the floors or walls of a flooded home; repair the roof of a wind-damaged home; replace floors, drywall, roofs, or ceilings; or paint.

Mercy Ships

P.O. Box 2020
Garden Valley, TX 75771
(800) MERCYSHIPS or (903) 939-7000;
Fax (903) 882-0336
E-mail: info@mercyships.org
Web site: www.mercyships.org

Project location: Africa, the Caribbean, Latin America, and 17
administrative offices located worldwide.
Project type: Medical and relief work in developing nations.
Project costs: $40 application fee. Volunteers provide their own
transportation to and from the ships. On board, they pay
$100 per week for room and board.

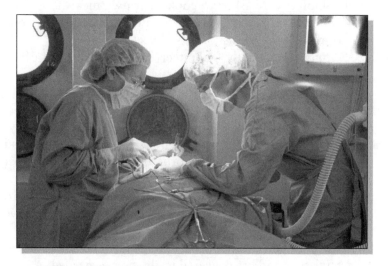

Life-changing surgeries such as this one are performed every day by volunteers, helped by the light coming through the portholes of a Mercy Ship.
(Photo courtesy Mercy Ships)

Project dates: Year-round. Volunteers may stay from two weeks up to one year.

How to apply: Contact Mercy Ships at the address listed above and request an application.

Work done by volunteers: Relief projects, water and sanitation development, surgeries, village medical and dental care and education, administrative and support services, information technology, marine and technical operations, training, communications, and graphics.

Special skills or requirements: Volunteers must speak English, be in good physical health, and be at least 18 years old unless accompanied by an adult. All skills and skill levels are useful.

Commentary: Mercy Ships, a Christian charity founded in 1978, utilizes oceangoing vessels to bring hope and healing to the poor and needy in port areas around the world. The organization fosters change by mobilizing volunteers to serve others through medical care, relief, development, evangelism, and training.

Michigan Nature Association (MNA)

Box 102
Avoca, MI 48006-0102
(866) 223-2231; Fax (810) 387-3717
E-mail: mna@greatlakes.net

Project location: One hundred and fifty-nine nature sanctuaries in fifty-four counties throughout Michigan. MNA projects take place in preserves and sanctuaries that protect rare and endangered species, unique scenic vistas, critical wetlands, old growth forests, shorelines, bogs, geological formations, and other natural features that make Michigan unique. Twenty-nine of Michigan's thirty native habitats are represented superbly on MNA lands. Volunteers get to explore some of the unique regions of Michigan.

Project type: Ecology, conservation, and education.

Project costs: Volunteers are responsible for their own travel and living costs.

Project dates: May through August.

How to apply: Call or write to the vice president at the address listed above.

Work done by volunteers: Sanctuary maintenance, trail work, exploration for new land preservation projects, photography, and leading field trips. Volunteers may also "adopt" a particular sanctuary to monitor.

Special skills or requirements: Volunteers need to have access to a car. They should be interested in preservation of natural areas. There is no minimum age requirement for volunteers.

Mingan Island Cetacean Study, Incorporated (MICS)

378 Bord de la Mer
Longue-Pointe-de-Mingan
Quebec G0G 1V0 Canada
Tel/Fax (418) 949-2845
E-mail: mics@globetrotter.net
Web site: www.rorqual.com

Project location: Mingan Island, in the Gulf of St. Lawrence, and Loreto, in Baja, California.

Project type: Marine mammal research, with emphasis on rorquals.

Project costs: Volunteers are responsible for transportation to the project and approximately $155 per day to cover research and living costs.

Project dates: Various times during the year; generally between June and October in the Mingan Island study area, and in March in Baja, California.

How to apply: Write or call the office listed above.

Work done by volunteers: Assisting scientists in research as required.

Special skills or requirements: Some experience handling or working on boats is required. A degree in biology is required for full assistants.

Commentary: MICS is best known as the first organization in the world to carry out long-term studies on the blue whale.

Sample projects: In the past, volunteers have conducted a photo identification of blue, fin, humpback, and minke whales to help determine the distribution, migration patterns, population estimates, behavioral attributes, and genetic makeups of the various populations.

Missouri Department of Natural Resources

Division of State Parks
P.O. Box 176
Jefferson City, MO 65102
(573) 751-2479 or (800) 334-6946; Fax (573) 751-8656
E-mail: moparks@mail.dnr.state.mo.us
Web site: www.mostateparks.com/volunteer.htm

Project location: State parks and state historic sites throughout Missouri.

Project type: Campground host, interpreter, park aide, and trail worker

Project costs: Volunteers are responsible for their travel and living expenses, as well as for providing and paying for their own housing.

Project dates: March to October for hosts. Park aides, interpreters, and trail workers may be year-round.

How to apply: Contact the volunteer program coordinator at the office listed above, or visit the organization's Web site.

Work done by volunteers: Volunteers are expected to perform at the same standards as paid employees. Volunteers are scheduled according to availability and park needs. Campground hosts serve a minimum of four weeks and are provided free full hookups for collecting fees, issuing permits, and assisting visitors.

Special skills or requirements: Volunteers must be physically able to perform assigned tasks. There is no minimum age for volunteers; one-year-olds (accompanied by their parents, of course) have volunteered as re-enactors. Trail crews are usually made up of volunteers who are at least 13 years old.

Commentary: Many of Missouri's state parks are located in the Ozark Mountains or near large man-made reservoirs.

Monkey Sanctuary

Looe, Cornwall PL13 1NZ United Kingdom
(01503) 262 532
E-mail:info@monkeysanctuary.org
Web site:
www.ethicalworks.co.uk/monkeysanctuary/index2.htm

Project location: Looe, Cornwall, in southwestern England.

Project type: Winter work includes maintenance of enclosures as well as general duties in the sanctuary. During the summer when the sanctuary is open to the public, volunteers work in the shop and at the gate.

Project costs: Volunteers are responsible for travel; there is a weekly charge of £35 for room and board (£25 for students and unemployed people). The sanctuary charges a £10 booking fee upon confirmation of a reservation; this fee gets the volunteer a biannual newsletter about the monkeys, the sanctuary, and other related issues.

Project dates: Year-round, with stays from two weeks to one month.

How to apply: Write to the volunteer coordinator at the address listed above. Enclose an envelope with an international postal coupon.

Work done by volunteers: Maintenance is done during the winter, as is cleaning enclosures. The same work, plus shop and gate duties, are done in the summer.

Special skills or requirements: A pleasant nature and a willingness to work and mix with groups is required. The sanctuary prefers volunteers who are at least 18 years old. An interest in animal welfare and conservation is essential.

Commentary: The Monkey Sanctuary is situated in a beautiful wooded setting overlooking Looe Bay. For 25 years, the Victorian house and gardens have been the home of a natural colony of woolly monkeys. The initial aim of the sanctuary was to provide a stable setting in which woolly monkeys, rescued from lives of isolation in zoos or as pets, could live as naturally as possible. The work now focuses on the need for rehabilitation projects and public education on local and global conservation and animal welfare, including the unsuitability of captivity for primates.

Morrow Mountain State Park

49104 Morrow Mountain Road
Albemarle, NC 28001
(704) 982-4402
E-mail: momo@vnet.net
Web site: www.ncsparks.net, select
Morrow Moutain State Park

Project location: Albemarle, North Carolina.
Project type: Trail work, interpretation, maintenance, and resource management.
Project costs: None. Barracks-style housing is provided, meals are not. Transportation to the park is not included.
Project dates: Year-round.
How to apply: Contact Larry Hyde, Park Ranger/Volunteer Manager, by phone, mail, or e-mail.

The Morrow Mountain State Park has volunteers who work on trail renovation, building maintenance, and giving interpretive programs to visitors. (Photo courtesy of Morrow Mountain State Park)

Special skills or requirements: Requirements and skills depend on the type of assignment, but an interest or skills in park settings is preferred. There is no minimum age for volunteers.

Commentary: References, preferably of past volunteer or park-related projects, are required.

Sample projects: Trail renovation, building maintenance, litter and trash removal, restroom cleanup, and giving interpretive programs to visitors.

Mount Vernon Ladies' Association

Archaeology Department
Mount Vernon, VA 22121
(703) 799-8626 or (703) 799-6303
E-mail: ewhite@mountvernon.org or
archaeology@mountvernon.org
Web site: www.mountvernon.org

Project location: Mount Vernon, Virginia.

Project type: Archaeological excavation and artifact processing.

Project costs: Participants must pay all transportation, room, and board.

Project dates: Most volunteer opportunities are from June through September. Volunteers are needed for special projects during other months. Please inquire for specific dates.

How to apply: Contact Ester White, Archaeologist, or Christy Leeson, Assistant Archaeologist, at the office listed above.

Work done by volunteers: Excavation and recording in the field and artifact washing, labeling, and cataloging in the lab.

Special skills or requirements: A willingness to work hard and a time commitment of one day or more are required. Volunteers must be at least 16 years of age or accompanied by a parent or guardian.

National Audubon Society

700 Broadway
New York, NY 10003
(212) 979-3000; Fax (212) 979-3188
Web site: www.audubon.org

Project location: Throughout the United States.
Project type: Habitat restoration, trail building, guide work, and visitor-center work.
Project costs: Depends on the individual project.
Project dates: Vary according to project.
How to apply: The national office of the Audubon Society does not place volunteers, but state offices and local chapters often have programs in which volunteers are used. Visit the organization's Web site for access to local chapters, or contact the state offices listed below for information.
Work done by volunteers: Depends on the project; mainly ecological work and work in the visitor centers and as guides.
Special skills or requirements: Vary by project.
Commentary: The state offices are as follows:

Alaska State Office
308 G Street, Suite 217
Anchorage, AK 99501
(907) 276-7034

Arkansas State Office
Heritage West, Suite 450
201 East Markham Street
Little Rock, AR 72201
(501) 244-2229

California State Office
555 Audubon Place
Sacramento, CA 95825
(916) 481-5332

Connecticut Representative Office
P.O. Box 1028
Old Lyme, CT 06371
(860) 526-4686

Florida Audubon
102 East 4th Avenue
Tallahassee, FL 32303
(407) 539-5700

Iowa State Office
P.O. Box 71174
Des Moines, IA 50325
(515) 267-0701

Maine Representative Office
P.O. Box 524
118 Union Square
Dover-Foxcraft, ME 04426
(207) 564-7946

Minnesota State Office
26 East Exchange Street, Suite 207
St. Paul, MN 55101
(612) 225-1830

Missouri State Office
1001 Walnut Street East, Suite 201
Columbia, MO 65201
(573) 442-2583

Mississippi State Office
Finley Place
285 East Falconer Street
Holly Springs, MS 38635
(662) 252-4143

Montana Audubon
P.O. Box 595
324 Fuller Avenue
Helena, MT 59624
(406) 443-3949

Nebraska State Office
P.O. Box 117
Denton, NE 68339
(402) 797-2301

New Mexico State Office
Randall Davey Audubon Center
P.O. Box 9314
Santa Fe, NM 87504-9314
(505) 983-4609

New York State Office
200 Trillium Lane
Albany, NY 12203
(518) 869-9731

North Carolina State Office
720 Market Place
Wilmington, NC 28401-4647
(910) 251-0666

North Dakota State Office
Black Building
118 Broadway, Suite 502
Fargo, ND 58102
(701) 298-3373

Ohio State Office
692 North High Street, Suite 208
Columbus, OH 43215
(614) 224-3303

Pennsylvania State Office
100 Wildwood Way
Harrisburg, PA 17710
(717) 213-6880

Texas State Office
2525 Wallingwood, Suite 301
Austin, TX 78746
(512) 306-0225

Vermont State Office
Green Mountain Audubon Center
255 Sherman Hollow Road
Huntington, VT 05462
(802) 434-3068

Washington State Office
P.O. Box 462
Olympia, WA 98507
(360) 786-8020

National Meditation Center for World Peace

Route 10, Box 2523
Jacksonville, TX 75766
(903) 589-5706
E-mail: osensei@nationalmeditation.org
Web site: www.nationalmeditation.org

Project location: Cebu, Philippines.

Project type: This is a community action program, which is followed by a cultural tour.

Project costs: Volunteers pay for air travel, room, and board. Special packages may be available.

Project dates: May through June.

How to apply: Apply by e-mail to the address listed above. Include the phrase "volunteer culture tour" in the subject line.

Work done by volunteers: Various community action programs, from repairing a building to working with a local organization such as an orphanage.

Special requirements: Volunteers under the age of 18 must have parental permission. All volunteers are required to file for a visa if staying longer than 30 days.

National Trust for Scotland Thistle Camps

28 Charlotte Square
Edinburgh EH2 4ET United Kingdom
(44) 0131 243 9300; Fax (44) 0131 243 9301
E-mail: conservation@nts.org.uk
Web site: www.nts.org.uk

Project location: Throughout Scotland.

Project type: Practical conservation management.

Project costs: Currently about $40 per week for food and accommodations. Project cost does not include airfare.

Project dates: March to October, for one or two weeks.

How to apply: Write to the address listed above. Projects are frequently filled by April each year; apply early.

Work done by volunteers: Building fences, maintaining mountain footpaths, building drystone dykes, and participating in woodland management and farm work.

Special skills or requirements: Volunteers must be at least 16 years old, healthy, and prepared for hard physical work.

Commentary: Thistle Camps are organized by the National Trust for Scotland to help in the practical management of National Trust for Scotland properties.

National Trust Working Holidays

Wroxham
Norwich, NR12 8DH United Kingdom
(0870) 429 2428
E-mail: working.holidays@nationaltrust.org.uk
Web site: www.nationaltrust.org.uk/volunteering

Project location: Fifty-two locations throughout England, Wales, and Northern Ireland.

Project type: Countryside conservation, archaeology, construction, and botany.

Project costs: About $85 for most weeklong projects, inclusive of full board. Project costs do not include transportation to site.

Project dates: Year-round. Projects generally last for one week, but some are weekend projects.

How to apply: Write to the address listed above for a brochure. Enclose three international postal reply coupons.

Work done by volunteers: Outdoor conservation, archaeology, botany, and construction.

Special skills or requirements: Some botany and construction skills may be required, depending on the project.

Commentary: National Trust Working Holidays include Acorn Projects, for general outdoor conservation work; Construction Projects, for volunteers interested in building; and Oak Camps, for volunteers over 35 years of age. You may join the project that best fits your needs and interests.

Nevada Division of State Parks

1300 South Curry Street
Carson City, NV 89703-5202
(775) 687-4384; Fax (775) 687-4117
E-mail: stparks@govmail.state.nv.us
Web site: www.state.nv.us/stparks

Project location: State parks throughout Nevada.

Project type: Trail work, campground hosting, working as an interpretive assistant, and other common park jobs.

Project costs: Volunteers are responsible for their transportation and living costs. Free campsites with hookups are available to volunteers at some locations.

Project dates: Year-round, for varying lengths of stay.

How to apply: Send for the *Volunteer in Park* bulletin at the address listed above. The bulletin contains information about available positions and an application.

Work done by volunteers: All types of work are done by volunteers, from hosting campgrounds and surveying archaeological digs to patrolling the backcountry.

Special skills or requirements: Some positions require special skills, and these are specified in the bulletin. Volunteers under the age of 14 require adult supervision.

Commentary: As with most state park systems, Nevada relies heavily on volunteers to keep its system going.

Nicaragua Solidarity Network (NSN)

339 Lafayette Street
New York, NY 10012
(212) 674-9499; Fax (212) 674-9139
E-mail: wnu@igc.org

Project location: The five boroughs of New York City.
Project type: Activism.
Project costs: Participants are responsible for travel, room, and board expenses.
Project dates: Year-round.
How to apply: Send a resume and cover letter to the address listed above.
Work done by volunteers: Media networking, outreach, street theater, fund-raising, and producing a weekly newsletter.
Special skills or requirements: Volunteers should be familiar with Latin American issues and be interested in the progressive solidarity movement. Knowledge of Spanish is helpful, but not required.
Commentary: This organization has broadened its area of interest since the end of the civil war in Nicaragua. It produces *Weekly News Update on the Americas*, a publication covering news and information from all of Latin America and the Caribbean. NSN is also very active in work involving sweatshop issues and immigrant rights. NSN is a founding member of the Global Sweatshop Coalition and the Coalition for the Human Rights of Immigrants (CHRI).

Northern Cambria Community Development (NORCAM)

4200 Crawford Avenue, Suite 200
Northern Cambria, PA 15714
(814) 948-4444 or (888) 676-8781; Fax (814) 948-4449
E-mail: norcam@surfshop.net

Project location: West-central Pennsylvania.
Project type: House building and rehabilitation.
Project cost: $125 per week for housing and food.
Project dates: Year-round, generally for one week.
How to apply: Contact the office listed above for more information.
Work done by volunteers: Various types of construction work.
Special skills or requirements: NORCAM welcomes individuals, families, and groups of up to 40.
Commentary: This is an organization that does on a local level what Habitat for Humanity does internationally.

North York Moors Historical Railway Trust

Pickering Station
Pickering, North Yorkshire YO18 7AJ United Kingdom
(01751) 472 508; Fax (01751) 476 970
E-mail: admin@nymr.demon.co.uk
Web site: www.nymr.demon.co.uk

Project location: Along an 18-mile, mainly steam-operated railway in northern England.

Project type: All aspects of railway operation and maintenance.

Project costs: Basic accommodations are available in hostel-style facilities and converted railway carriages for a small charge—about £7.50 per night—to cover cleaning costs and upkeep. Volunteers are responsible for food and travel costs (self-catering facilities are provided).

Project dates: The main railway operating season is from the beginning of April to the end of October. Maintenance and engineering work takes place throughout the year.

How to apply: Write to the volunteer liaison officer at the address listed above.

Work done by volunteers: Painting, drainage, lineside clearance, building repairs, shop- and on-train sales, ticket inspecting, locomotive cleaning, administration, and customer services.

Special skills or requirements: All volunteers should be physically fit. Anyone with technical or railway experience, or who is able to give sufficient time to the project to gain experience (and be trained), may be given opportunities to become involved in skilled work. Volunteers who wish to operate and drive trains must be between 16 and 65 years old.

Commentary: Visiting groups may undertake special projects by arrangement.

Nothelfergemeinschaft der Freunde e.V.

Geschäftsstelle
Postfach 101510
52351 Düren
Germany
(0049) 0-2421-76569; Fax (0049) 0-2421-76468
E-mail: ndf-dn@t-online.de
Web site: www.nothelfergemeinschaft.de

Project location: Throughout Germany and Europe.

Project type: Work camps.

Project costs: Approximately $80 registration fee, plus transportation costs.

Project dates: Spring and summer for United States volunteers who are already in Germany.

How to apply: Write to Gerhard Fleming at the address listed above for more information and an application. Application should be received by the organization between March 1 and May 30.

Work done by volunteers: Volunteers spend three to four weeks working in social institutions like homes for the elderly or farms where handicapped and non-handicapped people live and work together. They help with construction or housekeeping and accompanying old people during their daily activities. Volunteers are often supervised by group leaders who are former work camp volunteers and who have attended work camp leadership seminars.

Special skills or requirements: A knowledge of English or German, an interest in people, and an interest in international exchange are required.

Oceanic Society Expeditions

Fort Mason Center, Suite E-230
San Francisco, CA 94123
(415) 441-1106 or (800) 326-7491; Fax (415) 474-3395
Web site: www.oceanic-society.org

Project location: The Bahamas, Belize, California, Midway Atoll,
the Peruvian Amazon, and Suriname.

Project type: Research social and family structure, distribution,
and abundance of free-ranging dolphins, primates, and man-
atees. Monitor sea turtle–nesting success, and help assess the
impact of human activities on whales and dolphins. Conduct
seabird population counts and monitor chick hatchlings.
Investigate an archaeology site, or restore native plant
species. Conduct snorkeling surveys of tropical coral reef
ecosystems.

Project costs: From $1,150 to $1,950. Some project fees include
airfare, but others do not. Room and board are covered by
most expedition fees.

Project dates: Most trips last for one week. Refer to the listing
of individual projects in the *Commentary* section at the end
of this entry.

How to apply: Contact the office listed above for an application.

Work done by volunteers: Participants photograph animals and
record behaviors, location of sightings, and habitat size. They
also assist biologists and other scientists with investigations.

Special skills or requirements: No research experience is needed.
An adventurous spirit, patience, respect of wildlife, and the
ability to follow instructions are necessary. Basic swimming
skills for water-based studies, snorkeling for Bahamas and
Belize dolphin studies, and scuba certification for scuba programs are required. Most expeditions allow children age 10
and above if accompanied by parent or guardian; some
research projects require a minimum age of 16 or 18. See
Web site for details.

Commentary: The specific programs and dates are as follows:

Amazon River Dolphins: Four eight-day trips in June, July, August, December, and January.

Bahamas Dolphins: July to August.

Belize Coral Reef Snorkeling Surveys: Weeklong trips in April, May, June, July, and August.

Belize Bottlenose Dolphins: Weeklong trips in January, February, March, April, May, June, August, October, and December.

Midway Dolphins: Weeklong trips from March through September.

Midway Seabirds: Weeklong trips year-round except May, September, and October.

Monterey Bay Dolphins and Whales: Six-day trips in September and October.

Suriname Sea Turtles: Nine-day trips in March, April, May, and June.

Operation Crossroads Africa

P.O. Box 5570
New York, NY 10115
(212) 289-1949; Fax (212) 289-2526
E-mail: oca@igc.apc.org
Web site: www.igc.org/oca

Project location: Africa and Brazil (Diaspora Program).

Project type: Work camp projects.

Project costs: $3,500. Project costs include room and board and airfare from New York. Volunteers are responsible for their own airfare to New York City.

Project dates: Mid-June to mid-August. Projects last seven weeks.

How to apply: Contact the office listed above for more information, or visit the organization's Web site.

Work done by volunteers: Volunteers perform a variety of work camp duties including education and training, community development and construction, agriculture and reforestation, community health and medical projects, and projects involving women and development.

Special skills or requirements: Volunteers must be at least 17 years old and interested in cross-cultural experiences.

ORDEX Cultural Exchange

Veintimilla y 12 de Octubre (esq)
Edificio El Giron, Torre—E, Mezzanine
Quito, Ecuador
(593) 2-2-502-345; Fax (593) 2-2-527-429
E-mail: info@ordex-ec.org
Web site: www.ordex-ec.org

Project location: Cerro Golodondrinas, Ecuador.

Project type: Forest conservation and demonstration of agro-forestry.

Project costs: $280 per month; $50 registration fee. Project fee includes room and board with a host family.

Project dates: Year-round; there is a required minimum one-month stay.

Work done by volunteers: Agricultural training, teaching, social work, and marketing.

Special skills or requirements: Basic or intermediate Spanish, as well as some training or experience in agriculture, are required. Volunteers should have the ability to work hard and live in primitive conditions. Volunteers must be at least 18 years old.

Oregon River Experiences, Incorporated

18074 South Boone Court
Beavercreek, OR 97004
(800) 827-1358 or (503) 632-6836
E-mail: info@oregonriver.com
Web site: www.oregonriver.com

Project location: Various rivers in the Northwest, including the Lower Salmon in Idaho and the Grande Ronde, John Day, Owyhee, and Rogue rivers in Oregon.

Project type: Educational white water river trips, many for senior citizens through the Elderhostel Program.

Project costs: Volunteers must pay their own transportation to and from the program site and provide their own sleeping bags, tents, and personal gear.

Project dates: The week-long Elderhostel programs run from May through September. Other programs of three to five days are scheduled from May through August.

How to apply: Send a letter and a resume, summarizing your qualifications, background, and experience, to the address listed above.

Work done by volunteers: Volunteers teach college-level mini-courses in subjects directly related to the river and the surrounding area. Typical subjects include geology, botany, ornithology, river ecology, local history, American Indian lore, archaeology, and astronomy. Lectures should be supported by appropriate handouts that the volunteers furnish for 25 students.

Special skills or requirements: Volunteers should have excellent verbal teaching skills and must be able to demonstrate a thorough knowledge of the subject. These are wilderness camping programs, so all participants should be in good physical condition. There is no age requirement, but since volunteers lecture about specific topics, it stands to reason that they be at least high-school graduates.

Commentary: Oregon River Experiences has been conducting educational river trips in the Northwest since 1977. They began doing Elderhostel programs in 1986.

Orkney Seal Rescue

Dyke End, South Ronaldsay
Orkney, KW17 2TJ, Scotland
(01856) 831 463
E-mail: selkiesave@aol.com

Project location: Dyke End, South Ronaldsay, Orkney, in Scotland.

Project type: Seal rehabilitation.

Project costs: £30.00 per week for food. Volunteer is responsible for transportation to site.

Project dates: May through December.

How to apply: Contact the office listed above by e-mail or postal mail and request a volunteer application form.

Work done by volunteers: Rescue, cleaning, feeding, and release of seals.

Special skills or requirements: Volunteers must be hard working and prepared to work with others in wet conditions, and be part of a small team of people dedicated to the rescue and rehabilitation of wildlife. Volunteers must commit to a minimum of four weeks.

Commentary: Meals provided are vegetarian.

Pacific Crest Trail Association

5325 Elkhorn Boulevard PMB 256
Sacramento, CA 95842-2526
(916) 349-2109; Fax (916) 349-1268
E-mail: info@pcta.org
Web site: www.pcta.org

Project location: Along the 2,650-mile Pacific Crest Trail, from Manning Provincial Park in Canada to the United States–Mexican border east of San Diego.

Project type: Trail building and maintenance.

Project costs: Minimal.

Project dates: Visit the organization's Web site for dates of work weekends.

How to apply: Visit the Web site for application information.

Work done by volunteers: Heavy physical labor building and maintaining trails in cooperation with the United States Forest Service, National Park Service, and private landowners.

Special skills or requirements: Good physical condition and a willingness to follow instructions while performing physical labor are required.

Commentary: The Pacific Crest Trail is one of the longest of the eight national scenic trails that are officially recognized in the United States. It runs along a high-altitude route on the ridges of mountain ranges along the west coast.

Pacific Northwest Trail Association

P.O. Box 1817
Mount Vernon, WA 98273
(877) 854-9415 or (360) 854-9415; Fax (360) 854-7665
E-mail: pnt@pnt.org
Web site: www.pnt.org

Project location: Various points along the Pacific Northwest Trail between northwest Montana and the Pacific Ocean in Olympic National Park in Washington State.

Project type: Construction of new segments of trail, repair and maintenance of existing trails, and other related work such as mapping and preparing a guidebook.

Project costs: Volunteers are responsible for transportation to and from the project site and for providing their own food.

Project dates: Summer.

How to apply: Write to Mike Dawson at the address listed above.

Work done by volunteers: Volunteers work at the site and maintain their camp.

Special skills or requirements: Knowledge of trails, backcountry living, guidebook writing, and mapmaking, and map and compass skills are required.

Commentary: The purpose of the Pacific Northwest Trail Association is to develop and maintain a 1,100-mile foot and horse trail as a showcase of the region.

Pacific Whale Foundation

101 North Kihei Road, Suite 21
Kihei, HI 96753
(800) WHALE11 or (808) 879-8811; Fax (808) 879-2615
E-mail: programs@pacificwhale.org
Web site: www.pacificwhale.org

Project location: Maui, Hawaii.

Project type: Research documenting the abundance and diversity of odontocetes (toothed whales and dolphins) off the coasts of Maui and the neighboring island of Lanai.

Project costs: $1,545 (includes lodging, all meals, transportation on Maui, and field project expenses). Transportation costs to Maui are not included.

Project dates: Volunteer projects run for varying lengths of time, all between June and September.

How to apply: Contact the office listed above for an application.

Work done by volunteers: Volunteers explore the area every other day in Pacific Whale Foundation's research vessel and help work on data analyses to learn about these whales and dolphins. Volunteers learn how to use a GPS (Global Positioning System) and laser rangefinders, and help record the behaviors of the whales and dolphins encountered during strip line transects. Researchers and volunteers will also opportunistically use a hydrophone (underwater microphone) and a DAT recorder to make recordings of sounds produced by whales and dolphins. Volunteers will work alongside research staff in the lab to help analyze photographic identifications of individual whales and dolphins collected during the previous five years of research. Information obtained during the study will provide wildlife management agencies important data on the size, range, stability, and long-term social dynamics of these species.

Special skills or requirements: Participants must be at least 18 years old and possess a basic knowledge of marine biology and good swimming skills.

Commentary: The mission of Pacific Whale Foundation is to inspire and promote the appreciation, understanding, and protection of whales, dolphins, coral reefs, and our planet's oceans. They accomplish this mission through public environmental education, by supporting and conducting responsible marine research, and by addressing marine conservation issues through activism and education. Maui and Lanai are home to populations of several hundred Hawaiian spinner dolphins, spotted dolphins, bottlenose dolphins, and species of less common small odontocetes including short-finned pilot whales, melon-headed whales, rough-toothed dolphins, and orca. Little is known about the distribution or abundance of these species in Maui County waters. Pacific Whale Foundation also offers longer and shorter term volunteer opportunities for Maui visitors. For more information, please call the office and ask to speak with the volunteer coordinator.

Passport in Time (PIT)

PIT Clearinghouse
P.O. Box 31315
Tucson, AZ 85751-1315
(520) 722-2716 or (800) 281-9176; Fax (520) 298-7044
E-mail: pit@sricrm.com
Web site: www.passportintime.com

Project location: National forests throughout the United States

Project type: Historic preservation, including archaeological survey and excavation, historic structure restoration, and lab and archival work.

Project costs: Volunteers are responsible for their own transportation to the projects. Services and facilities offered by the organization vary by project.

Project dates: Vary.

How to apply: Write to the address listed above for a newsletter and an application.

Work done by volunteers: Volunteers work directly with professional archaeologists and historians on excavations, surveys, lab work, building restoration, and oral histories.

Special skills or requirements: No previous experience is needed in most cases, although some projects may require special skills, such as carpentry or drawing.

Commentary: Passport in Time (PIT), a program of the United States Forest Service, gives the public an opportunity to work on more than 200 projects per year with professional archaeologists and historians in national forests and grasslands throughout the country. *The PIT Traveler* newsletter, published in March and September, lists current volunteer opportunities and may be obtained by contacting the office listed above.

Magic at Roundy Crossing

❖ by Catherine Jay Cowan ❖

Passport in Time

I am standing on ancient grounds, feeling the wind blowing
through my hair. Listening to the music of birds as they soar
overhead, my eyes gaze upon the vastness below. A real
magic occurs as I sense a people of long ago.

In the spring of 1999, I found myself working as a volunteer on my first Passport in Time (PIT) project at Roundy
Crossing, Arizona. On the first day, I met the forest service
archaeologist at 6:30 A.M. to head out on my journey. We
drove to the work center, an hour away, where most of the
other volunteers were, loaded our tools, buckets, gear, and a
lot of water, and headed to the site.

What a setting! No wonder these folks from long ago
(circa 1170 A.D.) chose this place to live. The view is incredible now; just imagine what it was like then! The pueblo,
comprising about 15 rooms, sits high up on a knoll. Its north
side is protected by ancient pecked images in the basalt cap
rock. Signs of terraced fields remain on the sloping hillside
west of the pueblo. To the east is what appears to be a farm-
stead, consisting of a couple of rooms and several dams on
the Show Low Creek for water control. What a handy work
place near the river for farmers tending their crops!

As my first day of work began, I ran out of breath, climbing up and down the knoll, using a pick and shovel, carrying
a five-gallon bucket of dirt to the screen, and moving heavy
rocks (or small boulders). By the last day of the month, I was
climbing the knoll without breathing hard, carrying two

buckets of dirt at a time, and learning the finer points and tools of the trade.

One of my own discoveries was a small pinch pot, with only a tiny piece of rim missing. It was so cute! As I held it in the palm of my hand, I thought of my four-year-old daughter and how she'd just love it. Then I thought of the possibility that I was holding the result of a child learning to make her first jar, or that it might have held small beads. I wondered how long it had been since anyone had held it.

It turned out the room I was working in was the kiva, a special place. The magic was sensed again, with a feeling of connection to these people of long ago.

The work was hard, the hours long, the weather ever changing. The rewards were constant: being involved in the efforts to fill in and preserve history, and developing friendships with the nicest kinds of people, old and young alike. This wonderful adventure was a crossing in my life, where the magic of growth and discovery took place.

Tennessee State University students wash artifacts while participating in a project to reconstruct the history and lifeways of Miller Grove, a Freed-Slave African American Community, located in the Shawnee National Forest in Illinois. (Photo courtesy Passport in Time)

Peacework Development Fund, Inc.

209 Otey St.
Blacksburg, VA 24060-7426
(540) 953-1376; Fax (540) 953-0300
E-mail: mail@peacework.org
Web site: www.peacework.org

Project location: Latin America, Southeast Asia, Eastern Europe, and Russia.

Project type: Short-term service with groups at established project sites.

Project costs: $700 to $2,000 all-inclusive expenses for a two- to three-week program.

Project dates: Throughout the year, typically coinciding with academic breaks.

How to apply: Contact the office listed above for information, or visit the organization's Web site.

Work done by volunteers: Basic building, repairs and renovations, agricultural projects, medial service, and more. All skill and support levels are needed.

Special skills or requirements: Only a genuine interest in service and cross-cultural experiences are required. Volunteers are mostly 18 and above, though there are some programs for youth as well.

Commentary: This program was begun to help bring residents of the former Soviet Union together with those of the United States on peaceful projects. Current programs have expanded, and today volunteers typically join groups of 10 to 20 people who work for two to three weeks on orphanages, schools, clinics, and other community service projects, and who also experience the culture and history of the host country. Some projects are emergency relief efforts; others are long-term development. All projects are organized, supervised, and sponsored by indigenous relief and development partners.

Peruvian Safaris

Alcanfores #459, Miraflores, Lima 18
P.O. Box 10088, Peru
(051 1) 447 8888, (051 1) 447 9475; Fax (051 1) 241 8427
E-mail: safaris@amauta.rcp.net.pe
Web site: peruviansafaris.com

Project location: Explorer's Inn lodge in the Tambopata National Reserve in the Amazon rain forest in southeast Peru.

Project type: Resident naturalist position for graduates in nature-oriented professions. Maintenance of bungalows, trails, bridges, and more for nonprofessionals.

Project costs: Resident Naturalists with research projects receive room and board in exchange for 10 days of guiding duties. Other scientists with long-term research projects receive substantial discounts for stay. Depending on their duties, nonprofessionals can have free lodging or substantial discounts.

Project dates: Year-round. Resident Naturalists work a minimum of three months, preferably six months. Nonprofessionals work a minimum of 30 days.

How to apply: Request an application form via e-mail.

Work done by volunteers: Resident Naturalists work on their own projects or assist others in ongoing programs; they also design and produce displays and posters for educational purposes. Nonprofessionals do maintenance work and assist management in its duties. They may also act as hosts or housekeepers at the lodge for periods of a minimum of three months, preferably six months.

Special skills or requirements: Applicants should be between 20 and 40 years old. Experience in construction, farming or gardening, arts and crafts, and recreation as well as previous group experience are all usefull. Resident Naturalist applicants must be graduates in nature-oriented professions.

Commentary: Peruvian Safaris owns the Explorer's Inn, a jungle lodge at the edge of the Tambopata National Reserve. With 26 years of operations, it claims the highest counts on earth of bird species (595) and butterfly species (over 1230) in only 5,500 hectares. The Explorer's Inn keeps a minimum of four resident naturalists doing research at the lodge.

Philanthrophy Host Families (Ghana)

P.O. Box 7781
Santa Rosa, CA 95407
(707) 569-8171
E-mail: benkeh1@msn.com

Project location: Ghana, West Africa.

Project type: Philanthrophy Host Families has different categories of programs year-round to provide for volunteers of varied skills and talents. The following is a partial list of projects and programs: health care and nutrition, HIV/AIDS education, social and child welfare, community organizing, working with disabled persons, agricultural and educational vocational, secondary, and primary education, pre-school assistance, and library services in schools.

Project costs: $600. A deposit of $200 must be submitted with the application two months prior to departure. The balance of $400 is to be paid in cash upon arrival in Ghana.

Project dates: Year-round.

How to apply: Contact the organization to receive an application and further information.

Special skills or requirements: None.

Commentary: Volunteers with disabilities are welcome.

Sample projects: Construction of classrooms at the Hohoe School of the Deaf, assistance at an HIV/AIDS education camp, and assistance with cultural activities.

Planet Drum Foundation

P.O. Box 31251
San Francisco, CA 94131
(415) 285-6556; Fax (415) 285-6563
E-mail: planetdrum@igc.org
Web site: www.planetdrum.org

Project location: San Francisco, California, and Bahia de Caraquez, Ecuador.

Project type: In San Francisco, administrative, editorial, and fund-raising projects support bioregional activities. In Ecuador, ecological restoration projects in a sustainable city are offered.

Project costs: Volunteers pay all of their own expenses.

Project dates: Year-round.

How to apply: An application is available on the organization's Web site.

Work done by volunteers: Administration, publication design, restoration projects, and more.

Special skills or requirements: Computer skills or an environmental background are helpful. Volunteers must be at least 18 years old.

Nature in the City

❖ **by Carey Knecht** ❖

Planet Drum Foundation

I joined up with Planet Drum and the Eco-Bahia project because I was deeply inspired by the task of integrating nature and a city. That is a task that requires not only reforesting one hillside, but actually changing culture. Sometimes I wonder how these projects are related. Sometimes I feel like the only nature I'm bringing into the city is in the mud on my boots. But sometimes the parallels jump out at me.

This past weekend, I participated in events that brought the reforestation work down from the hill into downtown Bahia, Ecuador, in a festive, concrete way. It was a celebration of the one-year anniversary of Bahia's Ecocity Declaration. The events of the weekend started with a parade through the town. The children in the Clubs Ecologicos marched in lines, holding signs with environmental messages. "Queens," decorated in skirts of leaves and flower necklaces, rode on *triciclos* festooned with palm leaves. This river of young life and vegetation flowed through the streets of Bahia for two hours.

After the parade, the *Fiesta Verde* began in an open park on the beachfront: theatrical acts and clowns; music including Latin rock, merengue, *cumbia*, and even the Police; the singing of Anja Light. The music and the party attracted a large group of onlookers, bringing ecology to the people.

The next day, nature came again to downtown Bahia. The patio under the *municiopio* (city hall) was filled with seedlings, demonstrations, and posters—an exposition of many ecological projects in Bahia. Enthusiasts brought tubs filled with mud and worms, samples of every seedling we're planting in the project and many more, and a formidable (meter-high) chunk of Paja Macho grass. Next to the composting-worm folks, we set up a display with posters showing where we're located, happy to finally be able to thoroughly explain what we're planting and where. At the same time, inside the building experts gave speeches on the wildlife of the region and the environmental law in Ecuador. Although the large venue left many seats open, I was surprised by the number of adults interested in listening to semi-technical information in the middle of a Saturday. Still, to me, more telling than the number of adults scattered throughout the back of the theater were the children, who filled the two front rows.

To finish off the weekend, Sunday and Monday were work days, full of short projects such as trying to create a healthy home for Miguelito la Tortuga, a tortoise from the Galapagos Islands, and ceremonially planting mangrove trees for the Dia de Mangles.

After the weekend, back to the hillside we went to plant again and to dig a hole, put a clump of grass in, cover it up, and wish it well—and to do this on a 75-degree slope of loose dirt clumps, or, even worse, wet clay. After three days of rain, I returned to a whole section of grass that had seemed completely dead. Out of every brown, dried-up clump of grass, every one, was one small green blade of grass—a new sprout.

This week, in two days we planted 924 seedlings—500 fruit and 424 *guayacan*—and three and a half truckloads of grass. Now, after three cool days of alternating rain and sun, when I walk on the hill, the ground no longer looks barren— I no longer envision it washing away. I imagine the sprouting stalks and the lines of grass merging into a forest.

Last weekend, in two days, the Eco-Bahia Celebration planted much more than 924 seedlings. Now, when I walk through town, it no longer looks barren—I no longer imagine the concrete winning. I remember the parading children, the dancing crowd. I imagine the seeds of thought they planted in the minds of the onlookers, blossoming into a town where nature is welcomed.

Potomac Appalachian Trail Club

118 Park Street SE
Vienna, VA 22180
(703) 242-0693, ext. 12; Fax (703) 242-0968
E-mail: info@patc.net
Web site: PATC.net

Project location: Shenandoah National Park and the George Washington National Forest, Virginia.

Project type: Trail building and maintenance.

Project costs: None. Travel expenses are paid by each volunteer. Housing and meals are provided at no charge.

Project dates: Shenandoah National Park: mid- to late-May and mid-August through mid-September. George Washington National Forest: mid- to late-June and mid-September.

How to apply: Apply via the Web site listed above, or call the organization and leave your name and address, and an application will be sent to you.

Work done by volunteers: Each trail crew works for five days. The work may include trail maintenance, improvements, or new trail construction. The work is often hot, sweaty, dirty, hard, and anything but glamorous. It is not a nature walk in the woods. However, volunteers do get to meet some fine people, to observe the beauty of the park and forest, and to eat some great food. They also might build up a few muscles.

Special skills or requirements: Given the large number of different projects, there are no specific required skills. Volunteers must be at least 18 years old or accompanied by a parent or guardian.

Commentary: Lodging arrangements at George Washington National Forest are tent or car camping. At Shenandoah National Park, there are accommodations at two cabins.

Sample projects: Rehabilitation of damaged trail sections, building new trails, and installing water control devices.

PRETOMA (Programa Restauración de Tortugas Marinas)

c/o Randall Arauz

1203-1100

TIBAS

San Jose, Costa Rica

E-mail: info@tortugamarina.org

Web site: www.tortugamarina.org

Project location: Punta Banco or San Miguel, Costa Rica (both on the Pacific coast).

Project type: Conservation—sea turtle protection programs in coastal communities.

Project costs: $600 for 2 weeks, $800 for one month, $1,200 for two months. Project costs include room and board, but do not include airfare.

Project dates: Mid-July thru mid-December.

How to apply: Contact the president of PRETOMA, Randall Arauz, at the e-mail address listed above.

Work done by volunteers: Patrolling beaches in search of nesting Olive Ridley turtles, tagging and measuring the turtles, collecting the eggs and placing them in the local PRETOMA hatchery, monitoring the hatchery, releasing baby turtles, and recording project data. Optional work includes educating the community about the program and teaching English at a local school.

Special skills or requirements: A strong interest in conservation, experience in marine biology, and basic Spanish skills are helpful, but not mandatory.

Commentary: Academic credit may be available for this project. For detailed project information and photos, please visit the organization's Web site.

Sample Projects: Since 1996, volunteers in the Punta Banco PRETOMA program have tagged, measured, and protected more than 1,000 nesting turtles and successfully released more than 60,000 hatchlings.

Turtle Tracks

❖ by Noah Anderson ❖

PRETOMA (Programa Restauración de Tortugas Marina)

It's 3:09 A.M. Who in his or her right mind is awake at 3:09 A.M.? You, the crickets, and the other volunteers. You join the six or eight other zombies in the dimly lit, open-air communal room. In semi-asleep stupors, no one's saying anything. Finally, somebody asks, "What's the schedule?" You're with Jorge on beach number three. Sweet. Less walking.

You all shuffle toward the door, toasting, "*Suerte*" (good fortune), to all as you go your separate ways, equipment bags slung over your shoulders. You and Jorge creep across the beachfront soccer field, dodging grapefruit-sized bullfrogs caught in the darting beam of your flashlight. You see the lights of the other volunteers flashing in the trees to the north. How still the town. You stop in the middle of the field and look up at the slowly moving starry sky. So bright. So black. And there's the Milky Way.

You suddenly notice the sound of the crashing waves that was always there but just now registers in your still sputtering brain. You can tell from the volume of the waves that the tide's about halfway in. Then . . . sand! Ahhh. There it is. The shift has officially started. Time to put thoughts of sleep behind, and keep your crusty eyes peeled for those telltale dents in the sand . . . turtle tracks. Down the beach you trod, dropping some questions to Jorge in an effort to practice your conversational Spanish, and getting who knows what for answers. But you nod and make affirmative sounding grunts just the same. No need for your flashlight tonight, as the starlight and phosphorescence are somehow lighting up the beach and bathing the overhanging palm fronds in a milky, unmistakable, quiet and still, middle-of-the-night glow.

"Ah ho! Tortuga!" says Jorge. "Huh?" you mumble, looking at the sand. But you know Jorge's right. Born here on the beach, he's got eagle eyes and almost seems sent from above to find turtles. And sure enough, 20 meters ahead, there she is, halfway up the beach, chucking sand this way and that, digging her nest. Nothing is going on except the sound of the waves, the stars, and Mama Tortuga doin' her thing.

Off comes the equipment bag, and then you and Jorge find a comfy place in the sand to sit and wait. When Mama's done digging her nest and starts to lay her eggs, she goes into a trance, so it doesn't hurt her as you tag her flippers and go about measuring her and collecting the eggs—all 100 of which you'll take to the program hatchery when all is said and done. You check her health, her shell, and her eyes as she's busily plopping her ping-pong-ball–sized eggs into her nice little pit nest—as completely unaware of your presence as you are unaware of what the heck Jorge is saying except for, "How beautiful. How peaceful." And his smile says it all.

So you've got the eggs as you watch Mama trundle her way back into the waves. "One down, how many more to go?" you wonder, as you feel the weight of the egg bag in your left arm. You score. It's a three turtle night, and as the predawn light engulfs the eastern sky above the jungle hills, replacing the stars' brilliance with a spectrum ranging from baby blue to royal blue to midnight blue that stops you in your tracks, and you can almost see the town yawning and rubbing its eyes, you and Jorge creep back across the dewy field, past a few still sleeping houses, to the hatchery (where you rebury the eggs) and then to your cabin, where you record your data as fast as you can and dive back into your bed fully clothed and fall back asleep despite the obnoxious morning calls of a toucan, perched in its favorite 5:30 A.M. spot just outside your bedroom window, and the gorilla-like roars of the howler monkeys, chatting about the previous night's gallivanting just a stone's throw up into the jungle. Hmmm, throwing a stone might not be such a bad idea. Nah, can't be bothered, and the snoring quickly sets in.

You wake again, without the aid of your alarm clock this time, at 9:45 A.M., with 15 minutes to get all primped for 10:00 A.M. breakfast—a huge plate of rice and beans with eggs or sausage, or pancakes, or maybe cereal with fresh, tree-plucked papaya or pineapple, or some fruit you've never seen before. And fresh-brewed Costa Rican coffee.

After breakfast you chill in the hammock for a bit, roll out, compare notes from the night's work, read, walk off your meal with a jungle stroll, play some beach volleyball with the locals, or some soccer, or Frisbee with the kids at recess, teach an English class at the one-room school house, check the hatchery for hatchlings and temperature readings, mingle with the locals in front of the "shop," have a snack, practice your Spanish or get a surfing lesson from the local expert, snorkel, chill on the beach under the palms, wash some clothes in the cabin sink, draw straws for who gets the late shift tonight . . . and by that time, you're ready for dinner, where you chat over pasta with homemade sauce and garlic bread about how many egg-stealing poachers you saw on the beach the night before.

After dinner, it's time to release about 100 baby turtles from the hatchery into the sea. Even though you've done it many a time, you still stand there, jaw on the ground, totally awestruck as the one-hour-old, three-inch-long little buggers disappear, drawn by instinct down the beach and into the crashing waves. When the last baby is washed out to sea, you head back to the pad to play a game of cards and try to put your middle-of-the-night shift out of mind. Oh me. But you're helpin' them turtles, you think as you blow out your candle, close your book and set your alarm. You're helpin' them turtles. Cheers.

Prime Care Network

P.O. Box OS 408
Accra, Ghana
(233) 21 761074 or (233) 21 783831
E-mail: primecare_net@yahoo.com or
mic_park61@hotmail.com

Project location: Ghana.

Project type: Education, environmental conservation, agro-forestry, health, cultural exchange, social work, and international solidarity.

Project costs: $500, which includes food and accomodations for a period of one month, as well as the registration fee. Volunteers are responsible for their own transportation costs.

Project dates: Teaching in schools occurs from January to April, June to August, and September to mid-December. Other programs are run throughout the year.

How to apply: Obtain a registration form from the address listed above.

Work done by volunteers: Teaching mathematics, English, or Bible studies in schools, storytelling, working with children in a communuty, assisting midwives and obstetricians, conducting education programs on drug abuse, teenage pregnancy, STDs and HIV/AIDS, promoting sustainable organic agriculture, working as orthopedic doctors, promoting women and development, or assisting local development projects.

Special skills or requirements: Volunteers must be at least 18 years old. No experience is required.

Commentary: An orientation program, conducted by Prime Care Network, is a compulsory part of each volunteer's work program. Volunteers are expected to arrive in time to begin this orientation, which is held two or three days before the start of volunteer work.

Quest

3706 Rhode Island Avenue
Mount Rainier, MD 20712
(301) 277-2514; Fax (301) 277-8656
E-mail: info@quest-rjm.org
Web site: www.quest-rjm.org

Project location: Haiti.

Project type: Established in 1971, Quest provides summer and year-long opportunities for lay and religious volunteers to live together in community and collaborate in ministry among the poor and marginalized. The goal of Quest is to provide concrete, realistic, and ongoing work with the poor in the context of a faith community, so that volunteers develop a critical social consciousness that will enable and enhance their effective work for justice.

Project costs: Summer volunteers: Room and board provided by Quest. Volunteers pay their personal expenses during service and provide their airfare to and from Haiti. A passport, vaccinations, and other health care needs are the responsibility of the volunteer. Long-term volunteers: Room, board, a small stipend, and medical insurance are provided by Quest.

Project dates: The summer program is from late June to early August. The long-term program involves a minimum of a one-year commitment and runs from August to August.

How to apply: Contact the Quest office by phone, fax, e-mail, or mail. Summer applications are due by April 15. Long-term applications are accepted on a rolling basis through July, with priority given to those postmarked by March 31.

Work done by volunteers: All summer volunteers serve as counselors at Kon Klodine (Kreyol for "Camp Claudine"). Long-term volunteers work in a variety of community organizing efforts in Haiti, including health care, gardening, education, youth groups, artisan groups, and reforestation efforts. There are many, many needs in Haiti, and volunteers and Haitians work together to meet these needs.

Special skills or requirements: For the summer program: Volunteers must be at least 18 years old. A high-school diploma is required, and a background in French is helpful. Fundraising is strongly encouraged. For the long-term program: Women aged 21 and older are considered. Flexibility, initiative, and a sense of humor are essential. French is helpful at both sites; Spanish is helpful at one of the sites. Prior service abroad is encouraged. A one-year commitment is required; a second year is encouraged. A high-school diploma is required; a college degree is necessary for some positions.

Rebuilding Together

1536 16th Street NW
Washington DC 20036
(800) 4-REHAB-9 or (202) 483-9083; Fax (202) 483-9081
E-mail: info@rebuildingtogether.org
Web site: www.rebuildingtogether.org

Project location: 880 communities across the United States.

Project type: Rehab and repair the houses of low-income homeowners, particularly the elderly, the disabled, and families with children.

Project costs: Volunteers pay nothing.

Project dates: Year-round, although 90 percent of rehab projects take place on the last Saturday in April (National Rebuilding Day).

How to apply: Find an affiliate near you via the Rebuilding Together Web site.

Work done by volunteers: All aspects of house rehabilitation.

Special skills or requirements: Projects always need some volunteers with special construction skills (roofing, electrical work, plumbing, and such). Volunteers must be at least 14 years old.

Commentary: On an annual basis, more than 8,000 houses and community centers are rehabbed by more than 250,000 volunteers for Rebuilding Together, the nation's largest volunteer organization that restores and revitalizes low-income homes and communities.

Religious Society of Friends, Philadelphia Yearly Meeting

Friends Weekend Work Camps
1515 Cherry Street
Philadelphia, PA 19102
(215) 241-7236
E-mail: Workcamps@pym.org

Project location: Philadelphia.

Project type: Inner-city work camp.

Project costs: $45 for a weekend work camp. Volunteers are responsible for all transportation costs. Room and board are included in the project fee.

Project dates: Weekend camps run monthly. Groups may call to arrange for a camp.

How to apply: Write to the work-camp director at the address listed above for more information and an application. Weekend camps are limited to 18 participants, so apply early.

Work done by volunteers: Volunteers perform a wide variety of activities, from preparing meals and taking care of children at a shelter for homeless women to visiting the elderly and helping people repair their homes.

Special skills or requirements: Anyone aged 15 or older can apply. The organization attempts to bring together as many people from different backgrounds, races, countries, and states as possible, so applicants from outside the Philadelphia area are encouraged to apply.

Commentary: The weekend work camps are an excellent way for volunteers to find out about the work camp experience without making a commitment to go to a foreign land for a longer stay.

Rempart

1, Rue des Guillemites
75004 Paris, France
(33) 1 42-71-96-55; Fax (33) 1 42-71-73-00
E-mail: contact@rempart.com
Web site: www.rempart.com

Project location: More than 150 sites throughout France.

Project type: Archaeological restoration and restoration of historical monuments and sites in France.

Project costs: Vary by site. Most of the sites provide room and board. Volunteers are responsible for transportation costs.

Project dates: Most projects are in July and August. Some sites accept volunteers for as little as one weekend, while some allow two-week stays, and others require volunteers to stay for the entire three-week session.

How to apply: Write to Delegation Nationale de l'Union Rempart at the address listed above for more information and an application. Rempart has a page of information about its organization in English. Program information and the application form are both available on the organization's Web site.

Work done by volunteers: A wide variety of restoration work is done at each site. Some sites also include archaeological excavations.

Special skills or requirements: Volunteers should know at least rudimentary French and be interested in hard work and the cultural heritage of France. Non-French residents must be at least 18 years old to volunteer; French residents may volunteer at age 13.

Commentary: Rempart is the largest organization in France that coordinates the excavation and restoration of historical monuments.

Romanian Children's Relief (Fundatia Inocenti)

P.O. Box 107
Southboro, MA 01772
E-mail: emmc2@aol.com
Web site: www.ultranet.com/~rcr/

Project location: Bucharest and Bistrita, Romania.

Project type: Provide training for staff or families involved with foster children.

Project costs: Volunteers pay all personal costs, including travel and housing.

Project dates: Throughout the year, but volunteer opportunities are extremely limited. Currently, only two are accepted annually.

How to apply: Interested degreed professionals should submit a written volunteer project plan (describe the type of training you will provide, and to whom) along with a resume and three references. Submissions should be addressed to the Board of Directors.

Work done by volunteers: Occupational therapy training (staff and foster families), early childhood education, early literacy training, physical therapy training, and more.

Special skills or requirements: Only degreed professionals are accepted as volunteers.

Commentary: Romania is a very difficult place to live and work. Experience in travel to third-world nations is extremely helpful.

Royal Tyrrell Museum: Day Digs

Box 7500
Drumheller, Alberta Canada T0J 0Y0
(888) 440-4240; Fax (403) 823-7131
E-mail: info@tyrrellmuseum.com
Web site: www.tyrrellmuseum.com

Project location: Drumheller Valley in Canada.

Project type: Dinosaur dig. Participants experience the various activities involved in excavating fossils.

Project costs: CAN $85 for adults, CAN $55 for youth age 10 to 15 (must be accompnied by an adult). Project fee includes room and board, but does not include transportation costs.

Project dates: June through September.

How to apply: Contact the bookings office at bookings@tyrrellmuseum.com.

Commentary: Day Digs fees include transportation to and from the museum and the work site, lunch, snacks, and admission to the Royal Tyrrell Museum. If the program is cancelled due to rain, an alternate indoor program will be made available.

Royal Tyrrell Museum: Field Experience

Box 7500
Drumheller, Alberta Canada T0J 0Y0
(888) 440-4240; Fax (403) 823-7131
E-mail: info@tyrrellmuseum.com
Web site: www.tyrrellmuseum.com

Project location: Dinosaur Provincial Park, a permanent field camp in southern Alberta, Canada. Digs at satellite camps are also offered.

Project type: Dinosaur dig. Participants join Tyrrell scientists and technicians to prospect for and collect fossils.

Project costs: Under CAN $1,000 per week.

Project dates: June through August.

How to apply: Contact the Field Experience coordinator at field-exp@tyrrellmuseum.com.

Special skills or requirements: No special skills are required other than a sincere interest in paleontology, although paleontology students are given priority. Participants range in age from 18 to 55.

Commentary: The program is rigorous and the work can be difficult, but Field Experience is the closest volunteers will come to experiencing the many aspects of paleontology without becoming a paleontologist. Weather permitting, all activities take place outdoors. Summer in southern Alberta can be hot and dry, and participants should be able to withstand the midday heat.

La Sabranenque Restoration Projects

Rue de la Tour de l'Oume
30290 Saint Victor la Coste, France
(33) 0-466 50-05-05; Fax (33) 0-466 50-12-48
E-mail: info@sabranenque.com
Web site: www.sabranenque.com
or
c/o Jacqueline C. Simon
217 High Park Boulevard
Buffalo, NY 14226
(716) 836-8698

Project location: Several sites in Saint Victor la Coste, near Avignon, in southern France. Two sites in Italy—one in Gnallo, a small hamlet in northern Italy, and one in Altamura, in the south.

Project type: Restoration of simple monuments, small structures, villages, and sites that are typical of the traditional regional architecture, such as medieval chapels, old village buildings, and other structures that are the property of villages and nonprofit organizations.

Project costs: $550 for a two-week project. Room and board are provided in the project fee, but airfare is not.

Project dates: Two-week sessions in June, July, and August. A three-week session is offered in July.

How to apply: Contact one of the addresses listed above for more information and an application.

Work done by volunteers: Volunteers participate directly in restoration projects, learn building skills on the job, and become part of an international team. Specific projects depend on the volunteer's time of arrival, since all projects are ongoing.

Special skills or requirements: No previous experience is necessary; very few volunteers have any previous building experience. The project organizers speak French, English, and Italian. Volunteers must be at least 18 years old.

Commentary: Projects offer participants the opportunity to enter into the life of Mediterranean villages while taking an active part in practical, cooperative, and creative projects. Volunteers live in houses in Saint Victor la Coste and at Italian sites.

Samaritans International

12302 East Beverly Boulevard
Whittier, CA 90601
(562) 568-0230; Fax (562) 695-6193
E-mail: Samsinternational@hotmail.com

Project location: Throughout the developing world, but primarily in Mexico.

Project type: Work camps and evangelical ministries.

Project costs: Generally between $200 and $500, plus transportation. Project fees include room and board.

Project dates: Mostly in the summer for one or two weeks.

How to apply: Write to Joyce Mullenbach at the address listed above for more information and an application.

Samaritans International volunteers begin construction of a church in Baja, California. (Photo courtesy of Samaritans International)

Work done by volunteers: Most projects involve building churches and chapels. Evangelism is a second major activity.

Special skills or requirements: Volunteers must be Christians who are interested in evangelism in the Third World. Volunteers under 14 years old must be accompanied by a parent or guardian.

Commentary: Although the Samaritans' ministry has been completely reorganized recently, it has been in service since 1967. With reorganization, it may be expanding its volunteer programs.

Santa Fe National Forest, Pecos–Las Vegas Ranger District, Wilderness and Trails Program

P.O. Drawer 429
Pecos, NM 87552
(505) 757-6121
E-mail: tgass@fs.fed.us

Project location: Santa Fe National Forest in Pecos, New Mexico.
Project type: Conservation.
Project costs: Housing or a trailer site might be available. A stipend is paid for backcountry work involving overnight stays. Camping gear is provided for overnight field work. All travel, food, and other normal living expenses are borne by the volunteer.
Project dates: Various projects are available at different times of the year. Field work is primarily during the summer and early fall.
How to apply: Contact Toby Gass or John Buehler at the phone number or address listed above.
Work done by volunteers: A wide variety of opportunities are available, including patrolling the Pecos wilderness, trail maintenance, trail reconstruction, entering and processing GPS or other data, inventorying conditions and collecting GPS data in the wilderness, maintaining horse tack and facilities and recreation signs, and cataloging old photographs.
Special skills or requirements: Depends on the job. Field work requires excellent physical condition and backpacking or horsepacking skills in a high-altitude alpine environment. Volunteers must be at least 18 years old.

Sierra Club National Outings

85 Second Street, 2nd Floor
San Francisco, CA 94105
(415) 977-5522; Fax (415) 977-5795
E-mail: national.outings@sierraclub.org
Web site: www.sierraclub.org/outings/national/

Project location: Throughout the United States and Canada in beautiful wilderness areas such as Grand Canyon National Park in Arizona, Glacier National Park in Montana, Acadia National Park in Maine, and the Canadian Rockies and Puerto Rico.

Project type: Cleanup, trail maintenance, research, and wilderness restoration.

Project costs: The average trip price is $275 to $755 and generally includes accommodations and most meals. Volunteers are responsible for all transportation to and from the trip sites.

Project dates: Year-round. Stays usually last for 7 to 10 days.

How to apply: Contact the organization via phone, e-mail, mail, or the Web site to make a reservation.

Work done by volunteers: Volunteers generally do manual labor such as trail building and maintenance, wilderness area cleanup and revegetation, archaeological work, campsite restoration, and wildlife research.

Special skills or requirements: Volunteers must be in good physical condition. Some trips require backpacking experience. Minimum age requirements vary from trip to trip, but family outings are available for people with children at least seven years old. See Web site for details.

Commentary: Sierra Club trips continue to be very popular among people who are interested in giving back to nature while simultaneously enjoying the beauty of the great outdoors. The club aspires to maintain the highest standards of conduct, regulatory compliance, and minimum-impact travel in the wilderness. Sierra Club trips are led by skilled volunteers and serve as a noncommercial means of educating people about the value of wilderness preservation and environmental protection. The Sierra Club is a non-profit organization. The Outings Program does not financially support other operations of the Sierra Club. Trip prices are comprised of the direct costs of operating the trip and an allocated portion of the indirect (administrative) costs associated with the operations of the Outings Program.

Sample projects: For a sacred experience among ancient ruins and artifacts, journey with the Sierra Club to the Southwest. Participants take part in trail work, archaeological preservation, and recording of primitive cultures in mystical areas such as Chaco Culture National Historical Park in New Mexico, Mesa Verde National Park in Colorado, Coconino National Forest in Arizona, and the vast canyon complex of Grand Gulch in Utah. For those who need to be near water, the National Lakeshore Service in Michigan, Green River Rafting Service in Colorado's Dinosaur National Monument, or Wild and Scenic Green River Service in Kentucky's Mammoth Cave National Park might be just the answer. Urban adventurers should consider the New York City Parks Service Trip: do park work in the city's natural spaces and enjoy the added bonus of comprehensive city tours and time off to explore the Big Apple. Wildlife lovers can put their skills to good use and get closer to nature's creatures on trips such as the Humpback Whales Service Trip on Maui, the Midway Dolphin or Seabird Research trip, or the Hawk Mountain Sanctuary Trip in Pennsylvania.

Service Civil International–International Voluntary Service (SCI/IVS)

3213 West Wheeler Street, #384
Seattle, WA 98199
Tel/Fax (206) 350-6585
E-mail: sciinfo@sci-ivs.org
Web site: www.sci-ivs.org

*Project location*s: Worldwide in approximately 70 countries.

*Project type*s: Work camps and medium- to long-term placements (three months to one year).

Project costs: There is an application fee of $65 for U.S. and Canadian camps, $125 for overseas camps. Transportation to the site is at the volunteer's expense, but room and board are provided.

Project dates: May through October, for two to four weeks. A few camps may be available during other months.

How to apply: Send a request for a free information booklet and list of summer work camps (published in late March) to the address listed above, or apply via the organization's Web site.

Work done by volunteers: Physical or social work; varies by camp.

Special skills or requirements: Campers in United States work camps must be at least 16 years old; in others, at least 18 years old. There is no upper age limit.

Commentary: SCI/IVS provides a way for people of different countries to develop close friendships in the process of doing valuable community service. Through practical and enjoyable work, volunteers live the challenge of international cooperation on a personal level.

The Share Centre

Smith's Strand, Lisnaskea
Co. Fermanagh, Northern Ireland BT92 OEQ
(0044) 28 677 22122
E-mail: info@sharevillage.org
Web site: www.sharevillage.org

Project location: Northern Ireland.

Project type: Work with the disabled, including participation in outdoor sports, arts and crafts, catering, and groundskeeping.

Project costs: Volunteers are provided food, shared accommodations, and a weekly stipend. Transportation to and from Ireland is at the volunteer's expense.

Project dates: April to October.

How to apply: Contact the volunteer coordinator at the address or e-mail listed above. Send a resume and a letter detailing your relevant experience and interests.

Work done by volunteers: Assisting staff in running art and outdoor sessions with guests of the Share Centre. Volunteers take part in all aspects of Share's work.

Special skills or requirements: Volunteers need to be motivated, enthusiastic, and willing to take on all types of work. Experience with outdoor sports is helpful. There is no minimum age requirement for volunteers.

Commentary: Volunteers are asked to work a normal 40-hour 5-day week, including weekends and some evenings as well.

Simon Community of Ireland

28–30 Exchequer Street
Dublin 2, Ireland
(00353) 1 671 1606; Fax (00353) 1 671 1098
E-mail: simon@simoncommunity.com
Web site: www.simoncommunity.com

Project location: Cork, Dublin, Dundalk, and Galway.

Project type: Working with the homeless.

Project costs: Volunteers must pay for their own airfare to Dublin both for an interview and to work. Room, board, and a small weekly stipend are provided to long-term volunteers.

Project dates: Year-round, for a minimum six-month commitment.

How to apply: Contact the office listed above for an application form.

Work done by volunteers: Residential work including befriending the homeless, housework, advocacy, and administration. Volunteers work as part of a team.

Special skills or requirements: Excellent communication skills, respect, and a commitment to working, in an empowering way, alongside people who have been marginalized and excluded. Volunteers must be at least 18 years old.

Sioux YMCAs

P.O. Box 218
Dupree, SD 57623
(605) 365-5232; Fax (605) 365-5230
E-mail: info@siouxymca.org
Web site: www.siouxymca.org

Project location: Sioux Reservation communities in North and South Dakota.

Project type: Community development, youth projects, and camping.

Project costs: Volunteers are responsible for travel and personal expenses. Room and board are provided.

Project dates: Volunteers are accepted quarterly for periods of no less than two weeks. Call for starting dates. (Starting dates are set by the YMCA.)

How to apply: Write or call for an application, or download one from the organization's Web site.

Work done by volunteers: Community recreation and support, youth projects, and fund-raising projects. Volunteers operate youth centers, organize community recreational events, assist in schools and Head Start programs, and serve as camp counselors.

Special skills or requirements: Experience working with children is required. Must be flexible, mature, creative, and able to work independently. Individual volunteers must be 18 or older. Groups can come with volunteers under 18 years old, but must have adult chaperones.

Commentary: These projects are sponsored by the only YMCAs operated by and serving primarily Native American people, and volunteers must realize that all projects entail a 24-hour, seven-days-per-week commitment. Because of problems caused by alcohol abuse on the reservation, all volunteers are required to abstain from drinking and drug use during their service. Persons of all religious faiths are accepted as volunteers, but they will be asked to respect and participate in the life of the community.

Siuslaw National Forest

4077 Southwest Research Way
Corvallis, OR 97333
(541) 750-7000; TDD (541) 750-7006; Fax (541) 750-7234
Web site: www.fs.fed.us/r6/siuslaw

Project location: Forest Service campgrounds and interpretive centers along the Oregon coast, between Tillamook and North Bend.

Project type: Campground hosting and maintenance and serving as natural resource and natural history interpreters.

Project costs: Volunteers are responsible for transportation to and from the Central Oregon coast. Housing may be provided to volunteers who meet minimum time commitment requirements. A small stipend may be available to volunteers. Campground hosts provide their own trailer or RV to live in, but are generally provided campsites with hook-ups. Volunteers must provide their own food.

Project dates: Most positions are from May to October for varying periods of time. There may be some year-round positions.

How to apply: For general information, descriptions of specific positions, and an application, those interested in being campground hosts in the South Zone should contact Wayne Gale at (541) 271-6080. For interpreter positions in the South Zone, contact the interpretive specialist at (541) 902-8526. Those interested in being campground hosts and interpreters in the Hebo Ranger District should contact Carol Johnson at (503) 392-3161.

Work done by volunteers: As campground hosts, caretakers, and natural resource and natural history interpreters, volunteers assist the Zone recreation and interpretation staff with visitor contacts and campground maintenance.

Special skills or requirements: Varies by positions. Volunteers must be U.S. citizens. Volunteers under 18 years old must have the written consent of a parent or guardian. All positions require good physical condition and some knowledge, skill, and experience in the outdoors. Good communication and people skills are preferred. An interest in off-highway vehicles is preferred in some campground host positions.

Commentary: The Siuslaw National Forest consists of the North and the South Zones (comprised of the Waldport and Mapleton Ranger Districts and the Oregon Dunes National Recreation Area on the southern end), and the Hebo Ranger District in the north. Campgrounds are generally traditional campgrounds, although some cater to off-highway-vehicle enthusiasts. There are two visitor centers in the South Zone. One is the Oregon Dunes National Recreation Area Visitor Center, located in Reedsport, Oregon; the other is the Cape Perpetua Visitor Center, located within the Cape Perpetua Scenic Area south of Yachats, Oregon.

Société Archéologique de Douai

191, Rue Saint-Albin
59500 Douai, France
(03) 27-71-38-90; Fax (03) 27-71-38-93
E-mail: arkeos@wanadoo.fr

Project location: Douai, France, and surroundings.

Project type: Archaeological excavations.

Project costs: Volunteers are responsible for all travel expenses, plus EUR23 for insurance and registration fees. Room and board are provided.

Project dates: July and August. Contact the organization for exact dates.

How to apply: Write to the address listed above for more information and an application. Applications must be received by June 1.

Work done by volunteers: Archaeological excavation work.

Special skills or requirements: No special skills are required, although experienced workers are welcome and will be assigned more complex tasks. Volunteers must be at least 18 years old. Volunteers will find French language ability to be helpful, but English is spoken widely in the camp.

Commentary: This project involves two excavations of medieval urban and small town sites. The work is an attempt to gain a better understanding of everyday life in towns during the Middle Ages.

Sousson Foundation

3600 Ridge Road
Templeton, CA 93465
(805) 434-0299; Fax (805) 434-3444
E-mail: info@sousson.org
Web site: www.sousson.org

Project location: Yosemite, Sequoia, Kings Canyon, Channel Islands (off California's southern coast), and Hawaii Volcanoes National Parks. Other parks are added periodically.

Project type: Conservation of habitats of endangered species and biodiversity preservation in the national parks.

Project costs: $595 and up, depending on the trip. The fee includes meals, camping equipment, and camping sites. Visit the organization's Web site for costs of specific outings.

Project dates: Most trips are held from April through early October for six to eight days. Trips to Hawaii are longer and are held year-round.

How to apply: Contact the office listed above for an application and information, or visit the Web site.

Work done by volunteers: Projects vary depending on the park. Typically, volunteers work on habitat restoration, revegetation, tree planting, construction, and restoring historic facilities and trails.

Special skills or requirements: No special skills are needed, although gardening and construction skills are always useful. Sousson Foundation accepts groups and individuals of any age or background. There are special programs for junior high and high-school teachers as well as for families. Children eight years of age and older are welcome.

Commentary: Trips are designed so that half of the week is devoted to working on the projects and the other half to enjoying the spectacular outdoors. Sousson Foundation strives to create a friendly environment where volunteers can get to know each other.

South Dakota Game and Fish Parks

523 East Capitol Avenue
Pierre, SD 57501
(605) 773-3391; Fax (605) 773-6245
E-mail: lynn.spomer@state.sd.us
Web site: www.state.sd.us/gfp/sdparks

Project location: Thoughout South Dakota.

Project type: Camp hosts, maintenance volunteers, special project volunteers, and special event volunteers.

Project costs: None. Volunteers are provided a free campsite with electrical hookup, but are responsible for their own transportation and food.

Project dates: April through October. Volunteers work a minimum of one month.

How to apply: Call or e-mail Lynn Spomer at the address listed above. Volunteers may also apply on-line via the organization's Web site.

Work done by volunteers: Cleaning, mowing, visiting with campers, selling firewood and park entrance licenses, working at the entrance booth, and trail maintenance.

Special skills or requirements: Volunteers must be able to positively interact with the public. There is no minimum age for volunteers.

Commentary: All volunteers except special project and special event volunteers are required to work 24 hours per week.

Student Conservation Association (SCA)

Conservation Crew Program
P.O. Box 550
Charlestown, NH 03603
(603) 543-1700; Fax (603) 543-1828
E-mail: crews@sca-inc.org
Web site: www.sca-inc.org

Project location: National parks, national forests, wilderness areas, and other conservation sites throughout the United States.

Project type: Environmental and cultural conservation and management of public lands and natural resources.

Project costs: SCA provides all food and group camping equipment during the project. Participants must provide their own individual camping gear and hiking boots, as well as travel to the site. Financial aid is available to assist with travel expenses. Those who are selected to participate must have a physical examination at their own expense.

Project dates: June, July, and August, typically for four to five weeks.

How to apply: Request an application from SCA. A list of projects is published in November/December and can be mailed, but it also available and regularly updated on the organization's Web site. The application deadline for projects is March 1; however, placements begin in early January. Apply early for optimal consideration.

Work done by volunteers: The work is usually physically challenging and may include trail or bridge construction, ecological restoration and revegetation, stream bank stabilization, and wildlife and fish habitat improvement.

Special skills or requirements: Applicants must be 15 to 19 years old and in high school (including graduating seniors), physically fit, and willing to undertake the challenges of hard work and rustic living conditions as part of a group.

Commentary: Through this program, SCA currently fields more than 600 volunteers each year with the National Park Service, the United States Forest Service, and other agencies. Volunteers serve in crews of eight to ten students with two trained adult SCA supervisors. They live in a tent camp, feeding and caring for themselves, usually in a remote location, for the duration of the work period. The work is followed by a one-week recreational trip, most often a hike, allowing the crew to explore its surroundings. This program offers unique rewards and opportunities for personal growth.

Sample projects: Projects change from year to year. In the past, volunteers have restored campsites and maintained trails on a roadless island on Lake Superior in Isle Royale National Park, Michigan. Others built a walkway for visitors inside Cottonwood Cave while camping on the surface in the Lincoln National Forest, New Mexico. Others have worked in the Pike/San Isabel National Forest, Colorado, constructing a segment of the Continental Divide Trail. Work sites are also in Hawaii, Alaska, Maine, and Wyoming.

How Volunteering in the Mojave Desert Really Did Change My Life

❖ by Jessie Tamayo (age 16) ❖

Student Conservation Association (SCA) Conservation Crew Program

I am not the same person I was just a few weeks ago; that's what a month in the Mojave Desert as a Student Conservation Association (SCA) Volunteer on a Desert Restoration Crew will do for you. It was awesome. It was so worth it!

Our job was to restore and occasionally just disguise areas of designated wilderness that had been trespassed upon and damaged by all-terrain vehicles, motorcycles, and bikes. We accomplished this through some innovative revegetation techniques. For example, some of us would form a Joshua Tree Crew that would "plant" huge, dead Joshua Trees in the middle of wide open areas because they did such a good job of disrupting the illegal trails that cut through the wilderness. Then there were the Texturites, crew members who would hack away with picks to create small holes in the ground to plant brush and cacti, and even smaller ones to catch seeds and serve as homes for tiny animals and insects, because we wanted nature to recapture these tracts of land. I'll never forget stepping back from repairing a route and looking at the before and after pictures. It was so clear we were making a difference.

We had the most deluxe camp ever. Perched atop a mesa, it featured a great kitchen area, two shade tents, an L.L. Bean mosquito net, and our own individual tents. But we never slept in tents. It was too beautiful outside. We would sleep out on tarps and watch the stars. I learned so much out there. I think a lot more about what I'm doing now and how my actions affect the world around me. I'm more conservation-conscious. In the desert we didn't have running water, just five-gallon jugs. That makes an impression on you. I've already convinced my family back in New Jersey to curtail their water usage. We also rely less on air conditioning—although that's kind of a controversial issue around the house. I returned home much more confident and aware of my abilities. I realize there's so much I can do with my life; I just don't know if I'll have enough time to do everything I want to do. Tops on my list is another stint with SCA. I'll never forget getting off the plane after landing in New Jersey. I looked up and said, "No! The stars! You can't see them at all!" And that's why I'll be back, SCA. I want to see the stars again!

Student Conservation Association (SCA) Conservation Internships

P.O. Box 550
Charlestown, NH 03603
(603) 543-1700; Fax (603) 543-1828
E-mail: internships@sca-inc.org
Web site: www.sca-inc.org

Project location: National parks, national forests, wilderness areas, and other conservation sites throughout the United States.

Project type: Environmental and cultural conservation and management of public lands and natural resources; positions in more than 50 disciplines are available. See the searchable database of positions on the SCA Web site for specifics.

Project costs: SCA provides a travel stipend to the service site, paid housing and related expenses, a weekly living stipend, free or low-cost accident and health insurance, academic credit, and AmeriCorps education awards of $1,180 to $4,725 (depending upon length of service). It may also provide a student loan deferment.

Project dates: Three- to twelve-month positions start throughout the year. There is a rolling admissions process, so apply anytime. More than 1,500 conservation internships are available annually.

How to apply: Obtain an application from SCA's Web site, or call or e-mail the office listed above.

Special skills or requirements: Applicants must be at least 18 years old and have a high school diploma or its equivalent. Individual position requirements vary; see specific position descriptions on the Web site for further details.

Commentary: Through this program, SCA currently fields approximately 1,500 conservation interns each year with the National Park Service, the United States Forest Service, and other agencies.

Sample projects: Some positions change from year to year, or may be added. In the past, SCA Conservation Interns have participated in fresh-water sampling research in Oregon; worked with policy makers on Capitol Hill with the House Environmental Committee; studied sea turtles and piping plovers in Georgia; developed environmental education programs for young people in coastal Maine; led tours and interpreted history along the route of the Lewis and Clark expedition in the Dakotas; educated the public on preventing forest fires; lead home inspections in Idaho or Nevada; and patrolled rivers by canoe, taking photographs of historic sites in New York's Hudson Valley.

Sunseed Desert Technology

c/o Xandra Gilchrist
89 Rugby Road
Milverton, Leamington Spa CV32 6DH, United Kingdom
Tel/Fax (0044) 1926 421380
E-mail: sunseedspain@arrakis.es
Web site: www.sunseed.org.uk

Project location: Almeria, in the province of Andalucia, in southeast Spain.

Project type: Organic gardening, desert reclamation, sustainable lifestyle research, practical environmental work, and low-tech research work developing technologies to assist people living on degraded land.

How to apply: Prospective volunteers are advised to first visit the Web site listed above, then write for more information. Send a large stamped, self-addressed envelope to receive an application form, up-to-date costs, and more information about the nature of the work that Sunseed does.

Project costs: Costs vary depending on length of stay, time of year, and whether the volunteer is otherwise employed. Longer stays are cheaper on a per-week basis, and it is less expensive to volunteer in winter. Costs range from £42 per week to £98 per week. Project fees include food, but volunteers are responsible for their own travel expenses. For more details, see the Web site or call the office listed above.

Work done by volunteers: Organic gardening; tree planting; maintaining renewable power systems, reed beds, and compost toilets; communal tasks such as cooking and cleaning (which all workers at Sunseed do); site maintenance and construction; and assisting with publications, publicity, and fundraising work. Volunteers with specific interests who want to stay for longer periods of time may be able to arrange projects to suit their interests. Students are also accepted to carry out their own projects, although no formal tutoring is offered. Each volunteer works under the supervision of a voluntary staff member and with the assistance of working visitors.

Special skills or requirements: None; all are appreciated. There is no minimum age to volunteer; fees for children under 16 are on a sliding scale by age.

Commentary: The work can be hard and the living conditions are basic. Volunteers should be prepared to share bathrooms and possibly bedrooms, and to use compost toilets. The research carried out is low tech; do not expect lab coats! An important part of volunteering with Sunseed is experiential learning, so volunteers learn about the technologies by living with them and using them.

Sample projects: Work completed by recent full-time volunteers includes the following: Claudia built a solar water heating system; Jos renovated and added to the wastewater treatment system; Helen wrote a small publication on solar water heating; Allan refurbished and extended two buildings using traditional local materials and techniques; and Sadie assisted in the running of the organic terrace gardens.

Tahoe Rim Trail Association

DWR Community Non-Profit Center
948 Incline Way
Incline Village, NV 89451
(775) 298-0012; Fax (775) 298-0013
E-mail: infol@tahoerimtrail.org
Web site: www.tahoerimtrail.org

Project location: Lake Tahoe in California and Nevada.

Project type: Trail maintenance on 164 miles of existing trail.

Project costs: Volunteers pay for all transportation and other expenses (including housing and meals). The association provides tools and training.

Project dates: July through mid-October.

How to apply: Contact the office for information.

Work done by volunteers: Trail maintenance consists of a beautiful hike to the work location, cutting brush, breaking ground for rerouted trails, moving rocks and stumps, cleaning up existing trail, removing hazards from the trail, and similar duties. The workday usually begins at 9:00 A.M. and ends at 3:00 P.M.

Special skills or requirements: Volunteers must be in good physical health to hike and work at 7,000- to 9,000-foot elevations. Volunteers must be equipped with work gloves, long pants, long-sleeved shirts, and sturdy boots. There is no minimum age requirement, but children under age 18 must have a waiver signed by a parent or guardian.

Commentary: The Tahoe Rim Trail is a 164-mile loop trail that stretches along the ridge tops of the Lake Tahoe basin. The Tahoe Rim Trail Association has used volunteers to plan and build the trail, which was completed in the fall of 2001. The organization has pledged to be the trail steward and caretaker, preserving it for hiking, mountain biking, and horseback riding.

Teaching and Projects Abroad

19 Cullen Drive
West Orange, NJ 07052
(888) 839-3535
E-mail: info@teaching-abroad.org
Web site: www.teaching-abroad.org

Project location: Mexico, Peru, Ghana, Togo, South Africa, India, Nepal, Mongolia, Thailand, China, Romania, Russia, and Ukraine.

Project type: Teaching, conservation, medicine, veterinary medicine, journalism, archaeology, volcanology, community action, and others.

Project costs: $1,595 to $3,295. Program fees include room and board, but do not include transportation costs.

Project dates: Year-round.

How to apply: Request an application and information packet from the office listed above.

Work done by volunteers: Teaching conversational English, conducting biodiversity studies, saving sea turtles, and various work experiences in media, medicine, and business.

Special skills or requirements: Volunteers must have university entrance qualifications and good spoken English. Volunteers must be at least 15 years old.

A volunteer lines up her class of kindergarten students and prepares to take them out into the yard to brush their teeth. All in a day's work on a small farm in South Africa! (Photo courtesy Teaching and Projects Abroad)

Third World Opportunities

1363 Somermont Drive
El Cajon, CA 92021
(619) 449-9381

Project location: Tijuana, Las Palmas, and Tecate, Mexico.

Project type: Awareness programs about the realities of poverty and hunger in the Third World, and short-term work projects.

Project costs: $225 for the six-day event, plus transportation costs.

Project dates: Awareness trips are year-round, and service projects are in the spring and summer.

How to apply: Contact the office listed above.

Work done by volunteers: Miscellaneous work-oriented service projects such as painting, building maintenance, gardening, road repair, and installation of playground equipment.

Special skills or requirements: Construction skills and a knowledge of Spanish are helpful, but not necessary.

Commentary: The work projects are conducted at two orphanages in Mexico: San Juan Bosco Home for Boys in Tecate, and Miracle Ranch Home for Boys in Las Palmas. These projects are done with volunteer groups of up to 25 participants per work project.

Transformational Journeys

P.O. Box 8571
Kansas City, MO 64114-0857
(816) 361-2111
E-mail: journey@qni.com
Web site: www.tjourneys.com

Project location: Brazil, Dominican Republic, Guatemala, Kenya, Honduras.

Project type: Various kinds of one- to three-week mission trips.

Project costs: $1,200 to $3,000, depending on destination and duration of trip. Project costs include room and board as well as airfare from a major city in the United States. Volunteers must pay their own transportation to the city of departure.

Project dates: Twelve trips are planned throughout the year; see the organization's Web site for details.

How to apply: Via the Web site.

Work done by volunteers: The following are example projects. In Brazil, volunteers developed and funded the Friends Forever Center in Recife, which offers educational programs for children in that area. In the Dominican Republic, volunteers worked on Habitat for Humanity home construction and led Vacation Bible Schools in Barahona and Paraiso. In Guatemala, volunteers erected four community centers for the people of San Lucas and San Andres. In Kenya, volunteers built a playground for the Sisters of Charity Orphanage in Nairobi. Currently they are also developing projects in Honduras.

Special skills or requirements: A desire to help others is essential. Volunteers under the age of 12 must be accompanied by parents.

Commentary: Transformational Journey's mission is to create vision, inspire compassion, and promote generosity through mutual service with people in other cultures.

Unitarian Universalist Service Committee (UUSC)—Just Works Workcamp Program

130 Prospect Street
Cambridge, MA 02139
(800) 388-3920 or (617) 868-6600; Fax (617) 868-7102
E-mail: justworks@uusc.org
Web site: www.uusc.org

Project location: Throughout the continental United States.

Project type: All projects relate directly to human rights and social justice. Specifically, projects include burned-church rebuilding (construction), farm-worker projects (migrant and permanent), youth and children education, and Native American projects.

Project costs: $275 per week. Some limited scholarships are available. Room and board are included in the project cost, but transportation to the work-camp city is the responsibility of the volunteer.

Project dates: Spring, summer, and fall; please contact the office listed above for exact dates.

How to apply: Contact UUSC for an application, or download one from its Web site.

Work done by volunteers: Playground construction, community development, church reconstruction, and tutoring.

Special skills or requirements: None required—training is provided when necessary. Most work camps have a minimum age of 16.

Commentary: Just Works Workcamp programs are short-term projects that help volunteers examine and understand the causes and damaging effects of injustice. Participants work directly with people in the communities they serve, experiencing social justice struggles firsthand. While learning about human rights issues and promoting intercultural understanding and reconciliation, volunteers are taught advocacy skills to address issues of poverty, discrimination, and racism. Participants may then make use of these skills in their congregations, campuses, and communities. The Just Works Workcamp program is an important element in the UUSC's mission to advance justice and protect human rights in the United States and around the world. Since 1996, the Unitarian Universalist Service Committee has operated more than 25 work camps across the United States. The program has provided hands-on learning for more than 2,000 people from around the country, as well as overseas, to work on issues of racial, social, and economic injustice.

Sample projects: In July 2001, 25 volunteers and staff participated in a community development project in the Yakima Valley of Washington to build playgrounds for farm worker's children. Over the last six years, volunteers have participated in 14 church rebuilding projects, reconstructing churches that were often victims of racially motivated arson. In August 2001, the UUSC worked on an educational program for children on the La Jolla Indian Reservation near San Diego, California.

A Playground Paradigm Shift

❖ by Heather Robb ❖

Unitarian Universalist Service Committee (UUSC)—Just Works Workcamp Program

The Scene: A stunning backdrop of watercolor skies and Maxfield Parish–esque blue and pink clouds.

The mountains stood tall and brown against the sky. The small town of Crewport, Washington sat nestled between the surrounding mountains. In a building in the town, a man stood expectantly in front of a group of 20-some youth and adults awaiting an answer that does not come. The question had struck us all dumb. For a rambunctious group of UUSC youth, we were miraculously quiet. Lyle wanted the answer that none of us were yet prepared to give. A sweet girl named Ellie had raised her hand and answered his previous question the way any of us in the room would have: "I want to help the people of Crewport because they are less fortunate than me. I want to learn about a new culture and share my experiences with my community at home." Lyle smiled knowingly at her response. "All right Ellie, and how do you think that answer would sound to the people of Crewport?" In retrospect, I don't see how a statement like Ellie's could have received the approving nods and muttered agreement that it had from myself and the rest of the youth. Suddenly Ellie's answer didn't sound so sweet—it sounded condescending, ignorant, and disrespectful. The rest of us were speechless, knowing we all would have answered the way Ellie had. We sat silently, searching desperately for an answer that didn't sound so patronizing. "Think of it this way," Lyle offered, "We are not saving poor destitute people who cannot save themselves. We are helping them build a community, because without community the world is nothing."

The scene: An hour-long bus ride through the irrigated desert.

Our destination—Crewport, our first day on the site. At that point, we had yet to be disillusioned of our benevolent, super-hero self-images. The majority of us still believed fully that we were on a noble mission to save the poverty-stricken from their dire straits. Our trite middle-class preconceptions of "poverty" were turned on their heads that first day in Crewport. We left not quite knowing what to think—the area did not appear the way many of us had pictured it would. The most common reaction: "They didn't seem all that poor." Poor, in this case, was a relative term. Until that day, our definitions of "poor" came from things we had only read about or had seen on television. We expected, I suppose, a scene not unlike those in the heart-wrenching television infomercials that portray small communities of makeshift shelters made of cardboard and dirty sheets, where people, half starving, drink out of dirty puddles and doe-eyed children stare blankly at the camera. We found a community that did not meet those expectations. The houses were not beautiful, but they were sturdy. The children were not starving, but energetic and enthusiastic, and very eager to help. There may have been dirty puddles, but they were hidden in the shadows of the lush, lovely gardens that flourished in every yard. It was not the kind of poverty we had seen on television. The poverty in Crewport was not easy to see. It did not throw itself in your face and solicit your immediate sympathy. It was much more subtle, making itself known in ways that weren't always easy to see upon first glance. Looking at one of the houses in Crewport, you would never have known that the family living inside had been without water for two days. You would never have known that its inhabitants, young and old, rose from the places they slept, in beds or on the floor, not knowing whether they would have a job that day. You would not have known that the children inside had watched their father get arrested and taken away by immigration, not knowing whether they would ever see him again. You would not have known that the people in these houses woke up every day in fear of their neighbors and all the people around them. By simply looking at Crewport, you would never know the painful conditions in which its inhabitants lived every day. So much was hiding behind the facade of their pretty white fences, sturdy roofs, and colorful flowerbeds.

The scene: The days passed hot and dry and on we worked.

Pulling, sawing, creating, growing, and building. Bit by bit the playground grew. Its progress seemed to manifest the unseen growth that was occurring on every level. The monkey bars took shape one day and that evening, at a fiesta we attended, I spoke Spanish with a Mexican woman as she taught me how to fry real taco shells from tortillas. I watched my peers laugh, smile, dance, and play with the children for whom they were building the playground. The next thing I knew, the swing set was up and running. It's amazing how quickly things can happen when people truly care about what they are doing and the goal they are working toward.

The truth: The work camp was a valuable experience on so many levels for every single person involved.

I know that the lives of the people in Crewport will improve because of the playground we built. And, as I said before, I am not giving our group full credit for that progress, but I do believe that our presence helped jump-start it. For those of us who volunteered, this experience was a reminder of how much goes on without our knowing. It reinforced the fact that we lead extremely sheltered lives and that, unless we make the effort to break out of our shells and learn what truly goes on in the world, we will live forever in our complacent ignorance. Crewport and other communities like it are overlooked by the government and society because the consensus seems to be that it is easier to simply ignore situations we label irrevocably doomed. My experience in Washington made me see that any effort, no matter how small or large, is significant in its own way. You don't have to reverse the effects of global warming or settle the disputes in the Middle East to have a positive impact on the world. Little steps toward a big goal are the best way to get where you're going—patience and perseverance are what will ultimately get you there. In the words of Margaret Mead, "Never doubt that a small group of thoughtful, committed citizens can change the world; indeed, it's the only thing that ever has."

We were not superheroes in Crewport—we did not swoop in and right every wrong in the community. We may have been the catalysts of some change, but we are not the ones who will ultimately make Crewport a better place. That will be done by the very people who live there. They have the will and the desire; our playground merely gave them inspiration. By the end of our first day in Crewport, I was convinced that the people living there are just as eager to help themselves as we were to help them. That was probably the most significant lesson I learned: sometimes the best way to help others is to give them the opportunity to help themselves.

United Children's Fund, Inc.

P.O. Box 20341
Boulder, CO 80308-3341
Tel/fax (888) 343-3199
E-mail: united@unchildren.org
Web site: www.unchildren.org

Project location: Kiwangala Village, Uganda, East Africa.

Project type: Education, medical assistance, village support, small cottage industry work, and building.

Project costs: Cost depends on length of stay. One month is $1,850.

Project dates: At this time, the project is ongoing, but it may be limited to summer months in the future.

How to apply: Contact the office listed above by mail or phone, or via the Web site.

Work done by volunteers: Teaching, construction, medical assistance, and help with local village projects.

Special skills or requirements: No skills are required, just the desire to help others.

United Nations Volunteers

Postfach 260 111
D-53153 Bonn, Germany
(49) 228 815 2000; Fax (49) 228 815 2001
E-mail: enquiry@unvolunteers.org
Web site: www.unvolunteers.org

Project location: Projects are located throughout the world; the organization's headquarters are in Bonn, Germany.

Project type: Various volunteer activities for peace, development, education, the environment, human rights, health, and more.

Project costs: Volunteer costs are paid by the organization. If selected, costs of the volunteer are covered.

Project dates: Projects typically range from two weeks to two years.

How to apply: Visit the Web site listed above, or send a resume to the e-mail address listed above.

Work done by volunteers: A wide variety of volunteer assignments range from technical and logistical work to community mobilization, electoral support, and conflict resolution.

University of Alaska, Anchorage, Department of Anthropology

3211 Providence Drive
Anchorage, AK 99508
(907) 786-6845; Fax (907) 786-6850
E-mail: afdry@uaa.alaska.edu

Project location: Broken Mammoth site, at the confluence of Shaw Creek and Tanana Rivers, 20 miles north of Delta Junction, Alaska.

Project type: Archaeological excavation.

Project costs: Participants are responsible for transportation to Anchorage and $30 per day for food and miscellaneous expenses.

Project dates: Generally around June, for five or six weeks.

How to apply: Write to David Yesner, Department of Anthropology, at the address listed above for an application. Applications must be received by May 1.

Work done by volunteers: Excavation of an eleven-thousand-year-old site containing extinct bison and elk bones and human artifacts.

Special skills or requirements: Volunteers must be at least 18 years old, have a high school diploma, and be in good health. An introductory knowledge of archaeology is helpful, but not mandatory.

Commentary: The project may be canceled if the field school does not have a minimum of 10 students registered. The department is also planning another project near Vladivostok, Russia, working on the earliest maritime site on the Russian Pacific coast.

University Research Expeditions Program (UREP)

University of California
One Shields Avenue
Davis, CA 95616
(530) 757-3529; Fax (530) 757-3537
E-mail: urep@ucdavis.edu
Web site: urep.ucdavis.edu

Project location: Worldwide.

Project type: Scientific research expeditions.

Project costs: Costs vary from $600 to $1,600, plus round-trip transportation to the point of departure.

Project dates: Most projects are held between June and September, but a few are held from January through March. Most are two to three weeks in length.

How to apply: Write to the address listed above for a catalog and an application, or download an application from the organization's Web site.

Work done by volunteers: Volunteers work alongside a project leader and staff, collecting and cataloging information. Fieldwork is often hard, tiring, and repetitive, but it can be very rewarding and exciting.

Special skills or requirements: Previous fieldwork experience is not usually necessary, but some general skills and experience are helpful in getting accepted by this program. Project leaders often ask for wilderness, photographic, drawing, and diving skills. Volunteers must be at least 18 years old; 16- and 17-year-olds can participate with approval from the Program Director and Project Leader.

Commentary: UREP is unique in that it sponsors projects led only by scientists who are employed by some branch of the University of California. Volunteers may be, and are, however, from anywhere in the world.

U.S. Army Corps of Engineers
Volunteer Clearinghouse
P.O. Box 1070
Nashville, TN 37202
(800) 865-8337
E-mail: gayla.mitchell@lrn02.usace.army.mil
Web site: www.orn.usace.army.mil/volunteer

Project location: Nationwide.

Project type: Conservation, outdoor recreation, and natural resources management.

Project costs: Volunteers are responsible for all personal expenses. A free campsite is provided at some locations, however.

Project dates: Year-round.

How to apply: Call the phone number listed above, or sign up via the organization's Web site.

Work done by volunteers: Serve as park or campground hosts, staff visitor centers, conduct educational programs, clean shorelines, restore fish and wildlife habitats, maintain park trails and facilities, participate in special events such as National Public Lands Day, and more.

Special skills or requirements: Friendly people are wanted for positions that involve the public; these volunteers will be trained for their duties. Other skills or requirements depend on the volunteer position. There is no minimum age requirement to volunteer.

U.S. Fish and Wildlife Service

Washington, DC 20240
(703) 358-2043
E-mail: volunteers@fws.gov
Web site: volunteers.fws.gov

Project location: Throughout the United States.

Project type: Conserving, protecting, and enhancing America's fish and wildlife and their habitats.

Project costs: Depends on the individual project.

Project dates: Varies according to project.

How to apply: For information about current volunteer listings, visit the the Web site listed above, or contact the office nearest where you wish to volunteer. The offices and the states they serve are listed in the *Commentary* section below.

Work done by volunteers: Biological and archaeological inventories, recreation planning, population censusing, habitat and facility maintenance, natural resource planning, clerical assistance, environmental education, and community outreach.

Special skills or requirements: Varies by project. There is no minimum age requirement.

Commentary: The United States Fish and Wildlife Service uses thousands of volunteers for a wide range of activities. Volunteers are valuable to the management of our nation's fish and wildlife resources and play a vital role in helping the United States Fish and Wildlife Service fulfill its mission. The volunteer program increases public understanding and appreciation through hands-on experience. The regional offices are as follows.

Volunteer Coordinator (AK)
U.S. Fish and Wildlife Service
1011 East Tudor Road
Anchorage, AK 99503
(907) 786-3542

Volunteer Coordinator (CO, KS, MT, NE, ND, SD, UT, WY)
U.S. Fish and Wildlife Service
Denver Federal Center, Box 25486
Denver, CO 80225
(303) 236-8145 ext. 606

Volunteer Coordinator (IA, IL, IN, MI, MN, MO, OH, WI)
U.S. Fish and Wildlife Service
1 Federal Drive, Federal Building
Fort Snelling, MN 55111
(612) 713-5167

Volunteer Coordinator (CT, DE, MA, ME, NH, NJ, NY, PA, RI, VT, VA, WV)
U.S. Fish and Wildlife Service
300 Westgate Drive
Hadley, MA 10135
(413) 253-8303

Volunteer Coordinator (CA, HI, ID, NV, OR, WA)
U.S. Fish and Wildlife Service
911 NE 11th Avenue
Eastside Federal Complex
Portland, OR 97232-4181
(503) 231-6121

Volunteer Coordinator (AL, AR, FL, GA, KY, LA, MS, NC, SC, TN, PR)
U.S. Fish and Wildlife Service
1875 Century Boulevard NW
Atlanta, GA 30345
(404) 679-4000

Volunteer Coordinator (AZ, NM, OK, TX)
U.S. Fish and Wildlife Service
P.O. Box 1306
Albuquerque, NM 87103
(505) 248-6635

U.S. Forest Service (USFS)—Volunteers in the National Forests

P.O. Box 96090, Room 1010 RPE
Washington, DC 20090-6090
(202) 205-1760
Web site: www.fs.fed.us

Project location: Throughout the United States

Project type: A wide variety of projects are available, including archaeological excavation, campground hosting, office work, trail work, tree planting, backcountry ranger work, and taking photographs.

Project costs: Volunteers are usually responsible for all transportation and living expenses, but if funds are available, incidental expenses such as transportation, lodging, subsistence, and uniforms may be reimbursed on a case-by-case basis.

Project dates: Varies according to project.

How to apply: Some offices of USFS are listed individually in the *Commentary* section, but all offices use volunteers extensively. If you are interested in a particular region, use the addresses listed below to contact that region's office directly.

Work done by volunteers: Varies by project.

Special skills or requirements: Varies by project.

Commentary: The regional offices are as follows:

USDA Forest Service
Northern Region (R-1)
Federal Building
200 Broadway, P.O. Box 7669
Missoula, MT 59807-7669

USDA Forest Service
Rocky Mountain Region (R-2)
740 Simms Street
Golden, CO 80401

P.O. Box 25127
Lakewood, CO 80225

USDA Forest Service
Southwestern Region (R-3)
333 Broadway, SE
Albuquerque, NM 87102-3498

USDA Forest Service
Intermountain Region (R-4)
Federal Building
324 25th Street
Ogden, UT 84401-2310

USDA Forest Service
Pacific Southwest Region (R-5)
1323 Club Drive
Vallejo, CA 94592

USDA Forest Service
Pacific Northwest Region (R-6)
333 SW First Avenue
P.O. Box 3623
Portland, OR 97208

USDA Forest Service
Southern Region (R-8)
1720 Peachtree Road NW
Atlanta, GA 30367

USDA Forest Service
Eastern Region (R-9)
310 West Wisconsin Avenue, Room 500
Milwaukee, WI 53203

USDA Forest Service
Alaska Region (R-10)
709 West Ninth Street
P.O. Box 21628
Juneau, AK 99802-1628

USDA Forest Service
Northeastern Research Station
11 Campus Drive
Suite 200
Newtown Square, PA 19073

USDA Forest Service
North Central Research Station
1992 Folwell Avenue
St. Paul, MN 55108

USDA Forest Service
Pacific Southwest Research Station
800 Buchanan Street, West Building
Albany, CA 94710-0011
P.O. Box 245
Berkeley, CA 94701-0245

USDA Forest Service
Rocky Mountain Research Station
240 West Prospect Road
Fort Collins, CO 80526-2098

USDA Forest Service
Southern Research Station
200 Weaver Boulevard
P.O. Box 2680
Asheville, NC 28802

USDA Forest Service
Forest Products Laboratory
One Gifford Pinchot Drive
Madison, WI 53705-2398

USDA Forest Service
International Institute of Tropical Forestry
Call Box 25000
Rio Piedras, PR 00928-5000

UPR Experimental Station Grounds
Botanical Garden
Rio Piedras, PR 00928

Visions in Action

2710 Ontario Road NW
Washington, DC 20009
(202) 625-7403; Fax (202) 588-9344
E-mail: visions@visionsinaction.org
Web site: www.visionsinaction.org

Project location: Tanzania.

Project type: Community development and sustainable environment projects.

Project costs: $4,400. The fee includes round-trip airfare, housing, food, travel and tour expenses, project funds, medical insurance, language training, and local support.

Project dates: June through mid-August.

How to apply: Contact the office listed above for an application packet.

Special skills or requirements: Visions in Action recruits volunteers from a broad base of skills and professions; those with manual, technical, and trade skills are just as valuable as individuals with professional certificates and academic credentials. Volunteers must have a commitment to social justice and improving the lives of the poor in the developing world. Language skill requirements vary by country. Volunteers must be at least 20 years old to apply; there is no upper age limit. Mid-career and retired professionals are specifically encouraged to apply.

Commentary: Visions in Action's summer programs include a one-week orientation followed by seven weeks of work and one week of vacation. The one week of orientation includes basic language instruction, an introduction to the country, and project training. Volunteers will be supervised by local staff members and a Visions in Action representative during the entire nine weeks. Volunteers will participate in various educational lectures and cultural exchange activities throughout the project period. After completion of the project, volunteers will then participate in a one-week visit to national parks or other attractions in the country. The one week of touring will include either a safari to Ngorongoro Crater and the Serengeti or a climb up Mount Kilimanjaro "to the roof of Africa" at 5895 meters above sea level. Inquire about other summer program destinations.

Sample projects: Construction of rainwater harvesting systems and filters at public buildings such as schools and churches in a semi-rural area. The project consists of building gutters that empty into a large concrete tank. Filters are contructed to purify the rainwater, which ensures that community members have access to safe drinking water during the dry season. This project especially benefits women and children of the community, as they are the ones responsible for collecting water, often from sources that are far away.

Voluntary Workcamps Association of Ghana

P.O. Box 1540
Accra, Ghana
(21) 663486; Fax (21) 665960
E-mail: volu@gppo.africaonline.com.gh
Web site: www.volu.org

Project location: Throughout Ghana, with some camps in adjoining countries.

Project type: Work camps.

Project costs: $200 for one camp; $300 for multiple camps. Volunteers are responsible for their own transportation to and from Ghana.

Project dates: June through October and November through February, for two to three weeks.

How to apply: Contact Volunteers for Peace, Inc. (see Index), or write to the address listed above for membership information.

Work done by volunteers: Volunteers conduct a wide variety of public service projects.

Special skills or requirements: Participants should be at least 16 years old and physically fit enough for heavy manual labor.

Commentary: Voluntary Workcamps Association of Ghana began in 1956 with a group of 11 men and women who wanted to direct the energies of young people in their country.

Volunteer Nepal Himalaya

P.O. Box 3665
Boulder, CO 80307
(888) 420-8822 or (303) 998-0101; Fax (303) 998-1007
E-mail: info@hec.org
Web site: www.hec.org

Project location: Nepal.
Project type: Education.
Project costs: $150 per month, plus a donation of $1,000. These
costs do not include airfare.
Project dates: September to December, and February to April.
How to apply: E-mail or call for the organization information.
Work done by volunteers: Run by the Himalayan Explorers Con-
nection, Volunteer Nepal Himalaya offers participants a
unique opportunity to teach English in a village school in the
Himalayas and to live as a family member in a local homestay.
Special skills or requirements: 25 hours of ESL teaching experi-
ence are required.

Volunteers for International Solidarity (Center for Creative Activities)

635 North 5th Street
Philadelphia, PA 19123
(215) 923-7635; Fax (215) 829-8954
E-mail: cca@libertynet.org
Web site: libertynet.org/cca

Project location: Philadelphia; international projects also available.

Project type: Housing rehabilitation, housing, education, and environmental work.

Project costs: $150 for a two-week session, which includes room and board. Volunteers are responsible for their own transportation costs.

Project dates: Projects take place during the summer.

How to apply: Via the organization's Web site.

Work done by volunteers: Volunteers do light construction work.

Special skills or requirements: There are no special skills or requirements. Volunteers from the United States must be at least 16; volunteers from other countries must be at least 18.

Sample projects: Renovating a computer school and cafe.

Volunteers for Israel

330 West 42nd Street, Suite 1618
New York, NY 10036
(212) 643-4848; Fax (212) 643-4855
E-mail: volunteers@vfi-usa.org
Web site: www.vfi-usa.org

Project location: Throughout Israel.

Project type: Volunteers work at Israel Defense Forces bases (civilian noncombat support activities), archaeological digs, Jerusalem Botanical Gardens, and hospitals.

Project costs: Between $900 and $1,300 on average, which includes airfare.

Project dates: Year-round; participants depart monthly for three-week programs.

How to apply: Applications may be downloaded from the organization's Web site. You may also e-mail the address listed above and request information; include a postal mailing address.

Work done by volunteers: Work may include general labor, maintenance and repair, warehousing, construction, painting, kitchen or laundry duties, gardening, or patient care assistance at hospitals.

Special skills or requirements: Good character, good mental and physical health, and enthusiasm and flexibility are required. Volunteers should be between 18 and 80 years old.

Commentary: More than 75,000 volunteers from the United States and 34 other countries have joined Volunteers for Israel since 1982. These individuals have provided hands-on help and significant moral support to the state of Israel, while gaining great insight into the culture and daily life of the Israeli people.

A Volunteers for Israel volunteer packages medical supplies. (Photo courtesy of Volunteers for Israel)

Volunteers for Outdoor Colorado (VOC)

600 South Marion Parkway
Denver, CO 80209
(303) 715-1010; Fax (303) 715-1212
E-mail: voc@voc.org
Web site: www.voc.org

Project location: Throughout Colorado.

Project type: Trail building, tree planting, revegetation, carpentry, improving wildlife and river habitats, and constructing boardwalks and wildlife viewing blinds.

Project costs: None. Most volunteers camp; food arrangements vary by project, but volunteers will be informed well in advance what meals (if any) will be provided. Transportation is at the volunteer's own expense.

Project dates: Various weekends during the spring, summer, and fall.

How to apply: Call or write the office listed above for project schedule.

Work done by volunteers: Trail building, tree planting, revegetation, and carpentry.

Special skills or requirements: There is no minimum age for volunteers. VOC has special opportunities for youth volunteers. See Web site for details.

Commentary: Volunteers for Outdoor Colorado is a nonprofit organization of volunteers working together to improve public lands. In both cities and remote wilderness areas, VOC has built miles of trails, planted thousands of trees, constructed whole-access boardwalks and nature trails, and improved wildlife and river habitats. VOC projects take place on weekends in the spring, summer, and fall, with 125 to 300 volunteers per project.

Volunteers for Peace, Inc. (VFP)— International Voluntary Service

1034 Tiffany Road
Belmont, VT 05730
(802) 259-2759; Fax (802) 259-2922
E-mail: vfp@vfp.org
Web site: www.vfp.org

Project location: In 70 foreign countries and throughout the United States.

Project type: International work camps.

Project costs: A $20 membership contribution is required. Membership includes a newsletter and the International Workcamp Directory, which contains listings of more than 2,000 work camps and is updated each year. Registration is $200 per camp, plus the cost of transportation to the camp.

A young group of volunteers process coffee beans in Tanzania. (Photo by Linda Kramer, courtesy of Volunteers for Peace)

Project dates: Ninety percent of the camps run for two to three weeks between May and September. Ten percent of the camps run year-round.

How to apply: Write, call, e-mail, or visit the Web site for information and an application.

Work done by volunteers: Volunteers perform a wide variety of community service projects.

Special skills or requirements: Most programs are for volunteers aged 18 and up. Three hundred are for those aged 15 and up. No special skills or foreign languages are required, but an interest in learning new customs, a willingness to live and work in an international group, sometimes under difficult conditions, and a cooperative spirit are all desirable.

Commentary: VFP is an organization with one goal—to find volunteers for work camps around the world. It is not a travel agency and does not book flights or tours of any kind.

Washington State Parks and Recreation Commission

7150 Cleanwater Lane
P.O. Box 42650
Olympia, WA 98504-2650
(360) 902-8500; Fax (360) 753-1594
E-mail: sarah.oldfield@parks.wa.gov
Web site: www.parks.wa.gov

Project location: One hundred and twenty-five parks throughout Washington State, from the Pacific Ocean through the Cascades into the dry eastern side of the state.

Project type: Volunteers perform a wide variety of park enhancement programs, including public relations projects, winter recreation projects, and assistance in a variety of other programs.

Project costs: Volunteers are responsible for all travel and personal expenses, but campground fees are waived. Most parks have full or partial RV hookups.

Project dates: Year-round. The length of stay varies with each project, but campground hosts must stay for one to four weeks.

How to apply: Send a request for an application to Volunteer Programs at the address listed above.

Work done by volunteers: Assisting at the office; trail building; park cleanup; acting as interpretive, campground, or marine park hosts; instructing boating safety; and general park maintenance. Volunteers do not collect fees or enforce park rules.

Special skills or requirements: Varies by project.

Commentary: State parks offer opportunities for volunteers of all ages and walks of life. Applications from families, singles, couples, groups, disabled individuals, and employed or unemployed people are welcome. The organization offers one-time projects as well as long-term and annual volunteer opportunities.

Washington Trails Association (WTA)

1305 4th Avenue, Suite 512
Seattle, WA 98101
(206) 625-1367
E-mail: trail_teams@wta.org
Web site: wta.org

Project location: The Cascades and Olympics Mountains in Washington State.

Project type: Conservation, trail maintenance, and construction.

Project costs: $75 per week includes all food. Volunteers provide their own camping equipment, and are responsible for their own transportation to the designated project meeting point.

Project dates: Trips begin in mid-April and end in early October.

How to apply: Applications may be downloaded from the Web site or requested via e-mail.

Work done by volunteers: Volunteers perform all types of backcountry construction using hand tools.

Special skills or requirements: All volunteers must provide their own backcountry camping equipment. Children are welcome as volunteers, but anyone under the age of 18 must have a waiver signed by a parent or guardian. Anyone under the age of 14 must be accompanied by an adult.

Commentary: WTA's volunteer trips are operated under three rules: safety first, fun second, and work third.

Sample projects: In the last few years, WTA has built several bridges and many turnpikes, steps, puncheons, and other trail structures. They have also cleared many miles, and built several new miles, of trail.

WTA Weeklong Vacation

❖ by Rachel Geissinger ❖

Washington Trails Association (WTA)

I arrived at the campground after a long drive on small, unnamed forest service roads. It was dark and a little rainy; I was tired, but excited. When I got out of the car, the Washington Trails Association (WTA) crew leader was there waiting for us all, introducing himself to each new volunteer and then introducing all of the volunteers to one another. He asked if I wanted anything—hot chocolate, coffee. I declined; I was ready for bed. I wanted a good night's sleep before the first day out on the trail. He helped me set up my tent and I fell asleep fast.

The next morning I awoke to the smell of pancakes being cooked . . . breakfast. I got ready in what was to be my home for the week (a tent) and went out to help with the meal. It was already almost ready, so I made my pack lunch from an array of choices and talked to the other half-awake volunteers. We ate a hearty breakfast and then headed out to work on the trail.

The first two days were spent on the Klickitat Trail, mostly cutting brush, cleaning and building drain dips, and other maintenance done annually on trails. It's rewarding work, especially at the end of the day when one walks back over the trail to see everything that was done. It's amazing what a group of eight volunteers can do in a day. On the third day we went back to the same trail. Since it was such a beautiful day, the forest service person who was working with us decided that we should hike to the top of the ridge to enjoy the beautiful views, and then work our way down in the afternoon. We all became excited, looking forward to some beautiful views. We hiked all morning through cool, amazing forests of cedar and Douglas firs. We made it to the top just before lunch. As the forest service person had said, the views were amazing. In one direction was Mount Adams, in another direction Mount Rainier, and in between it all, many named and unnamed peaks covered in forest splendor. We sat and ate lunch, enjoying it and trying to take it all in. We worked all afternoon, cutting out logs and rebuilding some trail tread, with beautiful mountain images stuck in our heads. It was a wonderful day, and the highlight of the week.

The week was great, with a lot of fun volunteers who became a mini family. We cooked and ate breakfast and dinner together, we sat by the campfire at night and told stories, and some of us keep in touch even now. Southwest Washington was a beautiful place for my first weeklong volunteer vacation.

I had so much fun the first time, I went back for a second week only one month later. This time, the camp was by Mount Rainier; the hike into the camp had an *amazing* close-up view of the mountain. That second week was spent with a small number of volunteers, building puncheons and bridges on the Pacific Crest Trail. It was another wonderful experience.

This summer I plan on going back, to enjoy new parts of the state and to meet a lot of other fun volunteers.

Welshpool and Llanfair Light Railway

The Station
Llanfair Caereinion
Powys SY21 0SF United Kingdom
(01938) 810 441; Fax (01938) 810 861
E-mail: info@wllr.org.uk
Web site: www.wllr.org.uk

Project location: Mid-Wales.

Project type: Operation of a narrow-gauge steam railway.

Project costs: Volunteers pay a small membership fee, airfare, and personal expenses. Free camping is available, and hostels are available for about £10 per week.

Project dates: Year-round.

How to apply: Write or phone in advance, or simply go to the office listed above and ask for the manager.

Work done by volunteers: The railway is run entirely by volunteers under a full-time manager. Unskilled work is always available, and training for skilled jobs, which includes locomotive operation, signaling, and crossing guard duty may be arranged in advance.

Special skills or requirements: None.

Commentary: This line is eight miles long and was built at the turn of the century as a cheap branch line. Run as a museum line for the past 30 years, it features locomotives and coaches from around the world.

Wild at Heart

15 Plantation Road
Hillcrest, 3610, Kwazulu-Natal, South Africa
(27) 31 765 1818; Fax (27) 31 765 72 45
E-mail: claude@wah.co.za
Web site: www.wah.co.za/volunteer.asp

Project location: Kruger National Park, South Africa.

Project type: Rehabilitating orphaned, sick, and injured wild animals.

Project costs: From $225 per week. Project costs include room and board and all transportation within South Africa; volunteers are responsible for their own transportation costs to South Africa.

Project dates: Each program starts on the first of every month.

How to apply: E-mail Claude for application forms at the address listed above.

Work done by volunteers: Volunteers may do any of the following: game tracking; inserting microchips into monkeys for satellite tracking; feeding lions, leopards, and crocodiles; rehabilitating cheetahs, hyenas, and wild birds of prey; building enclosures for snakes; game darting; game farm management; take a course leading to a Game Ranger Certificate; preparing food for animals; participating in antipoaching patrols; and general caring for the animals. Volunteers may choose to work in any or all of the following five locations: Wildlife Rehabilitation Center; African Reptile Park; Monkey Rehabilitation Sanctuary; a private game farm, or Kruger National Park.

Special skills or requirements: There is no minimum age or language requirement to volunteer.

Commentary: Wild at Heart offers a hands-on volunteer experience; therefore, volunteers should have an interest in helping the wildlife of Africa.

A volunteer works with a restless young alligator in the African Reptile Park in South Africa. (Photo courtesy of Wild at Heart)

Wildlands Studies

3 Mosswood Circle
Cazadero, CA 95421
Tel/Fax (707) 632-5665
E-mail: wildlnds@sonic.net
Web site: www.wildlandsstudies.com/ws

Project location: Alaska, Montana, Washington, California, Canada, Costa Rica, Hawaii, Nepal, Kenya, New Zealand, and Thailand.

Project type: Resource management, wildlife study, cultural ecology, conservation, biology, study of endangered species, and study of the impact of tourism.

Project costs: $464 to $940 for United States programs and up to $1,900 for non–United States programs. The project cost is an academic fee. Volunteers are responsible for their own transportation and room and board, but room and board costs tend to be minimal because projects are field-based and students are usually camping.

Project dates: Year-round.

How to apply: Contact the office listed above for information, or visit the organization's Web site.

Work done by volunteers: Full participation in research activities.

Special skills or requirements: Volunteers must be high school graduates, and most participants are college students. There is no language requirement.

Commentary: Participants can earn college credit for participation.

Sample projects: Volunteers have worked on endangered wolf and whale species studies, studied ecological problems in wilderness areas and national parks, studied wild rivers in Montana, and examined cultural ecology and the impact of tourism in the South Pacific.

Willing Workers on Organic Farms (WWOOF) Australia

Mount Murrindal Co-op
Buchan, Victoria 3885 Australia
(3) 5155-0218; Fax (3) 5155-0342
E-mail: wwoof@wwoof.com.au
Web site: www.wwoof.com.au

Project location: Throughout Australia and all other countries that do not have an existing WWOOF group.

Project type: Organic farming and living and working with a family on a cultural exchange.

Project costs: Volunteers are responsible for travel costs. Membership fees for Australian projects are $50 for individuals and $55 for couples, including postage overseas. WWOOF membership includes accident insurance while with a WWOOF host in Australia. The Worldwide List of Hosts costs $27 including postage overseas.

Project dates: Year-round.

How to apply: Contact the office listed above for information or for a list of farms and other organizations that take volunteers.

Work done by volunteers: Volunuteers perform all types of farm work, including reforestation of unused land, conservational planting, weeding, harvesting, rain forest regeneration, stock handling, and assisting at bed-and-breakfast establishments, exotic fruit farms, horse trail riding businesses, alpaca and llama farms, and more.

Special skills or requirements: Enthusiasm and a willingness to participate are a must. Volunteers must be at least 17.

Commentary: In Australia, there are more than 1,400 hosts whose aim is to give volunteers an organic farming and cultural experience. There are more than 350 hosts in other countries worldwide.

WWOOF Canada, WWOOF USA, WWOOF Hawaii

4429 Carlson Road
Nelson, BC, Canada, VIL 6X3
(250) 354-4417
E-mail: wwoofcan@shaw.ca
Web site: www.wwoof.ca and www.wwoofusa.com

Project location: Throughout Canada and the United States, including Hawaii.

Project type: Farm and garden help on organic farms.

Project costs: There is a $30 membership fee. Members receive a booklet describing the organizations' various projects. Volunteers are responsible for all transportation and personal expenses. Room and board are generally provided by hosts.

Project dates: Anytime, but spring through fall has the most opportunities.

How to apply: Apply via the organization's Web site or by mail.

Work done by volunteers: Outdoor-related farm and garden jobs.

Special skills or requirements: Volunteers do not need to have any farm experience, but do need to have a willingness to learn, laugh, and try their best. Volunteers must be at least 16 years of age; children under 16 may volunteer if accompanied by parents or guardians.

Commentary: E-mails from prospective volunteers are welcomed and encouranged.

Winant-Clayton Volunteers, Incorporated

109 East 50th Street
New York, NY 10022
(212) 378-0271; Fax (212) 262-1781

Project location: Great Britain.

Project type: Social service.

Project costs: There is an application fee of $35. Volunteers are responsible for all transportation costs. A small amount of financial aid is available.

Project dates: Mid-June to late August. The application deadline is in late January.

How to apply: Contact the volunteer coordinator at the address listed above for information.

Work done by volunteers: Volunteers are placed full-time in the East End of London with community workers on projects dealing with people of all ages and with a variety of needs: on playgrounds, in rehabilitation programs, in neighborhood associations, and in community health programs.

Special skills or requirements: Involvement and interest in social services and the community are required.

Commentary: This is an exchange program between the United States and Britain, which was founded in the aftermath of World War II.

Wind Cave National Park

RR 1, Box 190 WCNP
Hot Springs, SD 57747
(605) 745-4600; Fax (605) 745-4207
Web site: www.nps.gov/wica/index.htm

Project location: Wind Cave in the Black Hills, South Dakota.

Project type: A variety of volunteer and intern positions are available that involve interpretation, campground hosting, visitor contact, and cave resource management.

Project costs: Volunteers are responsible for food and transportation, but housing is provided by the park. There are some stipends available for the intern positions.

Project dates: Year-round.

How to apply: Write to Phyllis Cremonini, Assistant Chief of Interpretation, at the address listed above for more information about volunteer and intern positions.

Work done by volunteers: Opportunities range from interpretive work in the visitor center to assisting resource management with cave- and prairie-related projects.

Special skills or requirements: Some positions require two or more years of college education in natural or physical sciences, communications, natural science interpretation, resource management, or park/recreaton management. Experience in interpretation, public speaking, environmental education, or caves is helpful, but not required.

Commentary: As with most national and state park units, Wind Cave desperately needs volunteers to enhance its offerings to the public.

Winged Fellowship Trust

Angel House
20-32 Pentonville Road
London N1 9XD United Kingdom
(0207) 833-2594; Fax (0207) 278-0370
Web site: www.wft.org.uk/index2.htm

Project location: Four vacation centers for people with physical disabilities in the United Kingdom.

Project type: Holidays for disabled people and breaks for caretakers.

Project costs: Room and board are provided; travel within the United Kingdom is reimbursed.

Project dates: Volunteers are needed for one to two weeks from February to December. Vacations for the disabled run throughout the year. Special weeks are offered for those interested in fishing, music, drama, outdoor pursuits, riding, and shopping.

How to apply: Write or call the office listed above to request a brochure and an application.

Work done by volunteers: Personal care of disabled guests, pushing wheelchairs on outings, and providing general companionship.

Special skills or requirements: Enthusiasm is important. The Trust feels that the greatest requirement for a volunteer is sensitivity to and awareness of a disabled person's needs. Volunteers must be at least 16 years old.

Wisconsin Department of Natural Resources

Bureau of Parks and Recreation
P.O. Box 7921
Madison, WI 53707
(608) 266-2152
Web site: www.dnr.state.wi.us/org/land/parks

Project location: All Wisconsin state parks and forests.

Project type: Parks, forests, trails, campgrounds, and visitor centers.

Project costs: Minimal. Volunteers are responsible for their own transportation and room and board, except campground hosts, who are given a campsite.

Project dates: Year-round. Project lengths vary, but it is appreciated if volunteers stay at least two weeks. Ski trail patrols are in the winter.

How to apply: Apply directly to the superintendent of the park or forest of interest. A list of parks and forests may be obtained via the Web site or by writing to the address listed above.

Work done by volunteers: Campground hosting; nature interpretation; ski, bike, or horsetrail hosting and patrol; trail, building, and grounds maintenance; habitat improvement; species inventorying; prairie restoration; historical research; visitor information; construction; litter control; and clerical work.

Special skills or requirements: Be able to communicate well with the public and have a strong interest in the parks. Volunteers with special skills, such as plumbers and electricians, are always appreciated. The minimum age to volunteer depends on the program; campground hosts must be at least 18. See Web site for details.

Worcestershire Lifestyles

Woodside Lodge
Lark Hill Road, Worcester WR5 2EF United Kingdom
(01905) 350686
E-mail: worcslifestyles@care4free.net

Project location: The counties of Herefordshire and Worcester-shire.

Project type: Working with disabled adults.

Project costs: Free accommodation is provided in Herefordshire or Worcestershire. A weekly allowance of £58.88 is paid to volunteers. Transportation to the site is the responsibility of the volunteer.

Project dates: Year-round. Placements are for a minimum of four months.

How to apply: Write, call, or e-mail, giving your name and address, for more information and an application.

Work done by volunteers: Volunteers usually work on a one-to-one basis assisting a disabled person to live independently in his or her own home. Duties may include personal care, household duties, and encouraging the person to access study, meetings, and leisure interests. Volunteers might enable the disabled person to go to the pub, the cinema, a football match, shopping, or swimming.

Special skills or requirements: Volunteers must be aged 17 or older and must be reliable, hardworking, and committed to the right of disabled people to live a life of their choice. No experience is required. Training is provided.

Sample projects: Supporting a disabled man with his daily living, which includes help with personal care and domestic duties, attending meetings, accompanying him to the pub, cooking meals, and being a companion. Supporting a disabled woman with her daily living, including personal care, domestic duties, accompanying her to a line-dancing outing, socializing, and being a companion.

World Challenge Expeditions

Black Arrow House
2 Chandos Road, London NW10 6NF England
(44) 0 20 8728 7200
E-mail: welcome@world-challenge.co.uk
Web site: www.world-challenge.co.uk

Project location: Australia, Belize, Canada, Costa Rica, Ecuador, India, Malaysia, Nepal, Peru, South Africa, and Tanzania.

Project type: Conservation, including reserve wardening; patrolling turtle nesting sites; trail clearance and maintenance; reforestation; building reserve facilities; assisting in biological research projects or environmental education programs; teaching various subjects such as English, math, or science in local primary or secondary schools; helping children and adults with special needs; assisting with community activities; and working with street children who are living in residential care. Some other work, such as farm work and medical suppport work, is also available.

Project costs: £1,700 to £2,385.

Project dates: Year-round. Most departures are in September and January. Project lengths range from two to nine months.

How to apply: Apply directly via the organization's Web site listed above or call for an information pack.

Special skills or requirements: A knowledge of Spanish is preferred for placements in South America. Volunteers must be between 18 and 24 years old, and are required to attend a Selection Course and Skills Training Course in the United Kingdom.

Sample projects: Teaching in Belizean primary schools in small rural communities around the Corozal, Cayo, and Orange Walk Districts. Volunteers will mainly be teaching children aged eight to fourteen or assisting with their classes. Volunteers will also be required to become involved with sport, music, drama, or art projects, as well as organizing events such as plays, carol concerts, and soccer leagues.

World Horizons International LLC

P.O. Box 662
Bethlehem, CT 06751
(203) 266-5874 or (800) 262-5874; Fax (203) 266-6227
E-mail: info@world-horizons.com
Web site: www.world-horizons.com

Project location: Rural Alaska, Hawaii, Utah, the Caribbean, Central America, Mexico, Puerto Rico, and Iceland.

Project type: Community service and cultural immersion.

Project costs: Approximately $4,000, which includes room, board, and airfare from Miami, New York City, or San Francisco, depending on the program.

Project dates: Late June to late July.

How to apply: Contact the office listed above for application information.

Work done by volunteers: Part of the program includes work done in groups, such as repairing and building local community facilities, establishing day camps for children, or working with senior citizens. The program in Iceland involves environmental volunteer work in reforestoration programs. The program in Utah involves animal rescue and rehabilitation work. The programs also include an individual component in which volunteers are paired with local people and shadow them in their work. In this capacity the volunteer might work as a reporter, baker, assistant to a physician, or on a radio call-in show, for example.

Special skills or requirements: Volunteers must be high-school students with an interest in intercultural exchange and community service.

WorldTeach, Inc.

Center for International Development
79 John F. Kennedy Street
Cambridge, MA 02138
(617) 495-5527 or (800) 4-TEACH-0; Fax (617) 495-1599
E-mail: info@worldteach.org
Web site: www.worldteach.org

Project location: Costa Rica, Ecuador, Namibia, and China.

Project type: Teaching English.

Project costs: $3,990 to $5,990 (a fundraising guide and limited aid are available). The fee includes round-trip airfare, health insurance, orientation and training, as well as in-country support. Host schools or communities provide housing for WorldTeach volunteers. Volunteers may live with a local family, share a house with other local or foreign teachers, or, in some cases, even have their own apartment. Volunteers in some countries live in traditional houses without running water or electricity; others have modern apartments with many of the amenities of home. Wherever volunteers are placed, they are likely to have their own furnished bedroom and access to a bathroom and kitchen or cafeteria.

Project dates: WorldTeach offers eight-week, six-month, and one-year programs.

How to apply: Contact the office listed above or visit the organization's Web site for information and an application.

Work done by volunteers: Volunteers teach English to adults or children, depending on the country and host institution. There also are opportunities to teach math and science, as well as to become instructors to nature guides in training.

Special skills or requirements: Participants on the year-long program must have a bachelor's degree. No previous language or teaching experience is required.

Commentary: This program promises intensive intercultural contact, and combines service, cultural immersion, and international development.

Wyoming Dinosaur Center

P.O. Box 868
Thermopolis, WY 82443
(800) 455-DINO or (307) 864-2997; Fax (307) 864-5762
E-mail: wdinoc@wyodino.org
Web site: www.wyodino.org

Project location: Wyoming.

Project type: Digging for dinosaurs.

Project costs: Dig-for-a-Day costs $125 per person or $300 per family of four. Kids' Digs cost $75 for a two-day session (for children aged 8 to 12).

Project dates: Dig-for-a-Day is offered from late spring to fall, weather permitting. Kids' Digs are offered during the summer.

How to apply: Contact the office listed above for information on current offerings.

Work done by volunteers: Normal excavation work.

Special skills or requirements: None but an interest in dinosaurs.

Commentary: This program is a great introduction to excavating for the whole family. The center is located in a small town only two hours from Yellowstone National Park. The town has plenty of facilities, including a hotel.

Volunteers dig for dinosaur bones in Thermopolis, Wyoming. (Photo courtesy Wyoming Dinosaur Center)

Wyoming Parks and Cultural Resources

Division of State Parks and Historic Sites
122 West 25th Street, 1E
Cheyenne, WY 82002
(307) 777-3680; Fax (307) 777-6472
E-mail: sphs@state.wy.us
Web site: wyoparks.state.wy.us/indexl.htm

Project location: Throughout Wyoming at state parks and historic sites.

Project type: Outdoor and recreational projects.

Project costs: Volunteers are responsible for all travel and living expenses, although there are free campsites for campground hosts.

Project dates: Year-round. Volunteers are most needed from May to September.

How to apply: Contact the personnel specialist at (307) 777-7010 or at 2301 Central Avenue, Cheyenne, WY 82002.

Work done by volunteers: Campground hosting, trail work, simple maintenance, visitor information services, and interpretive programming, including living history.

Special skills or requirements: Volunteers should be able to work well with the public, have mechanical or craft skills, and have an interest in the outdoors or history. Many volunteer positions in this park system are tailored to suit the particular needs and skills of the volunteers.

YEE Office

Ekologicke sentrum Toulcuv dvur
Kubatova 1/32
102 00 Praha 10 Hostivar, Czech Republic
(420) 2-71750643; Fax (420) 2-71750548
E-mail: yee@ecn.cz

Project location: Throughout Europe.

Project type: Environmental and nature studies.

Project costs: Vary, but are moderate in general.

Project dates: Year-round. Larger camps operate mainly during the summer months.

How to apply: Write to the address listed above for the camp list. Enclose two international reply coupons and a self-addressed envelope.

Work done by volunteers: Conducting nature studies and environmental projects.

Special skills or requirements: Most of these camps are for volunteers between the ages of 12 and 30, but some accept older participants. Campers should be interested in nature and environmental studies.

Commentary: YEE exists through the efforts of about 50 youth organizations throughout Europe that are concerned with nature and environmental studies. YEE attempts to spread information and knowledge about the environment through work camps and seminars, and is actively involved in lobbying and actions on behalf of the environment.

Sample projects: Recent projects include international training courses on environmental education in Turkey and conservation of rare species and forest protection in the Rhodope Mountains of Bulgaria.

Youth International

1121 Downing Street #2
Denver, CO 80218
(303) 839-5877; Fax (303) 839-5887
E-mail: director@youthinternational.org
Web site: www.youthinternational.org

Project location: Asia (including the Philippines, Thailand, India, and Nepal), Africa (including Kenya, Tanzania, Botswana, and Namibia), South America (including Peru, Bolivia, and Ecuador).

Project type: Education, housing, rehabilitation, health, and conservation.

Project costs: $7,500 for three and a half months. Covers all volunteer costs, including airfare.

Project dates: Every year from early September to mid-December and early February to late May.

How to apply: Download an application from the Web site or contact Youth International directly. Applications are taken at any time. Volunteers must undergo a reference check, followed by a telephone interview. Positions are filled on a first-come, first-served basis for those who are accepted.

Special skills or requirements: Volunteers must be high-school graduates.

Commentary: Youth International sends teams of 14 people between 18 and 25 years old to three or four countries in Asia, Africa, or South America for three and a half months. While abroad, groups travel extensively and participate in a wide range of activities. The focus of these experiences is on volunteer community work and short-term home stays. Outdoor adventure, such as trekking, deep sea diving, and safaris, is also an important element of the program. There is also some sight-seeing.

Sample projects: Renovating a school in Thailand; helping cook and clean for and entertain the sick and destitute in Mother Teresa's clinics in India; building a community garden in a Nepalese village; teaching English to Tibetan monks; helping to build a community water tank in Kenya.

A volunteer works with a member of the local community to build a community center in East Africa. (Photo courtesy Youth International)

Zoetic Research/Sea Quest Expeditions

P.O. Box 2424T
Friday Harbor, WA 98250
(360) 378-5767
E-mail: orca@sea-quest-kayak.com
Web site: sea-quest-kayak.com

Project location: The San Juan Islands, near the Washington State–Canada border and the Inside Passage of southeast Alaska.

Project type: Whale research.

Project costs: $399 to $999, depending on the project. In some cases this fee includes meals and accommodations. Transportation is not included.

Project dates: Between June and September, for three- or five-day trips.

How to apply: Visit the organization's Web site, or contact the office listed above for more information.

Work done by volunteers: The San Juan Islands project involves whale research and helping to mitigate the impact on orca (killer) whales by boat traffic in the Islands. Waterborn education and public outreach are performed in the presence of wild whale pods. In Alaska, volunteers help to investigate the ecology of humpback whales, especially their social behaviors displayed when cooperatively feeding with bubble nets.

Special skills or requirements: None but seaworthiness and an interest in whale research. For most trips, volunteers must be at least 16 years old. However, custom trips can accommodate younger paddlers in most destinations, and some trips are available to 5-year-olds. See Web site for details.

Additional Resources

American Birding Association (ABA)
www.americanbirding.org/opps/voldiindex.htm
Interested in volunteering in the area of bird conservation? The ABA has sites all over the United States and abroad that offer volunteer participation.

Archeology Abroad
www.britarch.ac.uk/archabroad
This organization publishes *Archeology Abroad*, which lists more than 1,000 volunteer positions located worldwide.

Archaeological Institute of America
www.archaeological.org/Publications/Publications.html
The Institute annually publishes the *Archaeological Fieldwork Opportunities Bulletins*, which lists volunteer opportunities on digs.

Catholic Network of Volunteer Service (CNVS)
www.cnvs.org
The CNVS has a database of thousands of full-time volunteer opportunities available through more than 200 member programs. You can search these opportunities on-line; the Web site allows you to define the limits of your search.

Coordinating Committee for International Voluntary Service (CCIVS)
www.unesco.org/ccivs/servvol/htm/basec.htm
CCIVS has links to many international volunteer organizations located throughout the world.

Council Exchanges
http://us.councilexchanges.org/opportunities/ivp/index.html
Council Exchanges places volunteers into small teams to conduct volunteer projects worldwide.

Council for British Archaeology
www.britarch.ac.uk
The Web site lists fieldwork opportunities in the United Kingdom.

Idealist.org
www.idealist.org
6,442 volunteer opportunities in 153 countries.

Institute for Archaeology at the Hebrew University of Jerusalem
www.hum.huji.ac.il/Archaeology/index.htm
For a list of archaeological digs in Jerusalem.

InterAction—American Council for Voluntary International Action
www.interaction.org/pub/gw2000.html
InterAction puts out the publication *Global Work*, which lists 70 organizations in 120 countries including the United States.

International Volunteer Programs Association (IVPA)
www.volunteerinternational.org
Utilize this search engine to find international volunteer opportunities.

International Year of Volunteers Country Profiles
www.iyv2001.org
Many countries, and some of the volunteer opportunities in these countries, are listed on this Web site.

Network for Good
www.networkforgood.org
The Network for Good Web site has a search engine that allows you to enter your zip code and find volunteer opportunities within your local community, or anywhere across America.

Quaker Information Center
www.afsc.org/qic/oportnty.htm
This Web site contains a listing of hundreds of volunteer opportunities of varying lengths.

St. Vincent Pallotti Center for Apostolic Development
www.pallotticenter.org/index.htm
This center publishes an annual directory called *Connections*, which lists 120 Catholic-based volunteer programs.

Volunteers in Technical Assistance (VITA)
www.vita.org/default.htm
Vita matches volunteers who have technical skills with Third World organizations that need those skills. This volunteer work is often done via mail, but occasionally on-site assistance is requested.

Index by Project Cost

$100 and under

Under $500

$500 to $999

$1,000 to $1,999

University of Alaska, Anchorage, Department of
Anthropology, 277
Volunteer Nepal Himalayas, 289

$2,000 to $2,999

$3,000 and above

Index by Project Length

Under One Week

One Week

Winged Fellowship Trust, 308
Wyoming Dinosaur Center, 314–15

Two Weeks

Three to Four Weeks

One to Five Months

Six Months or More

Length Varies by Project

Index by Project Location

Africa

Central America

Asia, South Pacific

Australia

Canada

Caribbean

Mexico

Worldwide

Index by Season

Fall

Spring

Summer

Winter

Year-round

Index by Project Type

Agriculture

Archaeology

Community Development

Construction

Education and Teaching

Environmental Protection and Research

Executive and Technical Assistance

Historic Preservation and Restoration

Council in International Education Exchange, 69
Friends of the Cumbres and Toltec Scenic Railroad, 104–5
Kansas Archaeology Training Program Field School, 153
Passport in Time, 213
Rempart, 235
Sabranenque Restoration Projects, La, 239–40

Marine Research

ARCHELON, The Sea Turtle Protection Society of Greece, 23
Caribbean Conservation Corporation, 46
Conservation, Education, Diving, Awareness, and Marine
    Research (CEDAM International), 53
Earthwatch Institute, 80–81
Marine Environment Awareness Program, 169
Mingan Island Cetacean Study, Incorporated, 183
Oceanic Society Expeditions, 202–3
Orkney Seal Rescue, 208
Pacific Whale Foundation, 211–12
PRETOMA (Programa Restauracion de Tortugas Marinas),
    225
Zoetic Research/Sea Quest Expeditions, 320

Medical and Dental

Amazon-Africa Aid Organization (3AO), 5
AmeriSpan Unlimited, 7
Amigos de las Americas, 8–9
Camp AmeriKids, 39
Dakshinayan, 77
Flying Doctors of America, 96
Fresh Start Surgical Gifts, Inc., 103
Health Volunteers Overseas (HVO), 128
Interplast, Incorporated, 142–43
Latin American Language Center, 157–58
Medical Ministry International (MMI), 170–71
Medicos Voladores, Los (LMV)—The Flying Doctors, 175
Mercy Ships, 180–81
Peacework Development Fund, Inc., 216

Monkey Sanctuary, 185–86
Oceanic Society Expeditions, 202–3
Orkney Seal Rescue, 208
Pacific Whale Foundation, 211–12
Peruvian Safaris, 217–18
PRETOMA (Programa Restauracion de Tortugas Marinas), 225
Royal Tyrell Museum: Field Experience, 238
Sierra Club National Outings, 244–45
Student Conservation Association (SCA), 259–60
University Research Expeditions Program, 278
Volunteers for Outdoor Colorado, 293
Wild at Heart, 301–2
Wildlands Studies, 303
World Challenge Expeditions, 311

Service Industry

Kalani Oceanside Retreat, 152
Monkey Sanctuary, 185–86

Social Justice and Amnesty

Bike-Aid, 26
BRIDGES (Building Responsible International Dialogue through Grassroots Exchange), 32
Casa de Proyecto Libertad, Incorporated, 51
Christian Peacemaker Teams, 62
Cross-Cultural Solutions, 70–71
Fellowship of Reconciliation—Task Force on Latin America and the Caribbean (Voluntarios Solidarios), 89–91
Nicaragua Solidarity Network, 198
Prime Care Network, 230
Quest, 231–32
United Nations Volunteers, 276

Social Service

C.A.I. Pina Palmera, A.C., 37
Camphill Special School, Beaver Run, 40

State and National Parks

Trail Building and Maintenance

Train Maintenance and Operation

Work Camps